Hervaeus Natalis

THE POVERTY OF CHRIST AND THE APOSTLES

translated by John D. Jones

"Is it heretical to assert that Christ and the apostles had none of the things that come into use in human life either in regard to ownership of or dominion over them?" From 1321 to 1323, debate about this question sparked a passionate and bitter controversy over the Franciscan doctrine of the "absolute" poverty of Christ and the apostles and hence of the basis of the Franciscan practice of poverty. The controversy pitted the Franciscan Order against Pope John XXII and the Dominican Order.

This volume contains a translation of two works from that controversy –Hervaeus Natalis's *The Poverty of Christ and the Apostles* and a Vatican scribe's summary of the positions of a several Franciscan clergy including those of two prominent cardinals: Vital du Four and Bertrand de la Tour. Hervaeus Natalis (d. 1323), a distinguished philosopher and theologian, was Master General of the Dominican Order during the controversy.

Hervaeus's work, which John XXII read and annotated, provides a comprehensive and rigorous analysis of the central philosophical, theological, and scriptural themes at the heart of the controversy. It presents a clear contrast to the positions held by the Franciscans.

In their works Hervaeus and the Franciscans treat a wide range of enduring themes in religious and social life: the nature of poverty; the relation of poverty and wealth to perfection; the interpretation of scriptural and patristic authorities; the relationship between ownership, rights, and use; the justification for making provision for the future; and so forth.

Apart from those of works by Thomas Aquinas, this volume presents the only English translation of a principal Dominican treatise on poverty.

It concludes with a bibliography and a comprehensive index.

D1594552

MEDIAEVAL SOURCES IN TRANSLATION 37

STUDIES IN MEDIEVAL MORAL TEACHING 2

Hervaeus Natalis

The Poverty of Christ and the Apostles

A translation, with introduction and notes, of the
Liber de paupertate Christi et apostolorum

by

John D. Jones

PONTIFICAL INSTITUTE OF MEDIAEVAL STUDIES

BV
4647
.P6
H4713
1999

Canadian Cataloguing in Publication Data

Hervaeus Natalis, d. 1323
    The poverty of Christ and the apostles

(Mediaeval sources in translation, ISSN 0316-0874 ; 37)
(Studies in medieval moral teaching ; 2)
Includes bibliographical references and index.
ISBN 0-88844-287-4

1. Poverty – Religious aspects – Christianity – History of doctrines –
Middle Ages, 600-1500 – Early works to 1800.   2. Dominicans –
Early works to 1800.   3. Franciscans – Early works to 1800.
I. Title.   II. Series.   III. Series: Studies in medieval moral teaching; 2.

BV4647.P6H4713 1999   248.4'7   C99-931523-4

Table of Contents

Abbreviations   vii

Acknowledgments   ix

Introduction   1

    A. Historical Background 2 □ B. Hervaeus Natalis 7 □ C. The Conceptual Foundation of Hervaeus's Treatise 8 □ D. Hervaeus and St. Thomas Aquinas 16 □ E. Text and Translation 18

HERVAEUS NATALIS

The Poverty of Christ and the Apostles   23

Question 1–The Relation of Poverty to Perfection   25

    Article 1–Whether Poverty Pertains Essentially to Perfection   25

    Article 2–Whether Poverty Pertains to Perfection Instrumentally   31

Question 2–Whether the Opposite of Poverty Diminishes the Perfection of Human Life   37

    Question 2A–Whether the Opposite of Poverty Diminishes Personal Perfection   37

    Article 1–Whether the Right to and Dominion over Temporal Things Can Be Separated from their Use   37

    Article 2–Whether Having a Right to and Dominion over Temporal Things Diminishes Personal Perfection   50

    Article 3–Whether Making Provision for the Future Diminishes the Perfection of Life   62

    Question 2B–How the Opposite of Poverty is Related to the Perfection of a State   77

    Article 1–Whether Having Things in Common Through Ownership Diminishes the Perfection of the Religious State   77

    Article 2–Whether Having Temporal Things Diminishes the Perfection of Prelates   87

Question 3–Whether It Is Heretical to Assert That Christ and the Apostles Had No Temporal Things in Common

in Terms of a Right to and Dominion over Them   91
Article 1–Whether Christ and the Apostles Had Some
    Temporal Things in Common in Terms of a Right to
    and Dominion over Them   91
Article 2–Whether it is Heretical to Assert that Christ and
    the Apostles Had Nothing Personally or in Common   112

Appendix. A Summary of Franciscan Positions Concerning the
    Poverty of Christ and the Apostles   117
        A Brief Summary of the Remarks of Cardinal Vital, Bishop
        of Albano 121 □ A Brief Summary of the Felicitous Re-
        marks of the Bishop of Capha 126 □ A Brief Summary of
        the Remarks of the Bishop of Lisbon 126 □ A Brief Sum-
        mary of the Remarks of the Bishop of Riga 127 □ A Brief
        Summary of the Remarks of a Teacher of the Franciscan
        Order 128 □ A Brief Summary of the Remarks of the Bi-
        shop of Badajoz 129 □ A Brief Summary of the Remarks
        of Cardinal B[ertrand] de la Tour 130 □ A Brief Sum-
        mary of the Remarks of the Archbishop of Salerno 138 □
        The Opposite Stance Argued through Authorities and Ar-
        guments 140 □ Response of the Lord Cardinal Vital to
        the Objection 140 □ Second Objection 140 □ Response
        of the Lord Cardinal Vital to the Objection 140 □ Third
        Objection 141 □ Response of the Lord Cardinal Vital to
        the Objection 141 □ Other Objections 141 □ Response
        of the Lord Vital, [Bishop of] Albano, to All of the Fore-
        going Objections 142 □ New Opposition 143 □ The
        Response of the Lord Vital to the Objection 143 □ Other
        Objections 144 □ Response of the Lord Cardinal Vital to
        the Objection 144 □ Another Objection 145 □ Re-
        sponse of the Lord Cardinal Bertrand de la Tour 145 □
        Other Opposition 145 □ Response of the Lord Cardinal
        Bertrand de La Tour 145 □ Another Objection 146 □
        Response of the Lord Cardinal Bertrand 146 □ Response
        of the Archbishop of Salerno 146

Bibliography   149
        A. Primary Sources 149 □ B. Secondary Sources 151

Index of Persons   155
Index of Citations to Scripture and Scriptural Glosses 159
Subject Index   161

Abbreviations

CCSL	*Corpus Christianorum, Series Latina*
CCCM	*Corpus Christianorum, Continuatio Medievalia*
CIC	*Corpus Iuris Canonici*
CSCO	*Corpus Scriptorum Christianorum Orientalium*
CSEL	*Corpus Scriptorum Ecclesiasticorum Latinorum*
PG	**Migne, J.-P.**, *Patrologiae Cursus completus, Series Graeca*
PL	**Migne, J.-P.**, *Patrologiae Cursus completus, Series Latina*
SC	*Sources Chrétiennes*

Acknowledgments

Several people have been most generous in providing assistance to me during the preparation of this volume. Special thanks go to Dr. Richard Taylor of the Marquette Philosophy Department and Dr. Mark Johnson of the Marquette Theology Department for reading substantial portions of the translation. Their many suggestions and modifications have greatly improved the quality of this work. I would also like to thank my philosophy colleagues, Dr. David Twetten and Rev. Roland Teske, S.J. for providing consultation on various points. I am also very appreciative of Dr. Kerry Spiers (University of Louisville, History) who provided me with copies of his own work on the poverty controversies, together with a number of important supplements to the bibliography. My research assistants Mr. John Simmons and Mr. Erik Richardson helped with production of the final draft of the typescript. Of course, I am most grateful to the Pontifical Institute of Mediaeval Studies, its staff, and readers for considering and producing this work.

Three grants made possible the publication of this work. I am most appreciative for the financial support provided by Rev. Edward Jackman, O.P. and the Jackman Foundation (Canada). Funding was also graciously provided through the Marquette University Christian Commitment Fund (administered by Dr. Francis Lazarus and, at present, Dr. David Buckholdt) and a Marquette Graduate School Faculty Development Grant administered by Rev. Thaddeus Burch, S.J. Editorial and production costs were also supported by the Medieval Moral Teaching Fund of the Pontifical Institute of Mediaeval Studies.

Introduction

"Is it heretical to assert that Christ and the apostles had none of the things that come into use in human life either in regard to ownership of or dominion over them?"[1] So reads the question that defines the subject matter of the two works translated in this volume. The first piece, *Liber de paupertate Christi et apostolorum*, was written by the Dominican Hervaeus Natalis.[2] The second, contained in the appendix, is a summary of the responses to this question given by several Franciscans.[3] These two works were part of a collection of treatises submitted to Pope John XXII. They provided expert opinions for his definitive bull, *Cum inter nonnullos* (1323). The specific doctrinal controversy surrounding this question is rooted in events that took place in 1321-1323. However, the conceptual issues raised by the question were embedded in the form of poverty practiced by St. Francis and the interpretation of that poverty by St. Bonaventure, Gregory IX, Nicholas III, and the Franciscan Order itself.[4]

---

[1] "Utrum asserere Christum et apostolos nichil habuisse in rebus temporalibus venientibus in usum humanae vitae quantum ad proprietatem et dominium sit haereticum."

[2] Hervaeus Natalis, *Liber de paupertate Christi et apostolorum*, Edited by J.G. Sikes, *Archives d'histoire doctrinale et littéraire du moyen âge*, 12-13 (1937-8): 209-97.

[3] F. Tocco, *La quistione della povertà nel secolo XIV*, Naples, 1910: 51-87. See the appendix for a brief discussion of this work.

[4] M.D. Lambert's *Franciscan Poverty* and Decima Douie's *The Nature and Effect of the Heresy of the Fraticelli* give the most extensive accounts in English of this controversy in its historical context. Lambert is especially helpful for understanding the complex philosophical and legal issues involved. Sikes gives a brief treatment of the controversy in the introduction to his edition of Hervaeus's treatise (207-219). For a very recent study on this matter, see Ulrich Horst's *Evangelische Armut und papstliches Lehramt: Minoritentheologen im Konflikt mit Papst Johannes XXII (1316-34)*. One should also consult the works of Gordon Leff, John Moorman, Patrick Gauchat, and Raphael Huber which are listed in the bibliography. Philip Mulhern treats the issue of evangelical poverty in the medieval Church in the broader context of a history of the Christian interpretation of poverty (*Dedicated Poverty* 97-132). Lester Little also gives

A. HISTORICAL BACKGROUND

In his Rule of 1223, St. Francis required that the brothers appropriate nothing for themselves.[5] This command expressed St. Francis's view that the brothers could best imitate Christ by being strangers and pilgrims in the world.[6] Francis was intensely drawn to follow the command given by Jesus to the disciples on their first preaching mission: "take nothing for the journey."[7] So Francis and his early followers wandered over Italy, owning no dwellings, refusing to use money, and accepting only what met daily needs. A number of the early biographies of Francis portray the near destitution in which he and his early followers regularly lived.[8]

However, the attempt to imitate strictly the life of St. Francis and these followers soon posed insuperable difficulties for the Order. Responsibility for ill and aging brothers, the rapid growth of the Order, as well as its engagement in the academic life of the universities could hardly be pursued by imitating the life style of itinerant mendicants. Moreover, external challenges to the Order as well as the technical demands of its administration increasingly required that the practice of poverty be conceptualized in the context of civil law and its categories of use (*usus*), dominion (*dominium*), ownership (*proprietas*), and right/law (*ius*).

---

a brief treatment of the Dominicans and Franciscans in the context of a social history of poverty in the middle ages (*Religious Poverty and the Profit Economy in Medieval Europe* 146-170). Hilarin Felder gives an excellent treatment of the experience and practice of poverty by St. Francis and his first followers (*The Ideals of St. Francis* 74-165). Although somewhat pietistic, Felder cites and discusses most of the relevant texts concerning Francis and poverty which are found in the early biographies and testimonies about Francis. W. A. Hinnebusch gives a good, but brief, account of the Dominican practice of poverty through 1275 (*The History of the Dominican Order* 1.145-168). A somewhat less satisfactory treatment in found in R. F. Bennett (*The Early Dominicans* 31-51).

[5]   In full, the rule reads: "Fratres nihil sibi appoprient nec domum nec locum nec aliquam rem" (*Regula bullata* VI (Esser 231; Habig 61). Cf. Lambert, *Franciscan Poverty*, 43.

[6]   *Regula bullata* VI (Esser 231; Habig 61). Cf. 1 Pet. 2:11.

[7]   Luke 9:3. See also, Matt. 9:10.

[8]   All of this material is contained in M. Habig's *St. Francis of Assisi: An Omnibus of Sources*. Of particular interest is the *Speculum perfectionis* (*The Mirror of Perfection*), as it was apparently composed in the early fourteenth century at the height of the controversy between the Spirituals and the Papacy (cf. Habig 1103-1265). For a portrait of the destitution of Christ and the apostles, see Bonaventure, *Apologia pauperum* VII.6-9 (Quaracchi VIII.273-279).

Pope Gregory IX played a crucial role in this process. Giving a juridical interpretation to Francis's dictum that the brothers appropriate nothing to themselves, Gregory required that the Order renounce common ownership of and dominion over all the goods it used:

> We say therefore that [the Friars] ought not to have *proprietas* [ownership] of things either individually or in common. But they may have the use of the utensils, books, and movable goods which they are permitted to have...[9]

Later, by means of the bull *Ordinem vestrum* (1245), Innocent IV transferred the ownership of the Order's goods to the Papacy, including consumable goods like food and beverage.[10] The claim that the use of goods could be separated from their dominion and ownership was implicit in these decisions. This view was particularly vulnerable to the objection concisely expressed by Gerard of Abbeville (1269), one of the secular clergy who launched a vigorous attack on the mendicant orders:

> To say that the use of [things consumed in use] is yours alone, and that the dominion pertains to those who have given them, until they are consumed by age, or until the food is taken to the stomach, will appear ridiculous to all, especially since among men use is not distinguished from dominion in things that are utterly consumed by use.[11]

St. Bonaventure sought to meet this and other challenges in his *Apologia pauperum* (1269) in the context of a comprehensive theological and scriptural justification of Franciscan poverty. In particular, he argued that the Franciscans renounced common as well as personal dominion over things.[12] Bonaventure made a crucial distinction between the apostles' renunciation of personal and common dominion on their first preaching mission and the renunciation of personal dominion alone that was practiced by the primitive Christian community in Jerusalem.[13] This distinction

---

[9] *Bullarium franciscanum* I.69.

[10] Ibid., I.401.

[11] "Dicere, vero, quod usus tantum vester est, dominium eorum, qui dederint, quoque vestustate consummantur, aut ciborum, quoque in ventrem reconditi fuerint, omnibus ridiculum videbitur, maxime cum eorum, quae per ipsum usum penitus consummantur, ab usu dominium nullatenus inter homines distinguatur." *Contra adversarium perfectionis Christiane.* Edited by S. Clasen, *Archivum Franciscanum Historicum* 32 (1939): 133. I use Lambert's translation (*Franciscan Poverty* 135).

[12] Cf. *Apologia pauperum* XI.1-6 (Quaracchi 310-312).

[13] In this community "all things were common to everyone" (Acts 4:32).

allowed Bonaventure to contrast Franciscan poverty with the poverty found in traditional monastic orders.[14] Within a few years, Nicholas III issued the bull, *Exiit qui seminat* (1279), which substantially legitimated Franciscan poverty along the lines developed by Bonaventure:

> the renunciation of all things, both personally as well as in common, for the sake of God is meritorious and holy, which Christ, showing the way of perfection, taught in words and confirmed by example.[15]

Indeed, Nicholas argued that the Franciscans retained only a *simplex usus facti* of things (a simple use of things in fact) without retaining any common dominion over them.[16] However, the bull did not explicitly take up the "consumables argument" posed by Gerard of Abbeville. This bull was of particular importance, since Nicholas III provided a crucial papal definition and legitimation of Franciscan poverty and, moreover, he prohibited glosses on the text and insisted that it be read literally.[17] The Franciscans believed that Nicholas III effectively closed off debate over the merits and nature of Franciscan poverty. One can gain an estimation of the importance of the bull by noting how frequently and approvingly it is cited in the works translated in this volume.

If the Franciscan Order was unified concerning the nature and legitimacy of the renunciation of all common ownership of goods as reflecting the poverty of Christ and the apostles, it was considerably divided over the nature and the legitimate scope of the use of goods. This issue had always been an administrative thorn. It formed a flash-point of controversy with the development of Peter John Olivi's doctrine of *usus pauper* which claimed that the restricted use of goods was an essential part of the Franciscan vow of poverty.[18] The Spirituals, who supported this position, were vigorously opposed by the Conventuals, who asserted that only the renunciation of dominion was part of the vow of poverty. Interwoven with other volatile issues, the controversy split the Franciscan Order from within and caused considerable friction between the Franciscans and the Church. The

---

[14] *Apologia pauperum* VII.4-5 (Quaracchi 273).

[15] "Abdicatio proprietatis huiusmodi omnium rerum non tam in speciali, quam etiam in communi propter Deum meritoria est et sancta, quam et Christus, viam perfectionis ostendens, verbo docuit et exemplo firmavit." Nicholas III, *Exiit qui seminat* (*CIC* II.1112).

[16] Ibid., 1113.

[17] Ibid., 1120.

[18] David Burr gives a detailed treatment of this matter in his work, *Olivi and Franciscan Poverty: The Origins of the Usus Pauper Controversy*.

controversy culminated in 1317 with the suppression of the Spirituals and the execution, by burning at the stake, of four unrelenting members of their faction.[19]

Pope John XXII and the Conventuals were fully aligned in the suppression of the Spirituals. However, the same pope's subsequent investigation into the poverty of Christ and the apostles unified the Franciscan Order solidly against him. The papal investigation was prompted by events in 1321 when a Dominican inquisitor in Provence, John of Belna, judged as heretical the view of a certain Beguin that Christ and the apostles owned nothing either personally or in common. This thesis was defended by Berengar Toloni, a lector in a Franciscan convent. When Toloni refused to comply with the Dominican's demand that he recant, an appeal was made, by both men, to the Apostolic See.[20] The pope requested various theologians to submit expert opinions on the matter. The case was brought before the pope in a consistory held March 6, 1322. The Franciscans defended Toloni as a proponent of sound Catholic doctrine. Moreover, they appealed to the bull, *Exiit qui seminat*, not only in light of its doctrinal authority, but also to render moot the discussion in light of the bull's final clauses forbidding further discussion of Nicholas III's determinations regarding Franciscan poverty.[21] On March 26, 1322, John XXII issued the bull, *Quia nonnumquam*, which effectively annulled Nicholas's prohibition of further discussion on the matter.

Following the issue of *Quia nonnumquam*, the Franciscans met in general chapter at Perugia. In the summer of 1322, they issued two letters which challenged the pope's right to abrogate *Exiit*. In the second letter, they also set forth a technical justification for their interpretation of the nature of Christ's poverty. It is worth noting two of these arguments, since Hervaeus treats them in his work. The first argument proceeded from the traditional position that the highest human perfection consists in the greatest removal of solicitude for temporal things.[22] According to the Franciscans, then, since owning even common possessions requires a solicitude for things, the highest poverty involves a renunciation of such ownership. As Christ and the apostles were most perfect, they too, therefore, renounced common as well as personal ownership.

---

[19] Sikes, 214.

[20] Sikes, 215.

[21] See the appendix, at page 129 below, where this point is forcefully made by the Franciscan bishop of Badajoz.

[22] See Hervaeus, page 51 below.

Lambert concisely summarizes the second argument in the following way. In light of Bonaventure's *Apologia pauperum*,

> *Exiit* had said that the Franciscans had renounced all the rights of the civil law, and had only a *simplex usus facti* in their goods. The [Franciscan] encyclical now took the doctrine one step further, and simply transferred the *simplex usus facti* to the life of Christ and the apostles. ...When Christ and the apostles held the [purse], or when in the early Church had all things in common, they were acting only as administrators. They had renounced all rights in the civil law; they had, for themselves, only a *simple usus facti*.[23]

The pope's response to the Perugia letters was devastating to the Order. In December 1322, Pope John XXII issued the first version of *Ad conditorem*, in which he permanently returned papal ownership of Franciscan goods to the Order. By so doing, he essentially undermined the papal administrative arrangement in effect since *Ordinem vestrum* (1245), which allowed the Franciscans to claim that they possessed nothing in common. Led by Bonagratia of Bergamo, the Franciscans appealed the first version of *Ad conditorem*. As Sikes notes, "war was virtually declared between the Pope and the Friars."[24] Indeed, Bonagratia of Bergamo, who had cooperated with Pope John XXII in the suppression of the Spirituals, was imprisoned for a year by the same pope.[25] The Franciscan appeal was followed in short order by a second version of *Ad conditorem* which John XXII substituted for the original version. Although less caustic in style than the first version, the pope basically reaffirmed his administrative decision and summarily rejected any attempt to separate the use of consumable goods from dominion over them.

The net effect of the two versions of *Ad conditorem* was to undermine the Franciscan claim that their Order practiced the highest poverty. *Ad conditorem* did not explicitly consider the question of whether Christ and the apostles owned nothing in common. The pope sought to deal definitively and dogmatically with this matter in the bull, *Cum inter nonnullos* (November 1323), in which he declared as heretical and erroneous the assertion that Christ and "his apostles in no way had a right to use the things that Holy Scripture testifies that they had, or that they had no right

---

[23] Lambert, *Franciscan Poverty*, 229-230. See Hervaeus, beginning at page 97 and beginning at page 113 below.

[24] Sikes, 217.

[25] Sikes, 213 and 217.

of selling, giving or exchanging them."[26]

One final note: as the question under investigation in this volume pitted the Franciscans and Dominicans against each other, a brief word is in order about the Dominican practice of poverty. Although both Dominicans and Franciscans were regarded as mendicant orders, there were substantial differences in their respective practice of poverty. The most radical view of religious poverty held by the Dominicans was set forth in the constitution of 1220 in which they renounced all common "possessions and revenues" (possessiones et reditus).[27] However, the Dominicans never renounced complete common dominion over things, since they took possessiones to refer largely to capital goods such as buildings and land which were devoted to agriculture or farming. They continued to retain dominion over their priories as well as over their movable and consumable goods. It is also worth noting that the intense confrontations in the latter part of the thirteenth century–e.g., between the Dominican Robert Kilwardby and the Franciscan John Pecham–contrast with the common ground formerly shared by the orders earlier in the thirteenth century. For example, a Franciscan story relates a meeting between Francis and Dominic in which the two founders expressed their admiration and esteem for one another.[28] Both orders presented a unified front against the criticisms of William of Saint-Amour and the other secular clergy in the 1250s.

B. HERVAEUS NATALIS

The distinguished French Dominican Hervaeus Natalis (Hervé Nédélec) entered the Order of Preachers in 1276 and commenced an active academic, literary, and administrative career at the turn of the fourteenth century. He was a regent master at Paris during 1307-1309. In 1309, he was elected provincial of the French province. In 1318, he was elected by unanimous vote as the Master General of the Dominican Order, a position he held until his death in 1323. He was a particularly devoted supporter and defender of Saint Thomas Aquinas. Over forty works, on a wide range of philosophical and theological topics, have been attributed to him.[29]

---

[26] "Eiusque apostolis [in] iis, quae ipsos habuisse scriptura sacra testatur, nequamquam ius ipsis utendi competierit nec illa vendendi seu donandi ius habuerint aut ex ipsis alia adquirendi." Bullarium Franciscanum V.257b-8a.

[27] W. A. Hinnebusch, The History of the Dominican Order, I.153.

[28] 2 Cleano 148-150 (Habig 481-83).

[29] See F. Roensch, Early Thomistic School, 110-117 and P. Glorieux, Répertoire des maîtres en théologie de Paris au XIIIe siècle, I.199-206, and Thomas Kaeppeli, Scriptores

Vollert cites the following testimony from a fourteenth-century manuscript as an estimation of Hervaeus's abilities: "a theologian second to none, a supreme metaphysician, a subtle dialectician, a most profound naturalist and keen debater, whose doctrine would gain for any disputant the assured prospect of academic victory."[30] He was nicknamed *Doctor Rarus*.[31]

Hervaeus's treatise on the poverty of Christ and the apostles was his last major work.[32] It is clear that Pope John XXII read and annotated this treatise.[33] It is worth noting that two key pieces of Hervaeus's analysis–the rejection of the view that use and dominion can be completely separated in relation to consumables, as well the claim that all just use of something implies at least the right to use it–were employed by Pope John XXII. Regardless of its effect on the pope, Hervaeus's work is interesting in its own right and, as I suggest below, in relation to Thomas Aquinas's analysis of poverty. *The Poverty of Christ and the Apostles* offers a fine example of scholastic thought–both philosophical and theological–regarding the nature of poverty and its connection with Christian perfection and religious life.

C. The Conceptual Foundation of Hervaeus's Treatise

Hervaeus divides his work into three questions. The first treats the relation of poverty to perfection. The second treats the relation of the opposite of poverty to perfection. The third applies the results of the first two questions to the issue at hand: the poverty of Christ and the apostles. Hervaeus offers nuanced and extensive analysis of a number of themes. However, two conceptual issues are central to his work and are worth a brief discussion here.

---

ordinis praedicatorum medii aevi, 2.242, N. 1916 for a listing of works by Hervaeus. Roensch gives the most extensive biographical sketch of Hervaeus available in English. Additional biographical and bibliographical sources can be found in the works by B. Hauréau and A. de Guimarães that are listed in the bibliography.

[30] "Nulli prorsus theologorum inferior, metaphysicus summus, dialecticus et terminista subtilis, naturalis profundissimus, acerrimus disputator. Qui enim sequitur, semper incuriosus et invincibilis erit." Cited in Cyril Vollert, *The Doctrine of Hervaeus Natalis on Primitive Justice and Original Sin*, 2.

[31] Glorieux, *Répertoire*, 199.

[32] A brief discussion of Hervaeus's treatise on poverty can be found in Ulrich Horst, *Evangelische Armut und Kirche: Thomas von Aquin und die Armutskontroversen des 13. und beginnenden 14. Jahrunderts*, 201-207.

[33] See Lambert, "The Franciscan Crisis under John XXII," 135, and Maier, "Annotazioni autografe di Giovanni XXII in codici Vaticani," 317-333. See also the work by Tóth listed in the bibliography.

The first issue has to do with Hervaeus's conceptualization of poverty. Following Aquinas and a much older tradition, Hervaeus distinguishes between poverty as a disposition of the mind (*praeparatio animi*) and poverty as an exterior effect (*exterior effectus*). Taken as a disposition of the mind, poverty signifies: "an inclination of the mind to renounce temporal things so far as they are impediments to charity."[34] In this sense, poverty is essential to human perfection, since it is a necessary expression of charity in our dealings with temporal things. However, this disposition of the mind bears no particular relation to the ownership or use of goods, since all people can and indeed are expected to exercise this disposition regardless of their condition or station in life.

On the other hand, poverty taken as an exterior effect[35] refers to a lack of temporal goods either in terms of their ownership and/or their use.[36] The reader should note the ways in which this conceptualization of poverty differs from more modern conceptions. In other words, we typically conceive of poverty in terms of a particular "standard of living" (e.g., mere subsistence contrasted with some socially defined minimum) or in terms of "inequality," that is, the degree to which poor people have less than others. Medieval thinkers, to my knowledge, never formally characterized poverty in terms of "inequality." Our approach to poverty in terms of "standard of living" is roughly analogous to medieval approaches to poverty in terms of the use of goods.[37] By way of contrast, we moderns do not conceptualize poverty formally in terms of the "possession of goods." Yet, the distinction between "possession" and "use" was crucial to medieval thinkers because many of the religious orders that vowed poverty in terms of a "lack of personal ownership of goods" were in fact quite wealthy. Their members often enjoyed a standard of living far superior to the ordinary poor of the day. The distinction between "use" and "possession" gained a special

---

[34] "Inclinatio mentis ad abdicationem rerum temporalium in quantum sunt impeditiva caritatis." See Hervaeus, page 28 below. Cf. Aquinas, *Summa theologiae* II-II.184.7.ad 1.

[35] Aquinas employs the phrase "renunciation of all personal belongings...in act" ("abraenuntio propriarum...in actu"), *Summa theologiae* II-II.184.7.ad 1.

[36] See Hervaeus, page 28 below.

[37] Of course, I am focusing on conceptualizing poverty principally in the economic domain. Medieval conceptions of poverty are not limited to this domain any more than are some modern conceptualizations. For example, St. Francis named his order the Friars Minor to emphasize its identity with the *minores*, the lower classes, and the marginalized. For him, poverty signified powerlessness and social disaffiliation/marginalization, not just economic deprivation.

significance for the Franciscans, since they claimed to renounce common as well as personal ownership of all the things they used, and indeed they faced ongoing criticism as to whether this was a defensible position, at least in relation to civil law.

At first glance, Hervaeus's second question seems to have a rather odd formulation: how the opposite of poverty is related to perfection. However, the formulation makes sense given that poverty can be defined in terms of the use and/or ownership of goods, and also that wealth can have more than one meaning. Hervaeus holds that people can experience something other than poverty either in terms of their use of goods, or the ownership of goods, or both. These ways of experiencing poverty can exist independently of each other. In particular, individual religious might be poor in so far as they lack personal ownership of goods, but they might not be poor in terms of their use of goods, or "standard of living."

Also, "wealth" can be taken as something contrary to poverty or as its opposite. For example, one of the objections Hervaeus considers is that having things necessary for sustaining life is the first degree of wealth.[38] Considered in this sense, wealth is the opposite of poverty: anyone who is not poor is wealthy in some sense. However, Hervaeus views this same condition as a mid-point between unqualified wealth and unqualified poverty.[39] In this sense, wealth is something that is contrary to poverty (as red is a color contrary to grey). That is, people are not necessarily wealthy even though they are not poor. Needless to say, both poverty and wealth are complex notions for Hervaeus and the medieval thinkers generally. It is often important to note shifts in the senses of these terms in order carefully and accurately to follow Hervaeus's arguments.

The second conceptual issue concerns the distinction between the use of things, on the one hand, and the right to ownership of or dominion over things, on the other hand. First, Hervaeus distinguishes between the power over something in fact (*posse facti*) and the licit power over something.[40] The former refers to the mere ability to act on or affect something. Such power occurs any time we act on, affect, or use something in some way. This sort of use need not be licit or just; it bears no essential connection to right, dominion, and ownership. By way of contrast, right, dominion, and ownership (which Hervaeus takes to be the same in reality [*in re*]) "signify

---

[38] See Hervaeus, page 79 below.

[39] See Hervaeus, page 34 below. Later, at page 86 below, Hervaeus asserts that, strictly speaking, the person who has the necessities of life is neither properly wealthy or poor.

[40] See Hervaeus, beginning at page 40 below.

nothing other than the power over something by which one is able licitly to use the thing or to transfer it–either in giving it away, or selling it, or in some other manner."[41]

Conversely, whenever someone licitly uses something, he or she has some sort of right to the thing–if only to its use (e.g., the person who rents a house has only a right to the use of the house but not to the house itself).[42] This analysis forms the backbone of his attack on the "absolute" poverty of Christ and the apostles. The attack has two prongs. The first is directed toward things not consumed in immediate use such as houses, clothes, utensils, and so forth. Even if Christ and the apostles did not own such things personally or in common, they still had a right to use them.[43] This prong is not necessarily fatal to the doctrine, since this kind of right would be qualified; it obviously does not constitute dominion over something in the full sense.

The second, and more deadly, prong aims at things consumed immediately in use, such as food, beverages, and money,[44] since when these things licitly come into a person's possession to be immediately consumed, the person must have dominion over them. Hervaeus rejects the idea that these things might belong only to God and not to the person who uses them. He affirms the traditional view that someone who transfers such things to another loses dominion over the goods when they are being consumed. Taken together, both prongs of the argument seek to establish the following claims. First, Christ and the apostles had at least a common right to things which they did not immediately consume. Secondly, they had full

[41] "Nichil enim aliud dicunt quam habere potestatem in aliqua re per quam possit licite re aliqua uti vel rem aliquam alienare, et hoc vel per donationem vel per venditionem vel per quemcumque alium modum." See Hervaeus, page 40 below.

[42] While Hervaeus regards dominion, right and ownership as the same in reality, he nevertheless notes a difference among them. "Dominion seems rather to signify power itself, while right seems rather to signify the circumstance of licit use. But, in fact, ownership signifies the thing to which someone has a right, where the thing does not belong to someone else." ("dominium magis videtur importare ipsum posse, sed ius magis videtur importare circumstantiam liciti; proprietas vero importat rem in qua quis habet ius, non esse alienum ab eo"). See page 40 below for this text. Consequently, he contrasts the right to use something with a right to the thing itself so that a person can have a right to use something without having a right to the thing itself. He never makes this distinction regarding dominion (which seems conceptually possible given that dominion refers to the licit power over something) or ownership (which is not conceptually possible given the meaning of ownership).

[43] See Hervaeus, page 98 below.

[44] See Hervaeus, beginning at page 98 below.

dominion over the things which they did immediately consume.

The second prong of Hervaeus's argument cuts directly to the heart of the Franciscans' claim that they enjoyed a *simplex usus facti* of things which was separable from right, dominion, and ownership. The term was introduced by Nicholas III in *Exiit qui seminat* where he distinguished it from ownership (*proprietas*), possession (*possessio*), usufruct (*ususfructus*), and the right of using something (*ius utendi*). For Nicholas III, *simplex usus facti* is the only legitimate means of having things which cannot be renounced by those taking a vow of poverty, since one must use things in order to stay alive. However, *simplex usus facti* gives the user of the thing no rights to it.[45] There is no clear consensus on how the term should be translated in English. Lambert leaves it untranslated. Moorman renders it as "simple use in fact"[46] while Douie[47] and Leff[48] offer the literal translation "simple use of fact." Huber suggests "simple use of a thing consumed."[49] Further, and more significantly, some have argued that the term has two different meanings.[50]

Hervaeus seems to interpret the difference between *usus facti* and the right to use something (*ius in uso*) in light of his distinction between *posse/potestas facti* and *posse/potestas licite*. *Posse facti* is exercised when someone uses something in fact (*uti de facto*) independently of whether the use is licit.[51] Hence, *usus facti* is distinguished from the right to use something (*ius in uso*).[52] Thus, although Hervaeus never explicitly identifies *usus facti* with using something *de facto*, it seems that *usus facti* can be understood as *usus de facto* and thus rendered as "use [of something] in fact."

Of course, the translation "use of fact" is literally faithful to the genitive construction of *facti*, but it is not clear what "use of fact" means. In English,

---

[45] *Exiit qui seminat* (*CIC* II.1113).

[46] *History of the Franciscan Order*, 180.

[47] *The Nature and the Effect of the Heresy of the Fraticelli*, 159.

[48] *Heresy in the Later Middle Ages*, I.90.

[49] *A Documented History of the Franciscan Order: 1182-1517*, 227.

[50] See Ockham, *Opus nonaginta dierum* 4 (1.303) and 6 (1.364-367) as well as Huber, 231. Cf. Marino Damiata, *Guglielmo d'Ockham: Povertà e potere*, 1.425-436 for a discussion of the notion of *simplex usus facti*, especially in Ockham.

[51] See Hervaeus, beginning at page 40 below for the texts discussed in this section. Hervaeus does not explicitly describe *simplex usus facti* as *posse facti*.

[52] Hervaeus employs this phrase and, at times, *usus iuris* rather than *ius utendi*. (These latter terms seem to be equivalent. See, P. Bulsano, *Expositio regulae fratrum minorum*, 377.) In the section under discussion, Hervaeus does contrast *posse facti* with *posse iuris*.

the phrase "use of x" suggests that x is the object used. So, too, in the Latin one would say *usus pecuniae* where the genitive *pecuniae* refers to the object, money, that is used. The phrase *usus facti* parallels the phrase *usus iuris*. Moorman renders the phrase *usus iuris* as "use of right." If one uses something because one has a right to it, one might be said to use the right. In this sense, *usus iuris* could mean the "use of a right." But a right is not something that is used, even though, as we saw above, Hervaeus describes a right as a power. In any event, we typically say "use of something by right" or "use of something with a right" rather than "use of right." However, if we construe *usus iuris* as the use of [a] right, then to what does *facti* refer as the object of a simple use? Huber's suggestion that *facti* refers to a consumable thing is plausible, although perhaps too narrow, since the Franciscans did not use only consumable things.

It is not completely clear what sorts of things are used in *usus facti*. In contrast to Huber, Ockham, as noted below, does not seem to restrict these things to consumables. Bulsano, following *Exiit qui seminat*, notes that *usus facti* concerns things used for personal subsistence, things which a living person cannot renounce. Hence, if *facti* refers to what is used in *simplex usus*, then *facti* might refer to consumables, subsistence goods, or anything whatever. Nevertheless, the contrast between use of right and simple use of something (regardless of what the something might be) seems obscure, since in the former case we have two uses, one of the right and the other of the thing, and in the latter only the use of the thing. This distinction seems rather different from Hervaeus's distinction between a simple use, which is indifferent to a right, and a licit use, which is a right. Hence, *facti* and *iuris* refer not to the things used, but rather to the "moral warrant," if any, with which they are used. I think that Hervaeus's distinction is more clearly brought out by translating *usus facti* as "use [of something] in fact," thereby contrasting it with use by/with a right (*usus iuris*) or a right to use something (*ius utendi*), even though this translation does invoke a more legalistic framework than Hervaeus might have intended.[53]

William of Ockham argued that John XXII had understood *usus facti* in this first sense. As Ockham notes, *usus facti* can be understood as an act of using something (*actus utendi*) when, for example, one eats, drinks, writes,

---

[53] It is perhaps worth noting that Hervaeus makes no explicit reference to civil law in his treatise. By way of contrast, the Dominicans, represented in the third section of Vat. Lat. 3740, and Bonagratia of Bergamo, in his *De paupertate Christi et apostolorum*, make numerous and explicit references to civil law in their analyses of the issues under discussion. My own sense is that Hervaeus formulates his position in terms of philosophical and conceptual, rather than legal, analysis.

clothes oneself, reads a book, and so forth. Ockham quotes a text from John XXII's bull, *Quia vir reprobus,* in which the pope maintains that *usus facti* refers to an individual's use of something which cannot be said of, or transferred to, another. For example, Peter's act of eating food cannot be predicated of anyone else, nor can it be transferred to anyone else. As Ockham notes, *facti* is added to *simplex usus* to distinguish this use from *ius utendi*–the right to use something that belongs to another.[54] Ockham's analysis certainly suggests the distinction between use *de facto* and use *de iure*. It provides further support for translating *facti* as "in fact" rather than "of fact," since the latter phrase appears to focus on the objects used in *simplex usus*. Yet, these objects *per se* are not the basis for Ockham's distinction between *usus facti* and *usus iuris*.

Ockham's analysis also suggests another rendering of *simplex usus facti* which is less legalistic than "simple use in fact." Given Ockham's identification of *usus facti* with *actus utendi*, we can understand *simplex usus facti* as a simple use of action: the simple use of something in actions such as eating, drinking, writing, clothing oneself, etc. Hervaeus himself implicitly seems to understand *usus facti* in this way. He initially identifies *potestas facti* with *potestas executionis* (power of action).[55] Later, he identifies *potestas executionis* (power of action) with a *potestas utendi de facto* (a power of using something in fact).[56] While I retain "simple use of something in fact" as the translation of *simplex usus facti*, the meaning of this first sense of the phrase is properly understood as "simple use of action" or "simple use of something in action."

Ockham argues that this first sense of *usus facti* differs from Nicholas III's meaning of the term. According to Ockham, Nicholas III did not simply construe *usus facti* as a mere act of using something (*actus utendi*) but as the power licitly to use something which does not necessarily carry a right allowing the user to claim the good in litigation.[57] Nicholas allowed the Franciscans only this kind of use of things. The standard Franciscan

---

[54] *Opus nonaginta dierum* 2 (1.302-3).

[55] See Hervaeus, at page 40 below.

[56] See Hervaeus, at page 46 below.

[57] *Opus nonaginta dierum* 6 (1.368). Lambert (*Franciscan Poverty* 144) describes *simplex usus facti* as "a license to use certain goods, revocable at the will of the conceder." Huber, 231, gives a somewhat different reading of the two senses of *usus facti*. According to him, "Nicholas III referred to things for which use and ownership can be separated and with respect to which the Franciscans had no civil rights. John XXII, however, referred to consumable things at the moment they are consumed and at which use can not be separated from ownership."

analysis contended that this *usus facti* was the kind of use enjoyed by slaves and children.[58] The crucial point remains that Nicholas III posited a licit use of things which was separable from any right to the things themselves. By way of contrast, as we have seen, Hervaeus virtually defines the "licit use" of something as a "right to" the thing. Although Bonaventure never employs the term *usus facti*,[59] Bulsano presents an interesting text from Bonaventure's *Commentary on St. Francis's Rule* of 1223 which clarifies the Franciscan understanding of the difference between *usus facti* and *usus iuris*. Bonaventure writes:

> The use of things is twofold. Some people use things according to personal authority, as does a master. Some [use things] by the authority of another, as does a slave. For the law says that the clothes which the slave uses belong to the *peculium* of the master. Elsewhere, the law says that what is acquired by the slave, is acquired by the master. In regard to the use of those things which people use by their own authority, the use of such things does not differ from dominion over them. But use differs from dominion in regard to other things [used by another's authority]. Since the Friars Minor have been made servile for the sake of Christ, they use things which they consume in use, but nevertheless they have no dominion over them. In this way, they imitate the Lord who ate food which belonged to others, continuously seeking shelter in other people's homes.[60]

Hence, *usus facti* concerns the use of things held by (and, hence, which can be withdrawn by) others while they are being used. Although one may translate this second sense of *usus facti* as "use in fact," I think that a better translation would be "simple use of what is permitted" (with the understanding that the permission carries no rights). This kind of use would then

[58] For the argument, see Hervaeus, p. 37 below.

[59] In the *Apologia pauperum* XI.5 (Quaracchi VIII.312), Bonaventure refers only to *simplex usus* which Nicholas III divides into *ius utendi* and *simplex usus facti*.

[60] "Duplex est usus rerum. Quidam enim utuntur rebus auctoritate propria, ut domini; quidam aliena, ut servi; quia, ut dicit lex, vestis, qua utitur servus, est de peculio domini, et alibi dicit lex quod res, quae servo acquiritur, domino acquiritur. In usu ergo illorum, qui sua auctoritate utuntur rebus huiusmodi non differt usus a dominio; in usu autem aliorum differt. Quia ergo Fratres Minores pro Christo serviles effecti sunt, utuntur rebus quas usu consumunt, nec tamen eis dominantur; et in hoc ipsum Dominum imitatur, qui cibo vescebatur alieno in alienis domibus continue hospitando." Bonaventure, *Expositio super regulam fratrum minorum* 6 (Quarrachi VIII.422), quoted in Bulsano, *Expositio regulae fratrum minorum*, 379.

contrast with *usus iuris*, which is the right to use or the use of things by one's own authority (even when the ownership of the thing still remains in another's hands). Of course, the focus here is not so much on the things used, but the authority by which they are used. As I noted above, Hervaeus and John XXII completely dismissed the possibility of a licit use of things for which there is no accompanying right to use the thing. The Franciscans and, apparently, Nicholas III wanted to posit such licit use of things. The reader's assessment of Hervaeus's views on this matter will have much to do with his or her acceptance of Hervaeus's (and hence the pope's) critique of the Franciscan doctrine of the poverty of Christ and the apostles and, perforce, the nature of the poverty which the Franciscans sought to imitate.

D. HERVAEUS AND ST. THOMAS AQUINAS

As I mentioned earlier, Hervaeus viewed himself as a defender and loyal follower of St. Thomas. This allegiance to Aquinas is evident in the overall approach which Hervaeus takes in discussing poverty. Indeed, his discussion on the relationship of poverty to the perfection of religious orders adheres very closely to that of Aquinas (*Summa theologiae* II-II.188.7). Actual poverty, or poverty as an exterior effect, is only a means to perfection. The relationship between poverty and perfection in religious life depends on the ends of the religious order in question. Consequently, as Aquinas writes, greater poverty in a religious order does not imply greater perfection. However, it would be a mistake to think that Hervaeus merely imitates Aquinas.

In the first place, the only definition of poverty given by Aquinas, at least to my knowledge, occurs in the *Summa theologiae*: "poverty is the privation of all property."[61] Although questions about the relationship between poverty, ownership of things, and their use constantly surface in Aquinas's writings, Aquinas himself never formally defines poverty with reference to the use of goods. The reason, in part, may be that the Dominican practice of poverty did not force the distinction between use and ownership of goods as sharply as did the Franciscan practice of poverty. Whatever the reason, Hervaeus's definition of poverty as the lack of things in terms of using them and/or in terms of a right to them gives Hervaeus's treatment of poverty considerably more formal, conceptual depth than Aquinas's definition of poverty. Consequently, Hervaeus is able to treat a variety of issues regarding poverty in a far more formal and systematic manner than did Aquinas.[62]

---

[61] "privatio omnino facultatibus." *Summa theologiae* II-II.188.7.

[62] For example, one can compare Thomas's discussion of the differing types of

In the second place, I do not believe that Aquinas offered a single and consistent treatment of poverty over the course of his career.[63] Two earlier "polemical" works from 1256 and 1269 respectively–the *Contra impugnantes dei religionem et cultum* (more commonly cited as *Contra impugnantes*) and the *Contra pestiferam doctrinam retrahentium homines a religionis ingressu* (or, *Contra retrahentes*)–offer a defense of mendicant poverty which seems very close to Bonaventure's defense. For example, the *Contra impugnantes* is similar in organization and content to Bonaventure's *Quaestio de paupertate*.[64] Both works were written to counter the attack on the mendicants launched by William of St. Amour. Two significant differences between Aquinas's polemical works and the treatment of poverty in *Summa theologiae* II-II.188.7 are worth noting.

First, Aquinas's view in the *Summa theologiae* that the perfection of poverty is dictated by the ends of a particular religious order implies that the lack of common possessions does not of itself produce greater perfection for an order. Indeed such a lack would undermine the perfection of an order if it thwarted the realization of its ends. Yet, in both the *Contra impugnantes* and the *Contra retrahentes*, Aquinas seems to hold a quite different view. For example, in the *Contra retrahentes*, he writes that "Among those who have followed the highest perfection, there will be no possessions....Thus if there is a congregation in which everyone tends to greater perfection, it is useful that they do not have common possessions."[65]

Second, in the *Contra retrahentes* Aquinas rejects as "altogether frivolous" the objection that "It is impossible that anyone possesses nothing personally or in common, since it is necessary that they eat, drink and be clothed. They cannot do this if they have nothing."[66] His retort: "The things

---

poverty for religious orders (or, institutes) in the *Summa theologiae* II-II.188.7 with Hervaeus's discussion beginning at page 96 below.

[63] For a discussion of Aquinas's analysis of poverty, see my articles listed in the bibliography. Also, see the works by Horst and Jan van den Eijnden for a critical discussion of all of Aquinas's major writings on poverty.

[64] *De perfectione evangelicae* II.1 (Quaracchi V.124-34).

[65] "Unde et apud illos qui illam summam perfectionem sectabantur, possessiones non erant...Unde si qua sit congregatio, in qua omnes ad maiorem perfectionem tendant, expedit eis communes possessiones non habere." *Contra retrahentes* 16,ad 1 (Leonine XLI.C73.10-1; 25-7). Cf. *Contra impugnantes Dei* 2.5(6).resp. (Leonine XLI.A99.474-4, A99,500-3, A100,519-21).

[66] "Hoc esse impossibile quod aliquis nihil in communi vel proprio possideat; quia necesse est quod comedant et bibant et induantur; quod facere non possunt, si nihil haberent" (*Contra retrahentes* XIV.obj. 9. (Leonine XLI.C68.92-6)).

which religious use to sustain their life are not theirs in terms of the ownership of one who has dominion, but these things are dispensed for the use of their necessities by those who have dominion over them, whoever they might be."[67] Since this retort is made to those who deny that people can possess nothing in common, it seems as if Aquinas is arguing that the licit use of goods can be separated from a right to them, both personally and in common. In any event, Aquinas's conceptual analysis of poverty in the polemical works is, at times, frustratingly unresolved. I have argued elsewhere that Hervaeus's treatment of poverty is at odds with Aquinas's treatment of poverty in the polemical works in a far more explicit and formal manner than is St. Thomas's own treatment of poverty in the *Summa theologiae*.[68]

E. TEXT AND TRANSLATION

The version of Hervaeus's text which Sikes termed "official" is found in a fourteenth-century Vatican manuscript (Vat. Lat. 3740, ff. 168^r-200^v).[69] The manuscript, divided into five parts, contains a set of documents relating to the question about the poverty of Christ and the apostles.[70] The first part contains the replies of various Franciscans. The second part, which I have translated in the appendix, contains a scribe's summary of these replies and contributions made by other Franciscans. The third contains the replies of fourteen cardinals who denied the Franciscan position.[71] The fourth con-

---

[67] "Ea quibus utuntur religiosi ad sustentationem vitae, non sunt eorum quantum ad proprietatem dominii, sed dispensantur ad usum necessitatis eorum ab his qui harum rerum dominium habent, quicumque sint illi" (*Contra retrahentes* XVI.ad 9 (Leonine XLI.C74.158-63)).

[68] See John D. Jones, "St Thomas Aquinas and the Defense of Mendicant Poverty," 189.

[69] In completing his edition of Hervaeus's work, Sikes also used two fifteenth-century copies (Rome, MS Chigi, A. VII. 222 and Venice, Bibliotheca Marciana, Lat. 142) and a fourteenth-century Parisian manuscript, Bibliothèque Mazarine, 3490 (1013)). Kerry Spiers, "A Significant Manuscript of Poverty Treatises by Hervaeus Natalis, O.P. and Pierre Roger, O.S.B., (Pope Clement VI)," discusses an additional manuscript of Hervaeus's treatise that was not available to Sikes, Vat. Lat. 4869, and its relation to other copies of the treatise.

[70] See Spiers, "Four Medieval Manuscripts on Evangelical Poverty," 330-342 for detailed description of the manuscript, particularly the listing of the complete contents of Vat. Lat. 3470.

[71] The second and third parts of the manuscript are published in Felice Tocco, *La quistione della povertà nel secolo XIV*, 51-87 and 88-173.

tains the views of various bishops who also denied the Franciscan view. The fifth, in which Hervaeus's text is found, contains replies of five regular clergy and others who also denied the Franciscan position.

I have tried to provide a fairly direct, rather than a highly idiomatic, translation of the Latin text. While this makes the English a bit cumbersome in places, I hope that it captures Hervaeus's analysis and language in a precise and appropriately literal manner. I have dealt with particular issues about the translation in footnotes. Page numbers from Sikes's edition are placed in double braces, $\langle\langle \rangle\rangle$, while line numbers from it are placed in single braces, $\langle\rangle$. In addition to the secondary literature cited in this volume, the bibliography contains a listing of selected primary and secondary sources relevant to the controversies over mendicant poverty. The books by Ulrich Horst, M.D. Lambert, and Odd Langholm, as well as the volume on Olivi edited by J. Schlageter, contain extensive bibliographies.

Sikes italicized passages that were quoted by Hervaeus; Tocco placed in quotes or italics passages that were quoted by the Franciscans. I have placed all such material in quotation marks. The reader should note two things. First, medieval authors frequently did not quote patristic or Scripture sources with the exactitude we expect when quoting material. They might alter word order, change case endings, or conflate texts without indication (where we use ellipsis marks). Of course, many of these changes are minor and do not affect the basic sense of the material quoted. Second, we do not always know exactly what sources medieval authors used for their material. Quoted texts may not conform with the original sources which are available to us, because the citations were drawn from other sources (e.g., the works of Bonaventure or St. Thomas, especially his *Catena aurea*). I have provided notes only for substantive differences between material quoted by Hervaeus and the Franciscans, on the one hand, and the sources available to us, on the other hand.

Compared with literature on the Franciscan tradition, scholarly literature on poverty in the Dominican tradition is scant, especially in English. Moreover, apart from the translations of Aquinas's works on poverty, there are no other significant Dominican texts on poverty that have been translated into English. The present volume, hopefully, will help to fill this lacuna in a modest way.

Hervaeus Natalis

The Poverty of Christ
and the Apostles

(Liber de paupertate Christi
et apostolorum)

The Poverty of Christ and the Apostles

Our ⟨⟨223⟩⟩ inquiry aims to clarify whether it is heretical to assert that Christ and the apostles had[1] none of the temporal things which come into use in human life in regard to ownership of and dominion over them.[2] For, not only do some people say that this assertion is not heretical, ⟨5⟩ they even say that it is true, namely, that Christ and the apostles had no owner-ship and dominion in the aforementioned manner, personally or in com-mon. Their arguments are based especially on the following: whatever pertains to the perfection of human life was in Christ and in the apostles in the most eminent manner. They say that the poverty of those who have nothing in terms of dominion or ownership, personally or in common, ⟨10⟩ pertains to this perfection.

In response to objections that Christ had a purse (as is evident in John 13),[3] and that "The disciples went into the city to buy food" (John 4),[4] and so forth, they say that what is meant is that Christ and the apostles had

---

[1] Variations of the phrase *habere temporalia* abound in this work. "To possess" is a more facile way to translate *habere* than "to have": "possess temporal things" rather than "have temporal things." However in English, "possess" connotes some form of ownership. Yet, what Hervaeus and his contemporaries are disputing is whether and to what extent the use of things is connected with ownership of them. Consequently, even though "to have" is a less felicitous translation than "to possess," I have used it throughout the translation. On occasion, I have used "held" rather than "had," since phrases such as "things were held" read more smoothly than "things were had."

[2] Variations of the phrase "habere temporalia quantum ad proprietatem et dominium" occur very frequently in this work. The literal translation: "have temporal things in regard to ownership and dominion" is incomplete in English, as one requires "have things in terms of ownership of and dominion over them." In English, we would probably say "have ownership of and dominion over things." However, for Hervaeus the accent is on having things, while dominion and ownership (as well as right and use) are ways of having things. Consequently, I have employed the translation: "to have things in regard to the ownership of and dominion over them." Similar considerations apply to "use" and "right."

Later, see page 42 below, Hervaeus distinguishes between a right to the use of something (*ius in usu rei*) and a right to a thing [itself] (*ius in [ipsa] re*). These latter rights seem to be the two ways in which someone can generally have a right to something.

[3] John 13:29.

[4] John 4:8.

such things, although not in regard to dominion over and ownership of them, but merely with respect to a simple use of them in fact. ⟨15⟩ Accordingly, it seems that our inquiry should be divided into three parts. The first treats the relation of poverty to the perfection of human life. The second considers how the opposite of poverty is related to this same perfection. The third part proceeds to the main question.[5]

---

[5] That is, whether the thesis under investigation is heretical.

[QUESTION 1–THE RELATION OF POVERTY TO PERFECTION][6]

In regard to the first part, there are two questions. The first is whether poverty ⟨20⟩ pertains essentially to the perfection of life. The second is whether poverty at least pertains instrumentally to the perfection of life.

[ARTICLE 1–WHETHER POVERTY PERTAINS ESSENTIALLY TO PERFECTION]

Let us proceed to the first article where it is argued that poverty pertains essentially to the perfection of human life.

1.   That which constitutes the state of perfection pertains to perfection essentially. ⟨25⟩ Poverty is something of this sort.[7] Therefore, etc. The major premise is evident, so it seems, since it appears that the state of perfection cannot be constituted except by what pertains to the being of perfection. The minor premise is readily apparent from the fact that the religious state, which is a state of perfection, is constituted by these three vows: obedience, chastity, and poverty.

2.   Just as the religious state is constituted ⟨30⟩ by the vows of obedience and chastity, so it is constituted by the vow of poverty. ⟨⟨224⟩⟩ Obedience and chastity pertain essentially to perfection. Therefore, etc.[8]

3.   Whatever is contained in the moral teaching of Christ seems to be a certain perfection or something that pertains to the essence of perfection. Poverty is something of this sort. ⟨5⟩ Therefore, etc. The major premise is evident, since Christ's instruction and teaching always pertained to the perfection of life. The minor premise is evident in light of Luke 14: "Unless a person renounces all his possessions, he can not be my disciple."[9]

4.   Any virtuous good pertains to perfection essentially. Voluntary poverty, which we are discussing, is ⟨10⟩ something of this sort. Therefore, etc. The proof of the major premise: a virtuous good pertains to virtue. Virtue

---

[6]   Although Hervaeus divides his work into questions and articles, no formal divisions are present in the text. I have made these divisions to provide a clearer organization to the work.

[7]   This marks the first of many occurrences of the following schematized argument form: A is B, C is *huiusmodi* (an instance of A). Therefore, etc. Hervaeus uses *huiusmodi* rather than repeat A. I have consistently translated *huiusmodi* as "something of this sort."

[8]   See the appendix, page 125 below, for the discussion of this argument.

[9]   Luke 14:33 (Sikes cites Luke 14:26).

is essentially perfection. Therefore, etc. The minor is evident as well, since a voluntary good refers to the goods that are in our power. Such goods are virtuous. As is self-evident, voluntary poverty is something of this sort. Therefore, etc.

5.   The ⟨15⟩ object of a vow seems to pertain to perfection essentially. Poverty is something of this sort, since it is the object of the third vow pertaining to religion. Therefore, etc.

6.   Blessedness is essentially perfection. Poverty is something of this sort. Therefore, etc. The major premise is self-evident. The minor premise is evident as well, ⟨20⟩ for it is written in Matthew 5, "Blessed are the poor in spirit," and so forth.[10]

ON THE CONTRARY: 1. Whatever is formally a privation is neither essentially perfection nor a part of perfection. Poverty is something of this sort. Therefore, etc. The major premise is evident, since privation cannot be something formally positive nor a part of it. However, every perfection formally signifies ⟨25⟩ something positive. Therefore, etc. The minor also is evident, since poverty formally signifies a lack of wealth.

2.   Perfection cannot exist without that which pertains to the essence of perfection. But even consummate perfection can exist without poverty. Therefore, etc. The major premise is evident, since nothing can exist without that which pertains to its essence. ⟨30⟩ The minor also is evident, since both Abraham[11] and David[12] were most perfect, and yet they had great wealth, which is the opposite of poverty.

RESPONSE: Three points must be treated to clarify this question. The first is to see what essentially constitutes the perfection of human life. The second is to set forth the general meaning of poverty. The third is to reply to the question.

In ⟨⟨225⟩⟩ regard to the first point, it should be noted that the perfection of human life essentially consists in virtuous habits and their acts, since virtuous habits and their acts are formally and essentially the very perfections of human life. We are not speaking of the natural life, which is the ⟨5⟩ soul itself, but of the moral life. We extend moral life to all the habits and acts for which we are responsible. In accordance with virtuous habits and acts, a person is deemed worthy of praise, while their opposite gives rise to blame. We are in some manner the cause of all our virtuous habits. It is somehow within our power to acquire them, since, although certain habits are infused in us, nevertheless ⟨10⟩ in some way we are able

---

[10] Matt. 5:3.

[11] Cf. Gen. 13:2.

[12] Cf. 2 Sam. 8:4ff.

to be their cause, namely, by disposing ourselves to them through a congruous merit. Such habits are also infused in us without our activity, as is evident in the baptism of children. Nevertheless, when we become adults, it
is within our power to conserve or lose these habits through our actions.

In ⟨15⟩ the first book of the *Ethics*,[13] where he says that virtue is what
perfects the one who has it and makes his work good, the Philosopher
makes it evident that the perfection of the moral life essentially consists in
virtuous habits and their acts. He is speaking about that which formally
perfects its possessor, that is to say, how that which is essentially perfection
makes ⟨20⟩ its possessor perfect. Augustine makes the same point evident
when he says, "Virtue is that by which one lives well, which no one uses
wrongly, and by which God acts in us without us."[14] The phrase "which no
one uses wrongly" should be understood in terms of what virtue brings
forth, since nothing is brought forth from virtue except a good act. Yet, in
an objective sense someone can use virtue wrongly, namely, when he considers himself ⟨25⟩ to be virtuous and is proud of it. The phrase "God acts
in us without us" is understood to refer to infused virtue that God is said
to produce in us without us. However, as has been said, this does not mean
that we contribute nothing to such virtue when we dispose ourselves to it
in a congruous manner. Rather, our acts are not a sufficient cause of the
virtue that is infused in us by God, who is its principal cause.

Nevertheless, all ⟨30⟩ virtues–whether theological or moral, whether
pertaining to the intellect or desire–belong formally and essentially to the
perfection of human life as that which is formally and essentially perfection. However, the virtues are not all equal in this regard. For among the
virtues, one pertains to perfection more than another and, in this regard,
one is nobler than another. ⟨⟨226⟩⟩ Charity is foremost among all virtues:
it unites us above all else to the highest good, especially with regard to the
state of merit; all other virtues have been joined in charity and in some way
are virtually and fundamentally contained in it, at least in regard to their
meritorious acts. ⟨5⟩ Charity is the virtue by which we are inclined to love
God above every love of friendship and to love our neighbor for God's sake.
Because of charity, we are inclined to choose and pursue all of the things
that are pleasing to God as well as profitable to ourselves and our neighbor,
especially with regard to salvation. So too, because of charity we are disposed to reject and shun what is contrary to these things.

---

[13] Aristotle, *Nicomachean Ethics* II.5.1106a22.

[14] Often regarded as drawn from texts of Augustine such as *De libero arbitrio* II.19
(*CCSL* 29.271; *PL* 32.268). However, the text is found in Peter of Poitiers, *Sententiarum* IV.2 (*PL* 211.1041). (See also, Thomas Aquinas, *Summa theologiae* I-II.55.4.)

Every ⟨10⟩ virtue is ordered to this end, namely, choosing and pursuing things that are pleasing to God and are advantageous to ourselves and our neighbor, and rejecting what is contrary to these things. In this way, every virtuous inclination, particularly with regard to the performance of acts, is virtually contained in the love of God and neighbor. So, the apostle writes in Romans 13: "Love is the fullness of the law."[15] ⟨15⟩ In speaking about the performance of acts, we refer to interior acts such as choosing and deliberating, and to exterior acts when they are within our power. Thus, the first point is evident concerning what essentially constitutes the perfection of human life: namely, perfection consists, first and principally, in the habit and act of charity as well as, consequently, in the other virtues and their acts that are ⟨20⟩ joined together in charity.

In regard to the second point that pertains to this question–namely, the meaning of poverty in general–it should be noted that poverty can be understood in two ways: first, in terms of a disposition of the mind, and second, in terms of an exterior effect.[16] Considered as ⟨25⟩ a disposition of the mind, poverty signifies an inclination of the mind to renounce temporal things so far as they are impediments to charity in which the perfection of human life essentially consists. In this renunciation, a person should be mentally disposed so that for the sake of acquiring or retaining any temporal thing, he would not consent in any way to something that is ⟨30⟩ contrary to the love of God or neighbor. However, considered as an exterior effect, poverty signifies a lack of temporal things either in regard to right and dominion, or in regard to their use, or in regard to both of them. Further, this lack can be greater or less in so far as things can be completely lacked or lacked to such and such a degree. Nevertheless, in general, all poverty formally signifies ⟨⟨227⟩⟩ a lack or privation [of things] in the degree and manner described.

In regard to the third point, I say that if poverty is considered in the first way–namely, as a disposition of the mind (as has been set forth)–then ⟨5⟩ poverty, so considered, pertains essentially to the perfection of human life. This can be proved by the following argument: whatever pertains essentially to charity, pertains essentially to the perfection of human life. As a disposition of the mind, poverty pertains essentially to charity. There-

---

[15] Rom. 13:10.

[16] The reference to poverty as an exterior effect is somewhat odd. Hervaeus is thinking of this mode of poverty as an expression of voluntary poverty and of the disposition of the mind which he just defined. However, the various ways of lacking things that constitute poverty as an exterior effect need not be connected with voluntary poverty; they would pertain to anyone who is poor in an everyday socio-economic sense, whether "voluntarily" or "involuntarily."

fore, etc. The major premise ⟨10⟩ is evident, since, as was said above, the perfection of human life consists essentially and principally in charity. The minor is proved in two ways. First, the same habit, which inclines the mind to one member of a pair of opposites, causes the mind to withdraw from the other. Charity inclines us to the divine good which is opposed to the love of temporal things in so far as they are impediments to charity. Therefore, ⟨15⟩ charity is the habit through which one is withdrawn from temporal things in so far as they are impediments to charity or the love of the divine. However, to withdraw from temporal goods in this way pertains to poverty as a disposition of the mind. Therefore, etc.

The same minor premise is proved in the second way as follows: each individual, through habit, denies himself what is contrary to that habit. However, ⟨20⟩ temporal goods are contrary to charity in so far as they are impediments to charity. Therefore, each individual, by virtue of the habit of charity, rejects temporal goods in so far as they are impediments to charity. Yet, the habit that inclines one to such a rejection of temporal things is called poverty when considered as a disposition of the mind. Therefore, when considered as a disposition of the mind, poverty pertains essentially to charity.

However, if ⟨25⟩ poverty is to be considered as an exterior effect, then it does not pertain essentially to perfection. This is evident for two reasons. The first is that no privation is something positive nor is it a part of something positive. Yet, perfection signifies something positive, while poverty, considered as an exterior effect, signifies a privation. Therefore poverty, considered as an exterior effect, ⟨30⟩ is neither a perfection nor a part of perfection. The major premise is evident, since no privation is something positive or a part of something positive. The minor also is evident, since, considered as an exterior effect, poverty is a lack of exterior things. Yet, it is the case that perfection is something positive.

The second argument is that whatever pertains essentially to perfection is either in ⟨35⟩ the intellect or in the will or in the sensible appetite. But, considered as an exterior effect, poverty does not exist in any of them subjectively. Therefore, etc. The major premise is evident, since every virtuous habit and the act it elicits is in one of the powers above.[17] But every perfection pertains essentially to such acts and habits. Therefore, etc. The minor also is evident, since poverty, considered as an exterior effect, consists in exterior things, because it is ⟨40⟩ the lack or privation of them.

In ⟨⟨228⟩⟩ opposition to the objections:

1. It must be stated, first, that the major premise is not necessarily true, since the state of perfection signifies not only what is essentially a

---

[17] That is, the intellect, the will, or some sensible appetite.

perfection, but also whatever contributes to perfection by disposing us to it. Thus, what constitutes the ⟨5⟩ state of integral perfection does not necessarily have to be what constitutes integral perfection itself. Or, it can be said that the three vows–obedience, chastity, and poverty–pertain principally to the state of perfection in that they are a disposition of the mind. In this sense, poverty is essentially perfection itself. Or, it can be said that the state of perfection is principally constituted by ⟨10⟩ these three vows–obedience, chastity and poverty–but that it is only secondarily, and not principally, constituted by the objects of the vows. Consequently, considered as an exterior effect, poverty need not be, either essentially or primarily, a perfection or a part of perfection. However, it does pertain[18] to perfection by disposing us to it in a manner that will be discussed below.[19]

2. ⟨15⟩ It is not necessary that everything pertaining to the state of perfection be related in the same way to perfection, since some things pertain to the state of perfection either as perfection itself or as what dispose us to perfection. Further, the things that dispose us to perfection do not dispose us to it in the same way. For, some ⟨20⟩ dispose us in a positive manner, such as works which, considered in themselves and their kind, pertain to virtuous deeds. Others dispose us in a negative manner by removing what holds us back from perfection. Thus, if obedience and chastity pertain to perfection ⟨25⟩ essentially and positively, then it does not necessarily follow because of this that poverty, considered as an exterior effect, pertains to perfection essentially and positively.

However, one should note that when considered as a habit of the mind, chastity signifies what is essentially a virtue. Nevertheless, considered as an exterior effect, it is formally a privation which is the lack of delight in sexual love. However, in this matter there is a difference between poverty and chastity: poverty more properly signifies an ⟨30⟩ exterior effect that consists in the lack of temporal things in the way we have indicated, while chastity more properly signifies an interior inclination to abstain from the pleasures of sexual love. On account of this, chastity is more properly regarded as something positive–that is, a virtue–while poverty is more properly regarded as a privation, namely, the lack of temporal things in the way we have indicated.[20]

3. The ⟨35⟩ major premise is false if considered universally, since Christ's moral teaching and instruction consisted not only of what is essentially perfection but also of what disposes to perfection whether in a

---

[18] Reading *pertineat* for *pertineant*.

[19] See the discussion beginning at page 34 below.

[20] See the appendix, page 125 below, for a discussion of this argument.

negative or positive manner. This will be discussed below.[21]

4. In one sense, something is said to pertain to virtue when ⟨⟨229⟩⟩ it is done through virtue. For example, giving alms pertains to the virtue of mercy. In another sense, shunning something on account of virtue pertains to a virtue. So, shunning temporal things in so far as they are contrary to it pertains to charity, while shunning sexual love and ⟨5⟩ lacking it pertains to chastity. In this way, not only do we call something done on account of virtue a virtuous (that is, positive) good, but we also regard shunning things which naturally impede perfection or virtue to be a virtuous good. The lack of such things is called good in the way that the lack of evil is good. In this way, poverty is called a virtuous good in an objective manner ⟨10⟩ in so far as it is a lack of evil. The reason is that poverty signifies the lack of temporal goods so far as they are impediments to virtue. In other words, it is virtuous not only to pursue what is appropriate to virtue; it also is virtuous to shun what is contrary to virtue.

5. The major premise is not universally true. For, ⟨15⟩ not only can the object of a vow be what is essentially a virtue or perfection, it can also dispose us to virtue, whether positively or negatively. For, a person can obligate himself not only to virtue but also to those things that dispose to virtue.

6. The poor are called blessed because poverty disposes to blessedness and not because poverty, ⟨20⟩ considered as an exterior effect, is essentially blessedness. Put another way: when we call the poor blessed, we are speaking of poverty as a disposition of the mind, which is charity rejecting temporal things for the sake of God, that is, in so far as they are an impediment to charity.

These ⟨25⟩ arguments against the objections prove that poverty, considered as an exterior effect, is not essentially a perfection or a part of perfection. However, they do not demonstrate that that sort of poverty, considered as a disposition of the mind, is not essentially a perfection.

[ARTICLE 2–WHETHER POVERTY PERTAINS TO PERFECTION INSTRUMENTALLY]

Let ⟨30⟩ us proceed to the second [article] and argue that poverty does not pertain to perfection even instrumentally.

1. No privation is an instrument for acquiring or conserving perfection. But poverty, at least when considered as an exterior effect, formally signifies a privation. Therefore, etc. The major premise seems probable, since what is ⟨35⟩ formally not a being is not the cause of anything, so it

---

[21] See the discussion beginning at page 32 below.

seems, and privation formally signifies non-being. Therefore, etc. The minor is evident from what has already been said.

2.   It seems that something cannot be an instrument for acquiring or conserving some perfection if it can exist together with an opposite imperfection. Rather, considered as an exterior effect, poverty ⟨⟨230⟩⟩ can exist with the opposite of charity, since many poor people are subject to such poverty, and they can exist without charity. Therefore, etc.

ON THE CONTRARY: since poverty pertains in some manner to perfection, it pertains either essentially or instrumentally. It does not pertain essentially, ⟨5⟩ as we have proved in discussing poverty considered as an exterior effect. Therefore, it pertains to perfection instrumentally. The minor premise is evident by means of a proof through division. The major[22] is proved because poverty consists in a rejection of temporal things, and the rejection of temporal things pertains to the perfection of human life. Therefore, etc. The major is evident. The minor is also evident, since it is written in Matthew 19: "If you ⟨10⟩ would be perfect, go and sell everything."[23]

RESPONSE: Three points must be treated to clarify this matter. The first concerns the manner in which something can contribute instrumentally or dispositively to the perfection of life. The second involves a continuation and elaboration of our previous discussion concerning poverty considered as an exterior effect. ⟨15⟩ The third involves responding to the question.

With regard to the first point, it should be noted that something can contribute to the perfection of human life instrumentally or dispositively in two ways: positively or by way of privation. For example, something can contribute positively to the perfection of what is brought forth from the earth, as heat and moisture do. ⟨20⟩ Something contributes in a privative manner by removing what is harmful to or impedes perfection, such as what removes spines and nettles, or as the removal or lack of things like them. The removal of these impediments is beneficial for things brought forth from the earth in so far as the power of the seed, once freed from what harms it, can act more perfectly and strongly than when it was impeded.

A similar distinction can be made with regard to the point under discussion: something can contribute in two ways to the perfection of charity which ⟨25⟩ principally constitutes the perfection of human life. Some things contribute positively such as precepts, counsels, admonitions to do good and, briefly, all those things that can lead us to the love of God, our neighbor, and to acts of the other virtues[24] which are joined in this love. On

---

[22] Reading *maior* for *minor*.

[23] Matt. 19:21.

[24] Reading *virtutum* for *virtutem*.

the other hand, some things are said to contribute to charity instrumentally or ⟨30⟩ dispositively, such as what also removes and prohibits us [from charity]. Everyone who denies himself or someone else the things that lead to the opposite of charity can be said to contribute to the charity that constitutes the perfection of human life. ⟨35⟩ These things include evil associations, a very excessive abundance of temporal things and, in short, all things that naturally lead the will to desire evil, or which naturally preoccupy the will to the exclusion of spiritual and divine matters. Thus, the lack of temporal things, in so far as they in some way naturally impede charity, is said to contribute to the charity which constitutes the perfection of human life. This discussion makes the first point evident.

With ⟨⟨231⟩⟩ regard to the second point pertaining to this question, it should be noted, as was said above,[25] that poverty entails a lack of temporal goods either in terms of a right to and dominion over them, or in terms of making use of them, or in terms of both. I make an additional distinction about the lack of temporal goods in terms of ⟨5⟩ right and dominion: the lack of a right to and dominion over such goods can be personal only or personal and common.

The lack of a right to and dominion over things is called personal when an individual lacks a right to temporal things and lack dominion over them as his personal property. This personal lack of a right to and dominion over things is the poverty which pertains to every form of religious life, since no ⟨10⟩ religious can own or have absolute or unqualified dominion over anything. However, it is possible for individual religious to have a right to things and dominion over them in a manner that will be discussed later.[26]

The lack of a common and personal right to and dominion over temporal things occurs when an individual has no right to or dominion over them as his personal property and ⟨15⟩ when he does not belong to a group that has such right or dominion. This situation exists if a group has no right to temporal things personally or in common. Thus, it is evident how poverty is understood in different ways according to the different ways of having temporal things.

Poverty also can be understood in different ways on the basis of the quantity of things held. ⟨20⟩ The greater[27] poverty that exists is the complete lack of temporal things, personally and in common, as well as in terms of right, dominion, and use in fact. Poverty in an unqualified sense

---

[25] See page 28 above.

[26] See the discussions at pages 43 and 48 below.

[27] *Maior paupertas.* The sentence makes more sense with *maxima paupertas*: "greatest poverty."

involves lacking temporal things in terms of right, dominion, and use so that a person lacks what is sufficient for life. ⟨25⟩ This lack can pertain to a community or a person. However, to have temporal things sufficient for life but not more than that–whether in common or personally–constitutes a certain mid-point between what is called unqualified poverty and what is called unqualified wealth. An individual person or a community in this condition should not be called poor or ⟨30⟩ wealthy in an unqualified sense. Thus, in regard to the text, "I will gather everything which is naturally mine,"[28] Basil writes that "If anyone takes what is sufficient for his needs and gives what is superfluous to those in need, then he is neither poor nor wealthy."[29]

Let us turn to the third point by responding to the question whether poverty, considered as an exterior effect, pertains ⟨35⟩ instrumentally to the perfection of human life. I make a distinction regarding how something can be said to pertain instrumentally to perfection. First, something can pertain to perfection as that without which it is simply impossible to have ⟨⟨232⟩⟩ perfection. Second, something can pertain to perfection as that by which someone is more disposed to acquire or conserve perfection. Taken in the first sense, as that without which perfection cannot be attained, ⟨5⟩ no poverty (when considered an exterior effect in any sense) pertains to the perfection of human life, speaking of the personal perfection now under discussion. For, no sort of poverty pertains necessarily to something that can be compatible with the opposite of any sort of poverty. However, the most perfect charity, in which is constituted the perfection of ⟨10⟩ human life, can be compatible with the opposite of any sort of poverty. Therefore, etc.

The major premise is evident, since one member of a pair of opposites cannot be compatible with the other. The minor is proved, since having great wealth (in the sense of full dominion over and use of it) is opposed to any sort of poverty both in regard to the manner of having things and in regard to the quantity of things held. But the perfection of ⟨15⟩ human life, namely, perfect charity, can be compatible with having wealth in this way, as is evident in the cases of Abraham and David in the Old Testament, and blessed Gregory in the New Testament. Therefore, etc.

If poverty is taken as the complete lack of temporal goods in terms of dominion and use, then poverty so considered does not pertain in any manner to the ⟨20⟩ perfection of human life which is possible in the present life. For, what is not compatible with the conservation of the present life does not pertain to the perfection which is possible in the present life. The com-

[28] Luke 12:18.
[29] *Homilia in illud Lucae "Destruam"* (PG 31.275).

plete lack of temporal goods that was previously mentioned is something of this sort. Therefore, etc. The major premise is evident, since the perfection which is possible in the present life ⟨25⟩ presupposes the present life. The minor is also evident, since to lack completely the use of temporal goods–namely, to lack food and clothing–can not be compatible with preserving the present life, and vice versa. Therefore, etc.

However, if poverty is taken as the lack of temporal goods with respect to personal right and dominion, and also if poverty is taken as the lack of excessive wealth in common, and ⟨30⟩ if that through which someone is better disposed to acquire or preserve perfection should be taken to pertain to perfection, then poverty in this sense pertains to the perfection of human life instrumentally, namely, in a privative manner. This is the position we maintained above.

To make this clear, it should be noted that temporal things, especially an abundance of them, naturally move us to an inordinate love of them. So Augustine writes in his letter to Paulinus and Therasia that "Worldly things actually possessed are more loved than those which ⟨⟨233⟩⟩ are desired. For, why did that young man go away sad except that he had great wealth? It is one thing not to wish to acquire what one does not have, and another to renounce what one already has. The former are rejected as something foreign to us; the latter are cut off like a limb."[30] In his commentary on Matthew, Chrysostom says that the possession of wealth kindles a ⟨5⟩ greater flame.[31] Again, wealth also moves us naturally to pride, as the Psalm says: "People boast who trust in their own strength and in their great wealth."[32] Temporal goods, which are held in this way, can engender distraction and the destruction of the mind. The first two [attitudes][33] are impediments to the habit of charity, and at times they are even its ⟨10⟩ destruction. However, the third[34] can impede some acts, specifically, the acts of the contemplative life.

Finally, one should note that having personal wealth and being anxious about it belong to a person's love for himself. Such love naturally turns one away from the love of God. However, having wealth in common belongs

---

[30] *Epistolae* 31.5 (*CCSL* 34(pt1).5; *PL* 33.124).

[31] *Homilia 63 in Matthaeum* 2 (*PG* 58.605).

[32] Ps. 48:7.

[33] Hervaeus's referent is unclear. He is possibly referring to items mentioned in Augustine's text, namely to wish to acquire what one does not have and to not relinquish what one has.

[34] Hervaeus's referent is unclear. He is possibly referring to what is mentioned in Chrysostom's text, namely, to possess great wealth.

more to the ⟨15⟩ love of our neighbor for the sake of God. Having wealth in this way does not naturally impede charity, although it can impede some of its acts. In light of these considerations, we can formulate this principle: the lack of things which naturally impedes charity pertains to the acquisition and preservation of charity both through deprivation, as we have said, and as the means by which one is better disposed to acquire and preserve charity. The lack of ⟨20⟩ personal dominion over temporal things, especially an abundance of them, is something of this sort, since, as has been said, these things naturally impede charity in regard to its habit as well as in regard to some of its acts. Therefore, etc. This discussion makes the third point evident.

In opposition to the objections:

1. It must be stated that the major premise is false. The reason is that, ⟨25⟩ when considered as an exterior effect, poverty does not positively contribute to anything. Nevertheless, in so far as poverty is a lack of what is harmful or an impediment, then, by removing the impediment, poverty makes it possible for virtue to work more perfectly.

2. The major is not universally true, since it is not true except in regard to the total and sufficient cause of perfection. However, poverty is not ⟨30⟩ a sufficient cause of human perfection, since it can coexist with wickedness or human imperfection.

[QUESTION 2–WHETHER THE OPPOSITE OF POVERTY DIMINISHES THE PERFECTION OF HUMAN LIFE]

Next, we will investigate the relation of the opposite of poverty to the perfection of human life: namely, whether the opposite of poverty ⟨35⟩ diminishes the perfection of human life. We will investigate this matter first with regard to ⟨⟨234⟩⟩ personal perfection and, second, with regard to the perfection of a state.

[QUESTION 2A–WHETHER THE OPPOSITE OF POVERTY DIMINISHES PERSONAL PERFECTION]

Since some say that the most perfect poverty requires total renunciation of a right to and dominion over exterior things as well as the renunciation of making provision for the future, except where evident need is pressing, we ⟨5⟩ must investigate three points. The first concerns whether the right to and dominion over temporal things can be separated from their use. The second concerns whether having a right to and dominion over temporal things diminishes personal perfection. The third concerns whether making provision for the future diminishes personal perfection.

[ARTICLE 1–WHETHER THE RIGHT TO AND DOMINION OVER TEMPORAL THINGS CAN BE SEPARATED FROM THEIR USE]

Let ⟨10⟩ us proceed to the first point and argue that the use of temporal things can be separated from the right to and dominion over them.

1. A monk cannot have ownership of or dominion over temporal things. However, he has use of them else he would not be able do eat, drink, or clothe himself, and so forth. The same point seems to apply to ⟨15⟩ a slave and a dependent child who do not have a right to temporal things, even though they have use of them.

It might be said that a monk has a right to temporal things; for although he cannot say that "This is personally mine" of what he eats or drinks, nevertheless he can say that "This is ours."

On ⟨20⟩ the contrary, one does not have a complete right to the things he shares with another. But a monk uses something completely as when he eats a whole piece of bread. Thus, in such use there exists a use of something without right or dominion.[1]

2. A person, who lives by means of what belongs to another person, uses that from which he lives without having dominion ⟨25⟩ over it, since no one has dominion over a thing that belongs to someone else. But it seems that those who live from alms, whether daily or annually, live by means of what belongs to another. Therefore, etc.

3. No person has dominion over the goods that are reckoned to be God's alone. However, the use of those goods that are reckoned to be God's alone ⟨30⟩ has been granted[2] to humans. Thus, in regard to such goods, use is separated from dominion. The major premise is evident, since something over which a person has dominion ought to be reckoned among the person's goods and, consequently, ought not be reckoned among the goods that are God's alone. The minor is proved in two ways. First, the fruits of this earthly paradise are not reckoned among any person's goods, but only among ⟨35⟩ the goods of God alone. Moreover, no one could speak of these fruits, saying that "This is mine" or "This is yours." However, their use was not only granted to humans, it was imposed on them. Therefore, etc. Second, ⟨⟨235⟩⟩ the same minor premise is proved in this way: the manna in the desert was not reckoned among the goods of anyone except of God alone. Yet, its use was granted to the children of Israel. Therefore, etc.

4. The fourth objection is argued chiefly in the following way: we are permitted to take hold of[3] that which ⟨5⟩ is reckoned among the goods to

---

[1]   See the appendix, page 137 below, for the discussion of this argument.

[2]   I have generally translated *concedo* as "grant," although at times I have used "permit" or "allow" when this provides for a smoother translation.

[3]   The term *occupo* has two relevant uses in Hervaeus's work. In one case, one can talk about the mind being inordinately occupied with something (e.g., "tempore indebito mentem inordinate circa talia occuparet") (p. 65 below). In this sense, *occupo* has the sense of being engaged with something or turning one's attention to something. I have translated this use of *occupo* by "occupy."

The other sense of *occupo* denotes a "physical" engagement with something as when one occupies a room. In this sense, *occupo* means to bring something within our reach in order to use it. However, *occupo* does not simply mean "to make use" of something, for the "occupation" of something seems to precede its use. As Hervaeus writes: "it is certain that no one uses such things before taking hold of them" ("Certum est autem quod nullus utitur talibus antequam occupet") (p. 50 below).

It would be simplest to translate *occupo* as "to possess" or "to take possession of"

which no one has rights. Since no one has dominion over a good that does not belong to anyone, this good is not granted to someone except for use. Therefore, the use of such a thing can be separated from dominion over it.[4]

5. In the case of someone who is capable of use and not dominion, ⟨10⟩ use is separated from dominion. Someone can be capable of use and not have dominion. Therefore, etc. The major premise is evident. I prove the minor not only in regard to children and brutes but also with regard to others: namely, people who have the use of reason. For, although a person can make himself unable to have dominion over things by means of a vow, no one can make himself unable to use things, otherwise ⟨15⟩ he would die of hunger and cold. Therefore, etc.

ON THE CONTRARY: anyone who uses something either uses it as his own or as someone else's. If he uses it as his own, he has a right to it, since in this case we can say that "This is mine" [or] "This is yours" in so far as you and I have some right to the thing. If he uses it as someone else's, then he ⟨20⟩ acts unjustly. Consequently, the licit or just use of something is inseparable from dominion over it.

One might say that this argument does not follow: namely, that if someone uses what belongs to another, he acts unjustly. For, using what belongs to another is not unjust unless it is done against the will of the owner, since if the owner grants the use of a thing, then it is not unjust. But this reasoning is not valid ⟨25⟩, since in granting the thing the owner either gives a right to the thing to someone or he does not. If he does, our original conclusion holds: namely, that the use of a thing is not enjoyed without dominion or right. If not, either he [the other person] has some licit power over the thing after the owner grants it which he did not have beforehand, or he does not. If he does, then he has some right to the thing which he did not have before the owner granted it. But this proves our original proposition. If not, then he does not ⟨30⟩ have more licit power to use the thing after the owner's concession than before. However, before the owner's con-

---

as *possidere* and *possessio* were used in one sense in Roman Law: mere physical control over something (cf. J. B. Moyle, *Imperatoris Iustiniani Institutiones*, 332). However, since the English verb "possess" all too readily connotes "ownership" (especially of a personal sort), it does not seem an appropriate translation of *occupo* in this context. Certainly, for Hervaeus, the *occupatio* of a thing is compatible with having a right to it. Indeed, a person's *occupatio* of a thing that does not belong to anyone else, gives the person a right to the thing. Still, "occupying" a thing seems prior to both the use of it and a right to it. Accordingly, I have almost always rendered the second sense of *occupo* as "to take hold of" in the sense that one takes hold of a pencil prior to using it.

[4] See the appendix, pages 137 and 143 below, for related discussions of this argument.

cession, he did not have any licit power over the thing itself or its use, since using something against the will of the owner is not licit. Therefore, the other person does not have any licit power after the thing has been granted. But this is false, since someone has some licit power to use a thing by virtue of the owner's granting it. This is what we call a right to the thing.

RESPONSE: ⟨35⟩ Three points must be treated to clarify this question. The first is to determine what is meant by dominion, right, and ownership with respect to temporal things. The second is to distinguish the different ways of having a right to and dominion over things. The third is to respond to the question.

With ⟨40⟩ regard to the first point, it should be noted that the words "dominion," "right," and "ownership" signify the same thing in reality. They signify nothing other than ⟨⟨236⟩⟩ the power over something by which one is able licitly to use a thing or transfer it—either in giving it away, selling it, or in some other manner. Thus, it should be noted that there are two powers by which someone can do something with a thing. First, there ⟨5⟩ is power in fact [*potestas facti*] or power of action. For example, a person can in fact eat food or drink a beverage whether or not it is his in regard to use and dominion. The other power a person may appropriately have over something is that by which he can not only in fact use or transfer a thing, but also can licitly use and transfer it as his own. ⟨10⟩ We call this power the power of right.

It is evident that this is the case, since a person does not have dealings with the things that come into use in human life except by means of these two powers: namely, power in fact (by which a person can use something in fact, whether licitly or not) or the power to use things licitly. Power only in fact does not signify the power of right to a thing. Therefore, the power to use something licitly signifies the power of right, or right itself. ⟨15⟩ The major premise is evident, since a person is not able to have some power over a thing except as an absolute power in fact or as a licit power. The minor also is easily proved, since what is common to the licit and illicit use of a thing cannot be called the power of a right to it, since what is done by means of a right is done licitly.

However, power in fact is common to both the licit and illicit use of a thing. Therefore, power in fact is not the power of ⟨20⟩ right. Thus, we have sustained the position that the power of right is the power to act licitly. Hence, it is evident that "dominion," "right" or "ownership" signify the power by which someone is able to do something licitly with the things that come into use in human life. Yet, dominion seems rather to signify power itself, while right seems rather to signify the circumstance of licit use. But, in fact, ownership signifies the thing ⟨25⟩ to which someone has a right, where the thing does not belong to someone else.

Thus, it should be noted that what belongs to oneself [*proprium*], deriving from ownership [*proprietas*], can be considered in so far as it is distinguished from what is [held in] common [*commune*] or from what belongs to another [*alienum*]. However, when what belongs to oneself is considered in terms of ownership in the sense we have discussed, then it is not distinguished from what is [held in] common, since a right to something can be held in common. But what ⟨30⟩ belongs to oneself, as it is considered here, is distinguished from what belongs to another, since that to which someone has a right does not belong to another. Therefore right, dominion, and ownership signify the power to use licitly or transfer the things that come into use in human life. This discussion makes the first point evident.

In regard to the second point, it should be noted that right and dominion ⟨35⟩ are understood differently in different ways. When we say that someone has a right to something, this right can occur in different ways, both in relation to the thing that is held and in relation to the one who holds it. Consider the thing that is held. If someone is able to have a right to the very use[5] of a thing that is held, then the right with respect to its substance remains in the hands of another. This is particularly evident in regard to things that are not consumed in their use, as for example, a house or a field. So, if ⟨⟨237⟩⟩ someone inhabits a house by means of rent or a gift, its ownership remains in someone else's hands. The reason is that if someone rents a house in order to inhabit it or if he inhabits it by means of another person's gift, then he has an unqualified dominion over its very use:[6] namely, inhabiting the house. ⟨5⟩ However, he should not be said to have a right to the house except in a relative sense: namely, he is said to have the house for habitation. Conversely, someone who rents a house to another for habitation does not have a right to its very use during the time the house is rented. However, he does have an unqualified right to the house itself.

---

[5] I translate *ipsius usus* by "very use" rather than "use itself" as the former phrase reads more smoothly in English. However, I translate *ipsa res* as "thing itself." Although the translation of *ipsius usus* as "very use" is a bit awkward, it is the most straightforward way of uniformly translating the Latin. At times, *ipsius usus* seems to mean "just the use" or "the use only" as in the present passage or when Hervaeus discusses whether the right to a thing can be separated from the very use of the thing (see page 44 below). At other times, Hervaeus seems to employ the phrase to mean "use itself," as when he frequently refers to things consumed in their very use (see page 46 below).

[6] *Simpliciter dominium in ipso usu.* In the present context, this phrase could also be translated as "a simple dominion over its mere use."

Thus, at times one has a right to the thing itself, at times to the use of the thing, ⟨10⟩ and at times to both, as when the owner of a house reserves its use for himself or when someone has a right to use a thing and the right to transfer it. Moreover, since there can be different ways of using and transferring the same thing, it happens that someone can have a right to use something in one way but not another, ⟨15⟩ and to transfer it in one way but not in another so far as it pleases the principal owner of the thing to grant this or that use or transference of the thing. For example, the principal owner of a house can grant someone the power to inhabit the house, or the power to sublet it, or both. Nevertheless, a person is said without qualification to have a right to and dominion over a thing if he can licitly use ⟨20⟩ the thing in regard to every use which naturally belongs to it. This discussion makes evident the different ways of having a right to and dominion over a thing in relation to the thing held.

There are different ways of having [a right to] something, both with regard to differences among those who have [the right] as well as with regard to the manner of having [the right]. Consider the differences among those who have something. Sometimes an individual person has [a right to] something ⟨25⟩ and, thus, he is said to have a personal right to something. However, sometimes a community has a right to something, as when we say that a monastery has a right to and ownership of the things that belong to the monastery. Yet, this right does not extend to a person within the monastery except in so far as he is a member of the community.

Accordingly, there are two ways in which a community has dominion over ⟨30⟩ something. One way is that the right to a thing pertains to the community accidentally, as is evident in the case of a community of merchants who gather together for trading. For, at the same time that the community has a right to and dominion over the goods of the community, in so far as they are objects of trade, nevertheless, this inherent dominion and right belong to the individual persons according to the prescribed share that ⟨35⟩ each one has of those goods. Conversely, there are times when the right to ⟨⟨238⟩⟩ and dominion over things initially and inherently pertains to the community but not to individual persons within the community, except accidentally and secondarily. This occurs in monasteries and communities of religious in which the community itself has the dominion over things, and the persons within the community do not, except ⟨5⟩ in so far as they are members of the community.

Furthermore, consider the manner of having a right to something. There can be different ways of having a right to things in relation to those who have these rights. First, someone may have a right to something, but not in his own name or on his own behalf. Rather, he has the right in another person's name and on another's behalf as determined and allowed by the principal owner. This takes place ⟨10⟩ when someone is a steward or administrator of something that the principal owner grants to him to administer, distribute, or dispense to others. We do not say that such a person has an unqualified right to this sort of thing; nevertheless, it can be said that he has the right to dispense or administer it. Second, someone can have a right to something on his own behalf but not in his own name. For example, someone might grant another person ⟨15⟩ his house for habitation or his grain or wine for eating or drinking as long as it pleases him. Having been granted the use of the thing, the other person has a right to the thing granted, while the principal dominion over it lies with him who granted it.

Also, it is not inappropriate that the right to a thing resides in the hands of many, provided that it resides with one person primarily and with someone else secondarily. ⟨20⟩ For example, dominion over things among those who live in common resides in the hands of the community itself, as in the hands of the one who has the principal dominion over the things of the community. However, dominion over community goods resides in the hands of the prelate, as in the hands of an administrator or steward who dispenses the goods of community life.

On the other hand, a right to these goods resides in the hands of monks, or any particular monk, ⟨25⟩ as one to whom the community or its steward owes the sustenance of life. The monastery is obligated to provide this sustenance if it has the wherewithal. The monastery also is bound to provide this sustenance to the prelate as it is bound to [provide sustenance to] the other monks. Similarly, a dependent child and a slave have the right to be provided with the necessities of life by the father and by the master ⟨30⟩ who are the principal owners of the things. However, the situation of a monk in relation to the monastery, a dependent child in relation to the head of the family, or a slave in relation to the master differs from the situation of someone to whom a right is granted as a favor by another person. The reason is that the monastery, head of the family, and master are obligated to provide the necessities of life to the monk, dependent child, or slave. Yet, this is not the case for someone who grants his things to another as a favor, as a ⟨35⟩ conditional gift, or out of sheer free-will, since one who grants things in this way is not obligated to the person to whom he made the grant, except to the extent that it pleases him.

If we ask how long the kind of right which we have been discussing ⟨⟨239⟩⟩ resides in the hands of the monk, dependent child, or slave, it must be said that they have the right to what sustains their life for as long as they remain a monk, dependent child, or slave.[7] Nevertheless, they do not

---

[7] Sikes provides the following note: "In his discussion of *paterfamilias* [head of the household], *filiusfamilias* [dependent child], and *servus* [slave], Hervaeus seems to refer to *Digest*, lex 25, lib. XV, tit.1; sec. 5, lib. XLI, tit. 1; lex 42, lib. XXXV, tit. 1; lex 4,

always have such a right to this or that specific thing until that right has been determined by the ⟨5⟩ monastery or its steward, whether this is the head of the family in relation to the child or the master in relation to the slave. However, if the use of a specific thing should be granted and the thing is not consumed by the use, then the unqualified dominion over the thing always remains in the hands of the principal owner. The owner can revoke the use of the thing ⟨10⟩ as he pleases provided that the necessary use of some similar thing is provided to the monk, dependent child, and slave. Yet, if the thing is something consumed in use, then for so long as it remains intact the principal right to it remains in the hands of the primary and unqualified owner who has the power to revoke it. However, in the context of actual use, namely, when the thing is naturally no longer able ⟨15⟩ to be used by another person, then the power, or right of revocation, does not reside in the hands of the one having principal dominion over it.

Consider something held merely on the basis of a conditional gift. The one to whom the use was granted has a right to use the thing. He retains it from the time the permission was given until the time the permission is revoked. However, this does not imply ⟨20⟩ that the right to and dominion over the thing do not remain principally in the hands of the person who granted its use. For these two conditions are compatible: an unqualified right to and dominion over a thing remain in the hands of one person in an unqualified way, while a conditional right to the same thing remains in the hands of someone else. Yet, suppose a person is granted something and uses it in such a way as to consume it. Then, because of this use, the principal owner loses the right ⟨25⟩ and the power to revoke it. Further, by completely using the thing, the person to whom the thing was granted ceases to have the right which he had to the thing, since the thing no longer exists. Can someone, to whom such a thing is granted and who retains it, act as a grantor and revoke the right to the thing which is granted? I say, "No," ⟨30⟩ since the thing is no longer intact and it cannot be used by someone else. This discussion makes the second point evident.

Let us proceed to the third point, that is, to the question of whether the use of temporal things can be separated from the right to them. It must be said that this question can be understood in two ways. First, ⟨⟨240⟩⟩ one might understand the question to be whether the use of such a thing can be separated from the right to its very use. Second, the question could be whether the use of the thing can be separated from the right to the thing [itself] that someone uses. If it is asked whether the use of the thing can be

---

lib. XLI, tit. 2; lex 93, lib. L, tit. 17. Cf. Bonagratia of Bergamo, *De paupertate Christi et apostolorum*, 502." For the Digest, see *Justiniani Digesta* in *Corpus juris civilis*.

separated from the right to its very use, then I would distinguish between the licit and illicit use of a thing. If one speaks of illicit use, taking licit and illicit in the sense ⟨5⟩ of just and unjust, then whenever something is used illicitly, the use is separated from the right to the thing by the very circumstances of the use. This follows from what has been said about illicit use, since the user does not have the power to use the thing licitly. However, the power to use something licitly is the same as a right itself or the power to exercise the right. Thus, in every illicit use of a thing, the use takes place without a right to the thing and, consequently, the use of the thing is separated from the right to it. This happens, for example, in the use of things in theft or ⟨10⟩ robbery, as well as in every case when something is used against the will of the person who is the owner of the thing and its use.

However, suppose we ask whether the licit use of a thing can be separated from a right, at least with respect to its very use, so that someone could use something to which he has no right in any of the senses we have previously set forth: ⟨15⟩ namely, [he does not have the right to the thing] in his own name, nor in the name of someone else, neither as principal owner nor through a favor or a conditional gift, nor in any of the other manners mentioned. But this is impossible, and the impossibility can be proved through two arguments. The first argument is drawn from the meaning of the term "right," since, as has been said, a right to a thing is the power to use it licitly or to transfer it. ⟨20⟩ Consequently, to have a right to the very use of a thing is to have the power to use it licitly. Because of this, it follows that there can be no licit use of something without the power to use it licitly, as this would imply a contradiction: namely, the use of the thing is licit, although the person using it does not have the power to use it licitly. Yet, to have the power to use something licitly is to have a right to the very use of the thing. Therefore, it is ⟨25⟩ impossible for licit use to be separated from the right to the very use of a thing.

The second argument arises from the different ways of having a thing which someone uses, and it goes like this: a thing which someone uses either ought to be reckoned among the goods that belong to God alone, and thus to no person, or it ought to be reckoned among the goods of a person. In the first case, a concession is made to the person who takes hold of ⟨30⟩ something that, by virtue of taking hold of the thing, he has a right to the thing and to its use. In this case, whenever someone uses such a thing, its use is not separated from the right to it or to the right to its use. However, if a thing is reckoned among the goods of some person, either it is reckoned among the goods of the one who uses it, or among the goods of another. If it is reckoned among the goods of the person who uses it, then it follows that this user has a right to the thing which he uses and, consequently, a right to its use, unless he ⟨35⟩ was obligated to someone else. Furthermore, it follows that such use is not without a right both to the thing and its use.

If, however, the thing which is used is reckoned among the goods of someone other than the person who uses it, then he uses it with the permission the owner, or he uses it without the owner's permission. If no permission is given by the owner, then this is not a case of the licit use we are now discussing. If, however, the owner of the thing gives someone else implicit or explicit permission to use the thing, ⟨⟨241⟩⟩ then I ask what sort of permission does the owner give? On the one hand, the owner gives the other person the power of action or the power of using the thing in fact. Yet, this is impossible, since anyone has this power by his nature unless he is impeded by another person. Moreover, this sort of power is common to both the licit and illicit use of a thing, yet we are here inquiring ⟨5⟩ about the licit use of a thing. On the other hand, the owner gives the other person the power to use the thing licitly. But, since the power to use something licitly signifies the power of a right to the thing or the right itself, then it follows that the user of the thing has a right at least to its use.

However, if one should ask whether the licit use of a thing can be separated from a right to the thing which someone uses, either we are speaking about things that are not consumed ⟨10⟩ in their use, such as a house and the like, or we are speaking about things that are consumed in their use, such as bread, wine and money. (When used, money is at least transferred from the one who uses it. For example, when something is bought with money, the money is transferred by the buyer.) In the first case, the licit use of a thing can be separated from the dominion over or a right to it, as is evident in the case of a house and its ⟨15⟩ inhabitation. The reason is that someone can have a right merely to inhabit a house, while the right to the house and its ownership remain with the principal owner. This is self-evident. However, the person who has a right to the very use of a house could be said to have a right to the house in a qualified sense, since he can be said to have a right to the house for the purpose of inhabiting it. Nevertheless, he cannot be said to ⟨20⟩ be the owner of the house in an unqualified way.

Consider things consumed in their use (namely, the means of subsistence that are consumed in being used). The right to them can be separated from their use, since the person who has a right to them need not always use them. On the other hand, however, the licit use of such things ⟨25⟩ cannot be separated from a right to the things themselves, which someone uses, in such a way that a person can licitly use these things and not have some right to them in one of the ways previously mentioned. Namely, he would not have an unqualified right to the things as their unqualified owner. He would not have the right appropriate to a monk, a dependent child, or a slave, or even to one holding a thing by favor or ⟨30⟩ conditional gift, as has been set forth.

The reason for this position is that a thing someone uses belongs to the person using it in these ways: he uses it as his own (that is, with a right to and dominion over it); it belongs to someone else as owner; or it belongs to no one. In the first case, it follows not only that the use of the thing is not separated from dominion over its use, but it also follows that the use of the thing is not separated from dominion over the thing. For, no one can say that something is his own in an unqualified way unless he ⟨35⟩ has a right to it. If the thing which someone uses belongs to another who grants the use of the thing, then either that person grants the use–retaining no aspect of the thing and no dominion over it–or he grants the use and retains some dominion over it. In the first case, it follows that in granting the use of the thing, he grants everything that he has of it, both in terms of its use and in terms of the right to it. It follows that this is the same as the first case above.

It ⟨⟨242⟩⟩ is impossible for someone who owns a consumable thing to grant its use and retain dominion over it, since when a thing is consumed no right to the thing remains for anyone. It might be said that while someone is using such a thing, it still exists in some manner and that someone other than the user can have a right to it. But ⟨5⟩ this is pointless, for after use has begun, the thing which is immediately consumed by use is no longer in a condition to be used by any one else. Moreover, it seems clearly laughable that someone would give another person a piece of bread to eat and, then, snatch it from his mouth so as to retain a right to it. It would not occur to anyone that he would be permitted only to begin consuming something but ⟨10⟩ not finish consuming it. Further, when this type of use is completed, the thing no longer exists, since it has now been consumed. Consequently, no one has a right to it and, furthermore, it follows that when something is used in these circumstances its licit use cannot be separated from dominion over it.

If, however, something is used that is not reckoned among the goods of anyone except the person who uses it, then it follows that the user has a right to it, ⟨15⟩ since he is permitted to take hold of it. Certainly, the person who actually uses something actually takes hold of it. The same point can be proved briefly. No one can transfer something for personal benefit except the person who has a right to it. But the person who consumes something in using it transfers that thing from the person who had the right to it, since when the thing has been consumed ⟨20⟩ no one retains a right to it. Therefore, etc.

Note that I speak about "personal benefit," since someone might well be commissioned by another to transfer a thing for the commissioner's benefit. However, the person who transfers the thing does not have a right to it. For example, someone can sell a thing at the behest of its owner so that the owner, and not the seller, ⟨25⟩ has a right to the thing that is sold.

However, it seems impossible that someone could transfer something for his own personal benefit and not have a right to it.

[Hence, we reply to the objections:]

1. It is evident from what has been said that the monk, the dependent child, and the slave have some right to the things that they use, although they do not have a full right to them or full dominion over them freely and in their own name. ⟨30⟩ Therefore, monks are said not to be able to exercise unqualified right and dominion over them in a way similar to a prelate among religious, although he has the right to administer the things of the monastery. Nevertheless, it cannot be said that a monk has an unqualified right to and dominion over any of these things, otherwise he would not be a monk. Yet, the situation of a monk differs on the one hand from that of a dependent child or from that of a slave, on the other hand, ⟨35⟩ for there are no situations in which a monk can have unqualified ownership of and dominion over things. Absolutely speaking, however, it is possible for a dependent child and a slave to have unqualified ownership of and dominion over things, since a dependent child is able to sell things,[8] and a slave can be freed. Consequently, they can have their own unqualified right to and dominion over things.[9]

2. So ⟨⟨243⟩⟩ far as people live from alms, whether on a daily or an annual basis, they are said to live by means of what belongs to another. This does not mean that they do not have a right to the things they use. Rather, they have this right as the result of the sheer kindness or generosity of someone else. Of course, this does not apply to someone who purchases goods or acquires them ⟨5⟩ through personal labor. It is certain that the keepers of churches, who live from predial alms, have a right to the things that they use.

3. There are two ways of understanding how the use of those things that are reckoned to be God's alone is said to be granted to a person. The first way has a composite sense: namely, ⟨10⟩ the use of these things was granted to human beings when the things were reckoned to be God's alone but before they were reckoned among the goods of some person. But this is false, since a person must have a right to the thing that he uses in so far as he uses it justly. Consequently, such things must be reckoned among the goods of a person who uses them justly. In this composite sense, then, the minor is false. ⟨15⟩ A divided sense underlies the other way of understanding the use of those things that are God's alone, but are granted to people: namely, the sense that things, initially belonging only to God, were subse-

---

[8] Reading *mancipare* for *mancipari*.

[9] See the appendix, page 137 below, for the discussion of this argument.

quently granted to people for licit use, that is, after they had taken hold of them. This reason is that we are permitted to take hold of such things in terms of having a right to them. In this way, the minor premise is true. However, the objection is based on the ⟨20⟩ composite sense and, as has been said, it is false.

In regard to the first proof of the minor premise, it must be said that its major premise is false, since the fruits of the trees of paradise were reckoned among the goods of humans even before they were used by humans. Accordingly, it is true that they held dominion over the things in common so that, consequently, even if there had been a thousand people [in paradise], they had common ⟨25⟩ dominion over the fruits of the trees during that time [before they made use of them]. Yet, they would have had dominion over something in particular after they had taken hold of it. For example, when the use of a forest is granted to a village, the members of the village have a common right to use the forest before they set foot in[10] it. However, in particular, they have a right to this or that tree after they have taken hold of it. Accordingly, it is true in a precise sense that no one ⟨30⟩ could say of the fruits of the trees in paradise: "This is mine" or "This is yours." However, any one of them was properly able to say that "This is ours." To claim the opposite would be contrary to Scripture when it says about every tree in paradise: "You may eat."[11]

With ⟨35⟩ regard to the second proof of the minor premise, it must be said once again that its major premise is false, since the manna was not among God's goods, but it was also reckoned among the goods of ⟨⟨244⟩⟩ the children of Israel. Accordingly, they had a common right to it in the sense attributed to [the people who had a common right to] the fruits of paradise. However, in particular, the children of Israel had a right to this or that piece of manna after taking hold of this or that piece. The manner in which religious ⟨5⟩ have a common right to and dominion over the goods that they use is more akin to the manner of people living in an earthly paradise and to the manner of the children of Israel living in the desert than to any other manner of living.

4.   Consider something which is not reckoned to be among the goods of some person. It must be said that during the time in which something is not reckoned among the goods of some person ⟨10⟩ either in terms of right or dominion, it does not belong to any person who has a right to or dominion over it. Before someone takes hold of something, there only exists what is God's alone, as is evident with regard to the fish in the sea and the

---

[10] "Set foot in" translates the verb *occupo* (to take hold of).

[11] Gen. 2:16.

birds of the sky. However, after a person has taken hold of such things, he has the right to them. Moreover, it is certain that no one uses such things before taking hold of them. Accordingly, ⟨15⟩ a right to such things[12] is not separated from dominion over them.[13]

5. In the case of people who lack the use of reason and who are unable to reason—either licitly or illicitly, or justly or unjustly—it is possible to separate the use of things from the right to them. But as has been shown, people who can reason—justly or unjustly, licitly or illicitly—cannot licitly use something without the right to it. Moreover, it does not seem ⟨20⟩ to me that someone like this should make himself unable through any sort of vow to have at least the right to use the things that are necessities of life.

[ARTICLE 2–WHETHER HAVING A RIGHT TO AND DOMINION OVER TEMPORAL THINGS DIMINISHES PERSONAL PERFECTION]

Let us proceed to the second article, where it is argued that to have something personally or in common, in terms of the right to and dominion over it, diminishes personal perfection.

[1.] The less one moves away from one member of a pair of opposites, ⟨25⟩ the less one draws near to the other. However, desire for temporal things and the charity that constitutes the perfection of human life are opposed to one another. Therefore, the less one recedes from a desire for temporal things, the less one draws near to charity and, consequently, to the perfection of human life. Someone who has something personally or in common does not recede completely from a desire for temporal things. ⟨30⟩ Therefore, he does not completely draw near to the perfection of charity, and consequently he draws near to it in a diminished manner. In light of this, it also follows that to have something personally or in common diminishes perfection.[14]

2. The perfection of life appears to be diminished by a manner of living in which the mid-point of human life is less like the extremes of human life. To have ⟨35⟩ something personally or in common causes the mid-point of human life to be less like the extremes of human life. Therefore,

---

[12] Something seems wrong in the text at this point: for, since "right" and "dominion" are equivalent, one expects *usus* rather than *ius*. That is, one expects the text to read: accordingly, the use of such things is not separated from dominion over them.

[13] See the appendix, pages 137 and 143 below, for related discussions of this argument.

[14] See the appendix, page 124 below, for the treatment of this objection.

etc. The major premise is assumed. The minor is proved, since the extremes of human life are death and birth, while the mid-point is the time of the present life. But in birth and death, a person has nothing either personally or in common. Thus, to have something either personally or in common makes ⟨40⟩ the mid-point of human life less like the extremes. This proves the minor.[15]

3.   Whatever causes discord and litigation among people diminishes the perfection of life. To have something personally or in common ⟨⟨245⟩⟩ is something of this sort. Therefore, etc. The major premise is obvious. The minor premise is proved by reference to Seneca who says that people will live most tranquilly if they get rid of the two words "mine" and "yours."[16] These words apply to having something personally. Similar considerations apply to "ours" and "yours," which pertain to having something in common.

4.   Whatever ⟨5⟩ increases solicitude and distracts the mind from spiritual things diminishes the perfection of human life. However, to have things personally or in common is something of this sort, since it is impossible for someone who has something personally or in common to be free of solicitude and the distraction of the mind. Therefore, etc.

5.   That which makes a person less able to transcend himself[17] ⟨10⟩ in relation to God diminishes charity and, consequently, the perfection of life. To have something personally or in common is something of this sort. Therefore, etc. The major premise is evident, since the effect of charity is to cause the movement [to God] that places a person outside himself, transformed in God. The minor also is evident, since someone who has something personally or in common ⟨15⟩ does not transcend himself to the degree of someone who has nothing. Therefore, etc.

6.   Whatever diminishes holy and meritorious poverty diminishes the perfection of life. Having something personally or in common is something of this sort. The major is self-evident. The minor is proved by reference to the decretal, *Exiit*, which says that "The renunciation of all things for the sake of God, ⟨20⟩ both personally as well as in common, is meritorious and holy."[18]

7.   The perfection of life is diminished by having temporal goods in a way that they more naturally move us to an inordinate love of them. To have temporal goods, whether in common or personally, in terms of a right to and dominion over them is something of this sort. Therefore, etc. The

---

[15] See the appendix, page 125 below, for a discussion of this argument.

[16] *De moribus* frag. 98 (ed. Hasse, Leipzig, III.63).

[17] "Go outside himself" is another possible meaning for *exire extra se*.

[18] Nicholas III, *Exiit qui seminat* (*CIC* II.1112).

major premise is obvious, since an intense love of ⟨25⟩ temporal things diminishes the love of God. The minor also is evident, since the most important way in which these things attract a love for them is that a person has dominion over and ownership of them.

8. The love of God, in which perfection consists, is diminished by loving something together with God that is not lovable for the sake of God. But temporal goods, ⟨30⟩ so it seems, are not lovable for the sake of God. Rather, so it seems, they always distract from the love of God and are incompatible with it. Therefore, etc. The major premise is evident as Augustine, speaking to God in *Confessions X*, says that "He loves you less who loves you with what is not loved for your sake."[19] The proof of the minor is this: whatever inflames the love for temporal things and ⟨35⟩ increases desire for them is not lovable for the sake of God. However, to have temporal things in regard to dominion over and ownership of them is ⟨⟨246⟩⟩ something of this sort. As Augustine says in his letter to Paulinus and Therasia, "Worldly goods actually possessed are more loved than those which are desired. For why did the young man go away sad?"[20]

9. That which cannot exist together with something better signifies an ⟨5⟩ imperfection. But the ownership of a thing cannot exist together with the use of the thing, which is better than the thing itself, since the use is its purpose. This is true for things that are consumed in their use. Therefore, etc.

10. What is less arduous [than something else] diminishes perfection. However, it is less arduous to retain something personally or in common than to ⟨10⟩ relinquish all things for the sake of God, which is more arduous. Therefore, etc. This argument is confirmed by the principle that what diminishes the difficulty in a work of virtue diminishes the perfection of the virtue, since virtue concerns what is good and difficult. To relinquish everything is more difficult than to retain something personally or in common. Therefore, to have something personally or in common diminishes ⟨15⟩ the perfection of virtue. So, Jerome says to Rusticus the monk: "The naked follow the naked Christ."[21] But the person who has something personally or in common is not naked and, therefore, does not follow Christ perfectly. This is confirmed through the similar authority of Gregory who, commenting on the text in Matthew 16, "If anyone wishes to follow after me,"[22] says that as the demons in this world ⟨20⟩ possess nothing of their own, we

---

[19] *Confessiones* X.29 (*CCSL* 27.176; *PL* 32.796).

[20] *Epistolae* 31.5 (*CCSL* 34(pt1).5; *PL* 33.124).

[21] *Epistolae* 125.20 (*CSEL* 56.102; *PL* 22.1085).

[22] Matt. 16:24.

ought to wrestle nude with those who are nude.[23] Therefore, etc.

11. That which is done out of condescension to the weak signifies an imperfection or a lesser perfection. Yet, the Lord made a condescension to the weak, speaking of a weakness of the mind. Thus, to have a purse, which is ⟨25⟩ to have something personally or in common, diminishes perfection.[24] The major premise is evident, since to condescend to someone's infirmity or imperfection shows the imperfection or lesser perfection of the one to whom the condescension is made. The minor is proved by Augustine in *On the Work of Monks*. Commenting on the Psalm text, "bringing forth hay for the beasts,"[25] he says: "With his customary mercy, our Lord sympathized with those who were weaker; even though the ⟨30⟩ angels were able to minister to him, he had or used to have a purse."[26]

ON THE CONTRARY: What diminishes the perfection of life, at least in a necessary way, cannot exist with such perfection. However as the preceding question made clear, having wealth, even abundant wealth, ⟨⟨247⟩⟩ can exist with any degree of the perfection of charity. Thus, to have wealth, even in respect to dominion and ownership, does not necessarily, at least, diminish the personal perfection of human life. Further, the power to use licitly the necessities of life does not diminish ⟨5⟩ the perfection of human life. The power to use licitly or transfer such things is nothing other than to have the right to and ownership of such things. Therefore, etc.

RESPONSE: To clarify this question two distinctions must be made, after which a response will be given to the question. With regard to the first point, a brief distinction must be made concerning perfection. Then, ⟨10⟩ a distinction must be made about imperfection, its opposite.

With regard to the first point, it should be noted, as we said above,[27] that perfection has two senses: personal perfection and the perfection of a state. The perfection of a state will be discussed below.[28] In regard to personal perfection, it should be noted, as we said above,[29] that charity as well as ⟨15⟩ other virtues and their acts pertain essentially to personal perfection, as essentially constituting perfection. However, other things contribute to human perfection itself instrumentally or dispositively in the man-

---

[23] *XL Homiliarum in evangelium* II.32 (*PL* 76.1233).

[24] Compare page 121 below in the appendix.

[25] Ps. 103:14.

[26] *De opere monachorum* V.6 (*CSEL* 41.539; *PL* 40.552).

[27] See page 37 above.

[28] See Question 2B, beginning at page 77 below.

[29] See page 28 above.

ner that we discussed in the first question of this treatise.[30]

On the other hand, in regard to the imperfection that is the opposite of this perfection, ⟨20⟩ it should be noted that imperfection can be taken in two senses, namely, in a privative and negative manner. In a privative sense, an imperfection is called the lack of privation[31] which is naturally fitting and which, in the circumstances, it is natural to have. Further, the lack of a perfection, which in the circumstances it is natural to have, can be understood in two ways: either as a complete lack of perfection itself, or as a lack of it to some degree. For example, ⟨25⟩ if someone unqualifiedly lacks charity in external matters in the wayfaring state, he would be called imperfect in an unqualified manner. Such a lack would be called an unqualified imperfection in a privative mode. However, if someone lacks charity to the degree that someone else has charity, he would not be called imperfect in an unqualified sense but in comparison to the one who has ⟨30⟩ charity in the greater degree. For example, if someone is lax in charity, he would not be called imperfect in an unqualified sense. Nevertheless, he would be called imperfect in comparison to one who has charity intensely.

Taken in a negative manner, imperfection is called the lack of perfection either because someone simply is not capable of perfection or because that person is not capable of it for a period of time. ⟨35⟩ In the first sense, every creature is called imperfect in a negative manner with respect to God. The reason for this is not that a creature lacks the perfection it ought to have, but because it lacks the degree of perfection which God has and of which it is not capable. In the second sense, a negative imperfection is called the lack of a perfection that something, which lacks it, is absolutely able to possess but not, however, at the time when it is lacked. ⟨40⟩ In this sense, the wayfarer who exists in the wayfaring state is called imperfect ⟨⟨248⟩⟩ in relation to the blessed, since, although the wayfarer absolutely is capable of blessedness he is, nevertheless, not capable of blessedness at the time he is a wayfarer.

Thus, it should be noted that in the wayfaring state a person has what is termed a negative imperfection in three ways: in regard to the intensity of charity, ⟨5⟩ in regard to the rootedness and unfailing character of charity, and in regard to certain defects of the body. [We have imperfection] with regard to the intensity of charity, since it is not natural for a person in earthly life to have the intensity of charity that he has in the fatherland. [We have imperfection] with respect to the rootedness [of charity], since

---

[30] See page 32 above.

[31] One would expect here *perfectionis* for *privationis,* reading "an imperfection is called the lack of a perfection...."

charity on earth is not as rooted or unfailing as ⟨10⟩ charity in the fatherland. Because of this imperfection, it is our lot that we can sin in this wayfaring state.

In virtue of both of these imperfections–the defect of our intensity of
charity, since charity does not totally occupy the mind of a person as it
does in the fatherland, and the defect of its rootedness–it is our lot that we
have an inclination to evil and a difficulty with doing good. Thus, with
ease, these defects ⟨15⟩ inordinately attract a person to wealth, pleasures,
and honors, and inordinately detract from what is opposed to them. All of
these things signify a negative imperfection: that is, the lack of perfection
that it is not natural to have in the wayfaring state.

With regard to certain operations of the body, it should be noted that
our said imperfection refers in a negative way to the fact that we need food
and ⟨20⟩ clothing, the use of which is not necessary in the fatherland. Moreover, we can not obtain these things at will, but we must obtain them as
the occasion allows (as will be discussed in more detail below).[32] This
bodily condition also pertains to our negative imperfection, since it is not
natural to have its opposite in the wayfaring state.

In light of these considerations, we can respond to the question about
whether the perfection of life ⟨25⟩ is diminished by having temporal things
in terms of a right to and dominion over them. This question should be
understood with regard to the perfection of life that it is natural to have in
the wayfaring state. Accordingly, I say that having temporal things does not
⟨30⟩ naturally diminish the perfection that it is natural to have in the
wayfaring state if we have them in terms of a right to and dominion over
them and also to a degree sufficient to sustain life according to the common course of nature. First, I will prove this by a general assertion in regard to all of the things that come into use in human life. Second, I will
prove the same with respect to the right to use things and with respect to
things that are immediately consumed in their very use, such as food.
Third, I will prove this same assertion in regard to things that are not immediately consumed in their very use.

The ⟨35⟩ first conclusion is proved in this way: the perfection of the
present life is not diminished by having the power to use licitly or transfer
the things that come into use in human life, so far as this assists in sustaining human life. Indeed, this power is necessary to the present life and, consequently, to the perfection that it is natural to have in this life. However,
having such power over the things that come ⟨40⟩ into use in human life is
to have a right to them. Therefore, etc. The major premise is evident ⟨⟨249⟩⟩
from what has been said. The minor is self-evident, since sufficiency in

---

[32] See the discussion on page 64 below.

human life cannot be had without the previously mentioned things. The argument for this is confirmed through what the Apostle says in [1] Timothy 4[33] where he reprimands people who said we should abstain from the food which God created to be ⟨5⟩ received with thanksgiving. Just as God created food for human use, and especially for the faithful, so too, he created other things for human use that pertain to the sustenance of human life. From this remark, one can argue that having the power to use licitly those things that God has created for human use in the present wayfaring state does not diminish ⟨10⟩ the perfection it is natural to have in the present life. However, to have this power over things is to have a right to these things. Therefore, etc.

[Second,] I prove the same conclusion with regard to the particular right to use things and with regard to the things that are consumed in their very use, since the perfection of human life is not diminished by having things in a way that is necessary to prevent their illicit use. However, it is illicit to use any sort of thing without ⟨15⟩ a right to use it. It also is illicit to use things that are consumed in their very use without a right to the things themselves.

Third, I prove the same conclusion in regard to things that are not consumed in their very use. First, from what has been said, the conclusion is evident in relation to the right to use a thing without which its use is not licit. In addition, I offer a proof of the same conclusion when the thing itself is ⟨20⟩ separable from its use. For, not only is the use of such things necessary or useful for human life, but it is also necessary or useful to transfer such things according to the circumstances and needs of those who possess them. The argument goes like this: the perfection of the present life is not diminished by having the power licitly to transfer things when circumstances or needs make it necessary or expedient for sustaining the life of those who have them. ⟨25⟩ However, it is not licit to transfer such things without a right to them. Thus, having a right to these things does not diminish the perfection of the present life. Hence, the fact that someone may have a right not only to use a house but also to the house itself does not diminish his perfection, since it is often possible that he can obtain what he needs by transferring the house [to someone else]. ⟨30⟩ Thus, it is evident that in order to have temporal things in terms of a right to and dominion over them (of course, for the sake of living licitly), one must have a right to these things and to their use.

However, while having a right to use such things does not, absolutely speaking, diminish the perfection of the present life, nevertheless a right to these things can be held personally and in common. As has been shown

---

[33] 1 Tim. 4:3.

above,[34] having a personal right to things naturally impedes ⟨35⟩ the development of charity, since it naturally moves a person to an excessive love of temporal things, an excessive care for them and even, at times, to pride. Yet, to have such things in common in regard to the necessities of life does not ⟨⟨250⟩⟩ seem to move a person in these ways by nature nor, consequently, does it diminish charity or impede its perfection.

In opposition to the objections, the following must be said:

1.   A distinction should be made concerning the desire for temporal things, since it can be considered as an ordered and ⟨5⟩ moderate desire for temporal things in regard to the necessities of life. In this sense, the minor premise is false, since such love is not opposed to charity. Indeed, for the sake of ourselves and our neighbors, charity demands that we have things for sustaining life.[35]

2.   The major premise is false, since, in regard to having or not having temporal goods, ⟨10⟩ the perfection of life does not require the mid-point of life be like its extremes mentioned earlier. For there is no comparable reason for needing things before birth and after death as for needing things in the middle of life. Moreover, we can draw the same conclusion concerning the use of things in fact that was drawn concerning the right to those things, because before birth and after death there is no need to use things in fact or by right.[36]

3.   The ⟨15⟩ cause of quarrels and discord diminishes perfection on the part of the person who promotes discord and quarrels. However, if someone takes what is his own, he does not, for his part, promote discord or dispute. This is done by the person who, for his part, unjustly wants to take or keep what belongs to someone else. If you say that having dominion over things is the cause, then ⟨20⟩ one must say "No," since the cause is having, or wanting to have, [things] unjustly. The same conclusion can be drawn in regard to using things in fact, since those who have the use of a thing in fact want to defend the thing they use in fact from being seized. So even brute animals, who have no capacity for justice or injustice, fight for food.

Yet, in Matthew 5, our Lord says, "However, I say to you ⟨25⟩ do not resist evil. But if someone strike you on the right cheek, offer him the other. And if he wants to contend with you in court over your shirt, hand him your coat as well."[37] But this text should not always be understood to

---

[34] See page 35 above.

[35] See the appendix, page 124 below, for the treatment of this objection.

[36] See the appendix, page 125 below, for a discussion of this argument.

[37] Matt. 5:39-40.

refer to an exterior effect in the sense that, if struck on one cheek, a person should immediately offer the other for a blow. Indeed, ⟨30⟩ as is written in John 18, the Lord himself, when struck on the cheek by one of the soldiers, did not immediately offer his other cheek but said, "If I have spoken evil, produce the evidence concerning the evil, but if I have spoken the truth, why hit me?"[38] Thus, the phrase "I say to you, 'Do not resist evil'" should always be understood to refer to a disposition of the mind in this sense: the person who is struck by another person is ⟨35⟩ mentally prepared to suffer more before being moved to inordinate anger or, in effect, to becoming inordinately vindictive.

4.   The ⟨⟨251⟩⟩ perfection of life is diminished by whatever increases solicitude superfluously beyond what is necessary in relation to temporal things. Yet, to have the proper solicitude for providing what is necessary–according to time, place and in a proper manner–does not diminish the perfection that it is ⟨5⟩ natural to have in this life.

5.   The major premise says that the perfection of life is diminished by what makes us less able to go outside ourselves in relation to God. This premise is true so far as the fragility of this life admits. But in this sense, the minor is false, since to have the necessities of life[39] in common does not diminish ⟨10⟩ a person's movement outside himself in relation to God according to place, time, and so far as the fragility of this life admits. The same point follows in regard to the use of things in fact, since we must have some solicitude for them unless a person expects that a morsel will be carried to him right up to his mouth.

6.   The minor premise is false. In order to prove this ⟨15⟩ in regard to the objection's claims about the renunciation of ownership of things, etc., it must be said that the renunciation of ownership can be understood in two ways, just as what belongs to oneself can be understood in two ways. On the one hand, what belongs to oneself can be distinguished from what is held in common. In this sense, having what belongs to oneself or having ownership of a thing means having dominion over the thing personally, but not at all in common. Understood in this way, not having ⟨20⟩ ownership of things is a holy and meritorious poverty that does not preclude having at least the necessities of life in common. On the other hand, what belongs to oneself can be distinguished from what belongs to another. So in this case, if someone has something, then not having what belongs to oneself is the same as having what belongs to another, which is the same as having something that does not belong to oneself. Yet, having something in this

---

[38] John 18:23.
[39] Reading *vitae* for *vita*.

way is neither holy nor meritorious. ⟨25⟩ Further, it does not pertain to perfection to renounce this sort of ownership of the things that a person uses, since it does not pertain to perfection to have what belongs to another. Indeed, just the opposite is the case. The decretal, [*Exiit*], may have said something implicitly about this and other matters.

7. The love of temporal things is twofold. In one case, ⟨30⟩ a person wants to have temporal goods necessary for life for the sake of God. [The objection] is not true in regard to such love. The major premise is obvious, since someone must desire either to have necessities of life for himself and for others whose care is imposed on him or to die of hunger. However, the other love of temporal things is illicit: namely, when someone has ⟨35⟩ an inordinate desire for temporal goods beyond a proper measure. In this sense, the major premise is true. Yet, the minor is false, since, when someone adheres to a proper measure that is necessary for sustaining human life, having dominion over temporal things does not bring about illicit love. So, too, having temporal things in order to use them does not move us more to a love of temporal things than does having dominion over them, since the end attracts us ⟨40⟩ more than the means to the end.

8.[40] The minor premise is false, at least in relation to a moderate possession of temporal things in common. The minor also is erroneous, since it is a fact that what can not be ordered[41] to the works of mercy and worship ⟨⟨252⟩⟩ is lovable for the sake of God. It is self-evident that temporal goods are something of this sort, since some temporal goods are given as alms, and this pertains to the work of mercy. These alms make churches possible as well as other things that pertain to the divine worship.

9. While ⟨5⟩ excessive wealth naturally kindles an inordinate love and moves us to it, and while it even at times moves us to pride, nevertheless in the nature of things, having the necessities of life does not naturally move us to pride or to excessive love.

10.[42] When speaking of things that are consumed in use, the minor premise–which claims that dominion over a thing ⟨10⟩ cannot be compatible with its use–is false, since the person who uses such goods has a right to them while he uses them. But no person other than the one using such goods can have a right to them, since in being used they are not fit to be used by someone else. Moreover, in using things up, neither the person using them nor anyone else has a right to them, since they no longer exist.

---

[40] Responses eight and nine correspond to objection eight above.

[41] Reading, in place of *inordinabile*, *ordinabile*: what can be ordered to works of mercy and worship....

[42] This response corresponds to objection nine above.

The major premise is not ⟨15⟩ universally true, since (as many say) faith pertains to the perfection of human life even though it cannot be compatible with what is unqualifiedly best in human life, e.g., blessedness. Accordingly, it might follow that the right to a thing could not be incompatible with its use. Nevertheless, this conclusion does not follow unless it pertains to the perfection of a possession that precedes use, since the possession of a thing becomes just and licit through a right to it. Without the ⟨20⟩ right to the thing, the possession of it would be illicit and unjust.

11.[43] The minor is false, since, when we speak in terms of a praiseworthy adversity, having nothing personally or in common is not more arduous than having a moderate degree of things in common. By way of proof, it must be said that not every sort of difficulty contributes to the perfection of virtue except for ⟨25⟩ the sort of difficulty which helps one attain the rational mean in respect to the proper end. For, if every difficulty in our activities increased the perfection of virtue, then living with very great wealth would pertain to the perfection of life, since in such cases it is extraordinarily difficult to attain the mean of virtue. Therefore, it must be said that difficulty in a work of virtue can be understood in two ways. ⟨30⟩ The first way is proportional in character and is determined by the relation of an activity to the power of the agent: namely, when in the nature of things the work produced by the agent greatly exceeds the power of the agent. For example, it is more difficult to carry 100 pounds than 50 pounds. The difficulties in such a work, as ordered to a good end, increase the virtuous perfection of a work. However, I say "as ordered to a good end" ⟨35⟩ for, although evil people at times undertake what is more difficult for them in order to carry out their evil intentions than what good people undertake to carry out their good intentions, nevertheless, what evil people undertake does not, absolutely speaking, increase perfection. Rather, it leads to a greater increase in defect and wickedness.

In the second sense, a difficulty can arise in actions which, in the nature of things, have no proportion between ⟨⟨253⟩⟩ act and agent. Rather, they are due to defects of the agent. For example, a sick person is not as easily able to act as is a healthy person. Therefore, suppose someone achieves a good end in a proper manner, and he experiences difficulty in the first sense, namely, in terms of the proportion of the work to the agent's powers, so that by its nature the work ⟨5⟩ exceeds his power in such a way that he can do it only with difficulty. In this case, the difficulty of the circumstances increases the perfection of the act and makes it virtuous itself. Virtuous works are accomplished either in relation to unfavorable things that repel desire, or in relation to delectable and profitable things that excessively

---

[43] Responses eleven and twelve correspond to objection ten above.

attract desire to them, especially sensuous desires. Therefore, ⟨10⟩ holding to the mean of reason or virtue in every work of virtue is difficult in the first sense, since it is difficult to hold to the mean of virtue and undertake unfavorable things that repel desire or repudiate profitable things that attract the desires.

When a difficulty arises from a defect of the agent, one can nevertheless ⟨15⟩ be weakened by it. For example, lacking virtue creates difficulties in acting virtuously, yet the increase of difficulty that comes about in this way does not increase perfection but diminishes it. Otherwise, work of a virtuous kind produced by someone who is not virtuous would be more perfect than the work of a virtuous sort that is produced by a virtuous person. This is false. Therefore, in response to the claim that the complete lack of temporal things in regard to ⟨20⟩ a right to and dominion over them increases the difficulty, one must say "No" when speaking of a virtuous difficulty. So too, the complete lack of temporal things in terms of using them in fact does not increase the virtuous difficulty, although it is more difficult to lack things than to have temporal things to a moderate degree. Indeed, it is never licit for a person to lack completely such things, otherwise it would be licit to kill oneself through starvation. However, ⟨25⟩ if you say "Yes," because it is possible to save one's life through the use of something in fact, then the initial claim does not follow, since, as has been shown, the licit use of something in fact is not possible without some right to it.

Thus, just as virtue consists in the mean for the other moral virtues, so too, the virtue of appropriately providing a measure of temporal possessions consists in this mean: ⟨30⟩ namely, there should be no notable defect in the necessities of life, and there should be no excess in relation to the manner of living that is appropriate to a person generally or in this or that condition. However, the mean in such things is one thing for a religious and another for a prince. Accordingly, the virtue attained in these and other matters is the mean ⟨35⟩ appropriate to each person according to his state.

Yet, it should be noted that in respect to extreme conditions, such as notable penury or need, and great wealth, it may happen that a person lives well and in a praiseworthy manner. This is evident in the case of Lazarus,[44] who was needy, and also Abraham and David, who had great wealth. However, ⟨⟨254⟩⟩ these conditions do not naturally and in themselves move people to virtue, as if this movement is caused by these conditions, since the movement is due to the perfection of the person who uses such things well. A person with perfect virtue uses such things well in the

---

[44] Luke 16:20-21.

midst of temptations, not because the ⟨5⟩ temptation leads to perfection but because of the opposite: namely, the perfection of the person who is tempted.

12. The nakedness of which blessed Jerome speaks should not be understood in regard to the total renunciation of temporal things personally and in common, otherwise people ought to lack ⟨10⟩ even clothes. Nor did Jerome himself practice nakedness in this sense. Thus, this nakedness should be understood in regard to the renunciation of abundant temporal goods, especially in the sense of personal renunciation. This nakedness should not be understood in the sense that such renunciation is always necessary for those who have outstanding perfection, as is evident in Gregory and Abraham. ⟨15⟩ Rather, this renunciation makes it easier for a person to have this perfection.

13.[45] The objection says that Christ had a purse for the sake of the imperfect. Yet, the imperfection, by which we are said to be imperfect in comparison with Christ, does not refer to an imperfection expressed in a privative way: namely, the lack of a perfection that it is natural to have ⟨20⟩ in the wayfaring state.[46] For, in the common course of things, one cannot remove the natural necessity to have or obtain temporal things in this wayfaring state although God might miraculously remove it. However, Christ, to whom the angels ministered and who could have had temporal things by means of creation, was not subject to the necessity ⟨25⟩ of providing or obtaining things. Augustine expressly says this in his commentary on the text in Matthew 6, "Be not solicitous for the morrow,"[47] which we will discuss in greater detail in what follows.

[Article 3–Whether Making Provision for the Future Diminishes the Perfection of Life]

Let us proceed to the following where it is argued that making provision for the future in regard to temporal things diminishes the perfection of life.

1.   Solicitude ⟨30⟩ for such provision distracts the mind. Reason offers the first proof for this claim: such provision cannot be made without solicitude for obtaining the storehouses and vehicles that are necessary to make provision for the future. This is not possible without distracting the

---

[45] This response corresponds to objection eleven above.

[46] Compare page 121 below in the appendix.

[47] Matt. 6:34. Cf. Augustine, *De sermone Domini in monte* II.17 (*CCSL* 35.159; *PL* 34.1294-5).

mind from spiritual things. Therefore, etc.

2. The authority of Sacred ⟨35⟩ Scripture proves the same point, since making such provision has regard for solicitude for the future. Yet, in Matthew 6, the Lord prohibits solicitude for the future when he says: "Be not solicitous for the morrow,"[48] and much less for the distant future. Therefore, ⟨⟨255⟩⟩ etc.

3. The same point is proved by the authority of the saints. First, there is the authority of Jerome, who speaks in the following way about present things, conceding therefore that we ought be solicitous while prohibiting thought about future things: "It suffices for us to think about things in the present; let us relinquish to God future things that are uncertain."[49] Thus, according to ⟨5⟩ blessed Jerome, solicitude for the future is forbidden, not just because it distracts the mind but because making provision for the future cannot be made without solicitude for the future. Therefore, etc.

[4.] The same point is proved by this consideration: those who make provision for the future seem to confide less in God. The argument goes like this: something apparently diminishes the perfection of life if it seems to lead ⟨10⟩ him to confide less in God than he should. But making provision for the future is something of this sort. Therefore, etc. The major premise is evident, since, by confiding in God less than one ought, one diminishes the perfection of life. The minor is proved through many authorities. First, consider the authority of Gregory. In his commentary on Ezechiel 43, he says that ⟨15⟩ "Another resolved to distribute all that he possessed to those in need, reserving nothing for himself and entrusting his life to divine governance alone."[50] But someone who makes provision for the future does not entrust his life to divine governance alone. Therefore, etc. Augustine makes the same point about the words of the Lord: "Nothing is so inimical to hope as to look back,"[51] i.e., to place hope ⟨20⟩ in things that are transient and will pass away. However, making provision for the future does this. Therefore, etc.

[5.] The same point is again made by Augustine in *The Conflict of the Virtues and the Vices*: "No one is secure in this life as is the person who embraces nothing besides Christ to possess everything that is necessary."[52] The minor is proved by this guarantee of security for those who trust in Christ. Yet, in making provision for the future it does not ⟨25⟩ seem that be

---

[48] Matt. 6:34.

[49] *Commentarii in evangelium Matthaei* I.6 (*CCSL* 77.41; *PL* 26.46).

[50] *Homiliae in Hiezechihelem prophetam* II.8 (*CCSL* 142.347; *PL* 76.1037).

[51] *Sermo* 105.5 (*PL* 38.621).

[52] Pseudo-Augustine, *De conflictu virtutum et vitiorum* 16 (*PL* 40.1099).

the action of embracing Christ alone one can have the necessities of life. Therefore, etc.

[6.] Once again, Chrysostom makes the same point when, in his *Commentary on Matthew*,[53] he says that the person who believes God to be a just ruler entrusts his nourishment to the hands of God. But those who make provision for the future do not entrust their nourishment to the hand of God. Therefore, etc.

ON ⟨30⟩ THE CONTRARY: Proverbs 6 says, "Go to the ant, O sluggard, study its ways and learn wisdom; for though it has no leader or ruler, it obtains its food in the summer and stores up its provision in the ⟨⟨256⟩⟩ harvest."[54] However, the wise man says this as an example of a good and praiseworthy act. So, such an act does not diminish the perfection of life. Therefore, etc.

Second, the perfection of life is not diminished by obtaining the necessities of life so far as they appear naturally suited to be obtained according to the disposition of divine ⟨5⟩ providence. Yet through the disposition of divine providence, temporal goods necessary for the present are naturally suited to be obtained[55] at one time for another time. Therefore, to obtain such goods at one time for another subsequent time does not diminish the perfection of life. However, to obtain such goods in one time for another pertains to making provision for the future. Therefore, ⟨10⟩ etc. The major premise is evident, since obtaining things according to the disposition of divine providence does not diminish the perfection of life. The minor is self-evident, since the necessities of human life are not present at every moment. Rather, they are supplied by God at certain times so that, according to the disposition of divine providence, they are naturally suited to be obtained at one time for another. ⟨15⟩ By obtaining things in this way, one makes provision for the future. Therefore, etc.

RESPONSE: To clarify this question, it should be noted that we are not presently discussing the perfection of a state. We are discussing the perfection of a person or personal perfection: namely, whether or not a person is in a state of perfection ⟨20⟩ in the sense we are discussing it. However, he must be in the state of Christian religion without which no perfection is possible (referring to the perfection under discussion). Further, we are also speaking about what is natural according to the course of nature. We are not speaking about what God could miraculously provide, since it is a fact that God could miraculously provide the necessities of life to anyone with-

---

[53] Pseudo-Chrysostom, *Opus imperfectum in Matthaeum* 16.32 (PG 56.724).

[54] Prov. 6:6-7.

[55] Reading *procurari* for *procurare*.

out that person having to make any sort of provision for the future. I say, therefore, that to make provision for ⟨25⟩ a future time does not diminish the perfection of life. First, I will show this in general: namely, I will show that the perfection of life is not diminished by making provision for the future according to need and what is proper to one's state. Next, I will prove the same point with respect to men dedicated to the contemplative life.

I prove the first point as follows: making provision for the future does not seem to ⟨30⟩ impede or diminish love for God or neighbor except in so far as the solicitude involved in making such provision leads us to prefer temporal things to spiritual things, to exceed the measure of what we should provide, or to occupy the mind inordinately with making provision for things in a way that the situation does not require. When someone acts for God and His service, observing a proper measure for what is necessary and what the situation demands, then, in making provision for the future with the intention of obtaining sustenance for himself and those in his care, ⟨35⟩ he incurs none of the impediments [to love] that have been mentioned. Therefore, etc.

The major premise is evident, since it does not seem that making provision for the future should impede or diminish our love for God and neighbor except under the following conditions. One prefers temporal things over spiritual things, especially by caring for temporal things over and above the love ⟨⟨257⟩⟩ one owes to God and neighbor. Or, one exceeds the measure of things to be supplied, since excess in these things quite naturally moves a person to love them inordinately and contrary to the love which one owes God and neighbor. Or, when engaged in such solicitude [for making provision for things], either the mind is occupied more with circumstances than ⟨5⟩ it ought, or it is occupied with circumstances with which it ought not be concerned, as is the case for one who is solicitous in January about crops to be harvested or grapes to be gathered. The minor also is evident, since a person does not incur these aforementioned impediments when he makes provision for the future according to a proper measure and as circumstances require, and when he also stands in a proper relation to God: namely, by disposing temporal things for the service of God.

I prove ⟨10⟩ the same claim more specifically in regard to those men dedicated to the contemplative life, especially those who have things in common. First, I show that making provision for the future does not diminish the perfection of such men. Second, I show that making no provision for the future diminishes the perfection of the contemplative life. The first point is proved as follows. If the ⟨15⟩ perfection of the contemplative life is diminished by having temporal things, which are the necessities of life, through making a proper provision for them (that is, by observing what circumstances require in place, time and in other concurrent matters), then the reason is that having things in this way diminishes the perfection of the contemplative life either in regard to its habits or its acts. But ⟨20⟩ making such provision for things diminishes the perfection of the contemplative life in neither of these ways. Therefore, etc.

The major premise is evident, since the perfection of life, whether active or contemplative, consists essentially in virtuous habits and their acts. First of all, I prove the minor by showing that making such provision for things neither impedes the perfection of life nor ⟨25⟩ diminishes it with regard to virtuous habits themselves. I prove the point as follows: temporal things that are provided in this way impede virtuous habits–namely, charity and the other virtues connected with it–either by reason of things themselves or by reason of what is joined to them. But temporal things do not impede virtuous habits in the first sense, since, because temporal goods can be ordered to God, they do not of themselves impede charity or the inclination ⟨30⟩ of the mind to God. Moreover, in regard to their substance, temporal things bear no wickedness that is opposed to any virtue.

Further, temporal things do not impede virtuous habits by reason of what is joined to them, for [the attitudes] joined to temporal things that have some opposition to virtue are the elation of the mind, the inordinate love of acquiring and conserving temporal things, or a preoccupation with and inordinate solicitude for them. ⟨35⟩ Yet, when someone has temporal things through making a moderate provision for them in the manner we have specified, he does not naturally, and according to the nature of things, assume one of [the attitudes] that are joined to temporal things. Therefore, etc.

The major premise is commonly assumed. The minor is proved, first of all, in regard to the elation of the mind, since elation of the mind does not naturally arise except in terms of what leads a person to think himself great. But merely having ⟨40⟩ the necessities of life–through making provision for them as the occasion requires and in terms ⟨⟨258⟩⟩ of the nature of things–does not naturally move a person to esteem himself great, since it is clearly unremarkable to have the mere necessities of life. Therefore, etc. Thus, speaking of the pride of wealth, the Psalm says that pride is joined not to wealth but to excessive wealth. ⟨5⟩ So, the Psalm says: "People boast who trust in their own strength and their great wealth."[56]

Second, I prove the same minor premise in regard to an inordinate love of temporal things. The fewer temporal things one has and the less one has in regard to those things, the less one is moved to an ⟨10⟩ excessive love of having things whether in the present or in the future. However, no one can

---

[56] Ps. 48:7.

have less of temporal things in regard to the necessities of life especially when they are held in common and according to the circumstances in which they are necessities. Therefore, according to the nature of things, having things in this way does not naturally move a person to an excessive love of them. Suppose someone responds that a person has less in ⟨15⟩ having temporal things for the present time only rather than for present and future, so that, consequently, the person who abstains from making provision for things has less of temporal things and is, consequently, less affected by them. We grant that it is true that someone who has things only for the present time has less than someone who has things for the present and future. But this [having] less is not the sort of [having] less[57] that can exist with an ⟨20⟩ appropriate sustenance of human life and the power to undertake virtuous acts tranquilly and without solicitude. For, the complete lack of temporal things in terms of using them in fact is the greatest lack of them. Furthermore, lacking things in this way should not be chosen since it is not compatible with the present life. Indeed, as we will see below,[58] having nothing for the future, to even the smallest degree, ⟨25⟩ is not compatible with an appropriate sustenance of human life that can be ordered to any manner of living.

Third, the same minor is proved in these terms: making provision for the future does not naturally induce an inordinate occupation and solicitude which hold the mind back from the perfection of charity. To ⟨30⟩ make this clear, note that a person cannot be completely freed from the care for those things that are necessary for the present life. Nevertheless, one can be freed from an inordinate and excessive care which impedes charity. I prove that making provision for such future things does not naturally induce this sort of inordinate love; for, when someone is naturally less ⟨35⟩ inordinately moved to something, then to that degree he naturally occupies himself less with an inordinate care. But, as I now say, having temporal things for the future in the previously specified manner does not naturally move someone to acquire or conserve such things excessively or inordinately. Therefore, etc. Thus, the first point is evident: ⟨⟨259⟩⟩ namely, making provision for the future in the manner specified does not diminish the perfection of the contemplative life with reference to the virtuous habits that pertain to it.[59]

---

[57] Note that "less" involves more than a quantitative factor, i.e., having fewer things. The person who has only the use of something that belongs to another person has less of something than the person who has the use of his or her own property.

[58] See the discussion beginning at page 69 below.

[59] See the appendix, page 134 below.

Next, let us turn to the second point in order to prove the same minor of the principal argument ⟨5⟩ in regard to the acts of the contemplative life. To make this proof clear, it should be noted that someone can be impeded in regard to the acts of the contemplative life in two ways. In the first way, someone may be impeded in his acts at a time and place in which he is obligated to carry them out either by precept, rule, his state, or his superior. Further, the concern, ⟨10⟩ with which he occupies himself and makes himself powerless in regard to the above-mentioned proper performance of such acts, is illicit. Another way [someone can be impeded] occurs when he ceases to carry out acts at a time and place in which a precept or some rule does not obligate him to perform them. Omitting [the performance of] such acts in this way can ⟨15⟩ take place in two ways. One way occurs through laziness and a superfluous care for temporal things. Omitting [the performance of] such acts would diminish the perfection of the contemplative life in regard to its acts (speaking of the perfection of life that it is natural to have in this life). This omission would be a defect of venial sin.

In another way, this omission could occur because of a necessary or even advantageous occupation with ⟨20⟩ temporal things according to the course of the present life. To omit, in time and place, acts of the contemplative life does not, in regard to the act, diminish the perfection of the contemplative life that it is natural to have in the present life, just as eating and sleeping do not diminish the perfection of life. The reason is that, since both eating and sleeping are necessary for the present life, ⟨25⟩ one must also provide necessities for oneself according to time and place. Since eating and sleeping are necessary for the present life, such acts are not said to diminish the perfection of the contemplative life that it is natural to have in this life. So too, they are not said to diminish the perfection of the contemplative life in regard to its acts. Therefore, etc. Thus, the ⟨30⟩ first conclusion is basically evident: having temporal goods, with proper provision for the future, does not diminish the perfection of the contemplative life which it is natural to have in this life either in regard to the habit and act of charity or in regard to other virtues.

Let us continue and set forth the second conclusion that pertains ⟨35⟩ principally to this article: lacking provision for temporal things under all circumstances and to any degree diminishes the perfection of the active life as much as of the contemplative life. To make this conclusion evident, it should be noted that there are certain necessities of human life that are not immediately consumed in their very use–e.g., a house, clothes, ⟨40⟩ books, utensils, and other similar things. There are also certain things that are immediately consumed in their very use–e.g., corn, wine, and money which at least is transferred[60] ⟨⟨260⟩⟩ in its very use. Therefore, given the common course of events that we observe in things, it does not seem possible to avoid making at least the slightest provision for the future in regard to the first group of things that are not immediately consumed in their use. The reason is that by lacking such things for ⟨5⟩ the future, no matter how briefly, someone needs to obtain these things for himself each day, indeed, each morning and evening. So, one ought reserve nothing for oneself for any future time, no matter how modest, or one ought lack such things completely.

First, in light of the course of events which we observe in things, it does not seem very possible to act in this way, especially for ⟨10⟩ many who live in common. It hardly seems possible for these people to make provisions anew each morning and each evening and, indeed, at each moment of the day. Second, the total lack of such things as clothing and housing would be unseemly, and it hardly seems possible. Thus, to abstain from making provision for things [not immediately consumed in use] seems neither appropriate nor even ⟨15⟩ possible for any sort of life.

Consider the things that are immediately consumed in use. First of all, it seems to me that the perfection of the contemplative life is diminished with regard to its act if one has nothing for the future in such a way that it can licitly be used (in the sense that this was explained earlier in the question concerning whether it is possible to separate a right to things from the use of them). ⟨20⟩ Secondly, it also seems to me that to have nothing for the future diminishes the perfection of contemplative life in regard to its habit. Thirdly, it seems to me that having nothing in this way is dangerous. Fourth, it would tempt God.[61]

The first point is evident, since the perfection of the contemplative life is diminished in terms of its act by a manner of living that demands a daily and, ⟨25⟩ as it were, continuous solicitude to obtain the necessities of life. However, the manner of living that lacks any sort of provision for future sustenance is something of this sort. Therefore, etc. The major premise is obvious, since the act of obtaining the necessities of corporeal life cannot take place at the same time as an act of the contemplative life in which the mind retreats ⟨30⟩ from an occupation with exterior things.

The minor also is easily made evident. Since it is necessary to have these necessities of life each day, those who totally lack them for the future will get them either by begging in order to obtain them or by other means. But this is not possible without daily solicitude, since people need these

---

[60] Reading *alienatur* for *alienantur*.
[61] Cf. Matt. 4:7.

things daily. Or, they will have these goods by obtaining nothing, but ⟨35⟩ by expecting that such goods will be offered to them without at all having to procure them. Yet, in light of the course of events that we observe, it is difficult to see how this can be. In fact, the opposite is the case, since, as experience daily teaches us, it is difficult for contemplative men ⟨⟨261⟩⟩ to be able to have what is sufficient for life entirely through begging. Thus, the lack of making any sort of provision for the future quite naturally serves to impede the acts of the contemplative life, and indeed for the greater part of the time.

The second point–⟨5⟩ that this manner of living naturally diminishes the perfection of the contemplative life in regard to its habit–is proved in the following way. A manner of living–which naturally increases the desire for temporal things and, at times, moves us to impatience–impedes the perfection of life in regard to the mind's readiness for what is good and, consequently, ⟨10⟩ in regards to [its] habit. But the manner of living which involves lacking everything for any future time is something of this sort. Therefore, etc. The major premise is evident, since it is self-evident that charity is naturally diminished by an increase in the love of temporal things–either in desiring to have them or by embracing things already held–and by a movement to impatience. ⟨15⟩ The minor also is easily shown, since need increases desire. But there can be no greater need than that of the person who has nothing for the future. Therefore, etc. As such need is continuous also, it naturally moves us at times to impatience.

The third point is evident, since it seems dangerous to entrust oneself to fortune in the things that are ⟨20⟩ necessary to life when a person can otherwise provide for himself. It seems that the manner of living in which nothing is provided for the future is something of this sort. Therefore, etc. The major premise is evident. I prove the minor, since in entrusting oneself to an uncertain eventuality when one can do otherwise, especially in regard to the necessities of life, amounts to entrusting oneself to fortune. But people who ⟨25⟩ provide none of these necessities for the future entrust themselves to an uncertain eventuality, supposing that they can do otherwise, namely, by providing for themselves in the future. Therefore, etc.

Since one might rejoin that these people do not entrust themselves to fortune but to divine providence, two responses against this [statement] are therefore added as a fourth point. In a certain sense it seems that one puts God to the test by not making provision for the future when one could do otherwise. The reason is that if someone expects from divine providence what is uncertain to him, then he appears to put God to the test when he can provide for himself through human industry without running afoul of divine providence. Moreover, the converse[62] does not appear to tempt God. Therefore etc.

The major premise is self-evident, so it seems. The minor also can easily be shown, since when a person is clearly able to provide ⟨35⟩ the necessities of life for himself, he tempts God with the expectation that these things will come to him from divine providence in a necessary manner. This expectation is implied by the rejoinder, since the person in this case can make provision for himself for the future, yet he expects what is necessary for him to come from divine providence in a necessary manner. Therefore, etc. However, there is an appropriate mode of making provision [for things] according to the course of events that we observe in human affairs and ⟨40⟩ in the circumstances where God supplies everything such as grain, wine, and so forth: a person should provide himself as well as he can with what is sufficient for his needs according to the common course of time.

In response to this, some initially say that this manner of living[63] does not ⟨⟨262⟩⟩ increase an inordinate desire or move a person to impatience, since, as the need is voluntary, a person assumes it voluntarily. They also say that by living in this way, a person does not expose himself to danger or put God to the test, since he does not belittle human help so far as it is ⟨5⟩ licit for him. For, he provides daily necessities for himself by begging, by means of the gifts of the faithful, or through manual labor for each day. Also, he reserves nothing for the future except in case of egregious necessity. He places hope in God that God will supply his necessities in some of these ways, ⟨10⟩ by moving the hearts of those people, who offer gifts or make grants to mendicants, to offer these necessities to him or grant them as alms, just as he moved the heart of the widow of Sidon of Zarephta to feed Elijah,[64] moved the raven to feed him,[65] and gave manna to the children of Israel in the desert.[66] God brings himself to help people in these ways.

In this connection, they cite the authority of blessed Augustine when, in ⟨15⟩ *On Grace and Free Will*, he speaks of God and says: "Not only does he direct the good wills of people to eternal life."[67] This [text] means that those things which conserve a creature, i.e., a person, are so subject to

---

[62] That is, making appropriate provision for things through one's own industry rather than expecting things from God.

[63] That is, not making any sort of provision for the future.

[64] 1 Kings 17:4ff.

[65] Ibid.

[66] Exod. 16:11ff.

[67] *De gratia et libero arbitrio* 20 (PL 44.906).

God's power that he does with them as he pleases, being inclined to bestow benefits on some or inflict punishments on others as he chooses. However, this ⟨20⟩ response does not seem to follow.

First, it does not seem to follow that such need is voluntary. Of course, some people live in a poverty that excludes full personal dominion over things, but allows only for dominion over things in common as well as the possession of a moderate amount of things that are necessities of life. (This poverty is the voluntary poverty to which the religious poor adhere.) ⟨25⟩ Nevertheless, the sort of poverty or need, in which someone is excluded from having to any degree what circumstances require, does not seem to be a voluntary poverty that should be assumed or chosen. This is because, as experience teaches us, the poverty which borders on harshness does not allow a person to live without significant and frequent penury. This sort of poverty naturally moves someone to an excessive desire for things, as is ⟨30⟩ evident in the case of a person suffering significant hunger. Moreover, such poverty naturally moves someone to impatience. Thus, such indigence should neither be chosen nor assumed.

However, it is true that if someone does not fall into such poverty and penury out of personal choice, he ought to bear it patiently, as is evident in the case of Lazarus who patiently bore both the grave infirmity and poverty into which he fell ⟨35⟩ even though he did not choose it. Thus, a person ought not of his own choice fall into such poverty any more than into other temptations; but, if he does, he ought indeed choose to have patience.

Consider the claim that a person who lives without making any sort of provision [for the future] does not expose himself to danger, disparage human assistance, ⟨40⟩ or test God. This claim does not seem well expressed, since, although such a person is ⟨⟨263⟩⟩ prepared to accept what is daily offered or to take what is granted, nevertheless he still disparages or neglects human help, anticipating uncertainty about receiving this help when he might otherwise provide for himself in the common course of events.

Further, ⟨5⟩ when it is said that God moves the hearts of people to supply things, then it must be said that God moves the hearts of people to do all the good things that they do. Nevertheless, when someone is uncertain about what God will move the hearts of people to do, or when God will move them, he ought not expose himself to uncertain events when he can otherwise provide for himself. Accordingly, since ⟨10⟩ we observe in the common course of events that people more readily share such temporal goods as God gives them with the indigent poor, then to expect these things at another time does not seem to be hope but rather presumption or a testing of God, as if someone were to expect to sow seeds in

August or to harvest in May.[68] If one refers to the woman and ⟨15⟩ the raven who fed Elijah or to the manna that was given to the children of Israel, then it must be said that the privilege of a few does not make a common rule. Thus, no one denies that God acts miraculously at times to affirm the faithful, whether by feeding them or in other ways. However, we are presently speaking about the common course of the world in which ⟨20⟩ many holy people are afflicted with hunger and thirst, and for them there is no help of this sort.

The words of the saints clearly show the truth of the claim that a moderate supply of temporal things for the future according to the state of each person does not diminish the perfection of life or of a state. In his commentary on Matthew 6, "Be not solicitous for the ⟨25⟩ morrow,"[69] Augustine writes: "When we see a servant of God taking care so that he does not lack necessities either for himself or for those in his care, we must be careful lest we judge him to be acting against the Lord's precept not be solicitous for the morrow. For even the Lord himself, to whom the angels ministered, deemed it worthy to have a purse to set an example. Also, in the ⟨30⟩ Acts of the Apostles, it is written that the necessities of life were obtained and reserved for the future on account of an imminent famine."[70]

Augustine expressly does not understand the saying, "Be not solicitous," to apply to every sort of provision, since the Lord himself did not hold such a view. After all, the Lord had a purse and, indeed, he had it as an example for us. ⟨35⟩ However, the phrase "as an example" means that the Lord had no necessity in himself to reserve something for the future, since he could have had things whenever he wanted either through the ministry of the angels or through creation. Augustine chose to take note of this when he said: "For the Lord, to whom the angels ministered, deemed it worthy to have a purse to set an example," ⟨⟨264⟩⟩ as if to say that it was not out of personal necessity that the Lord reserved money, since he could obtain the necessities of life from another source. Rather, he reserved money to give an example to those people who find it necessary to make provision for things, since they cannot have things that are prohibited.

---

[68] Spiers, "A Significant Manuscript of Poverty Treatises by Hervaeus Natalis, O.P. and Pierre Roger, O.S.B., (Pope Clement VI)," 12, cites the following variant for this text from Vat. Lat. 4869 (which Sikes did not have at his disposal): "Sicut si aliquis expectaret seminare in April et metere in Madio" ("as if one expects to sow seeds in April and harvest them in May").

[69] Matt. 6:34.

[70] *De sermone Domini in monte* II.17 (*CCSL* 35.159; *PL* 34.1294-5). See Acts 11:27-30.

In light of what is said later in Augustine's text about ⟨5⟩ having reserved the necessities of life for the sake of an imminent famine, some want
to say that making provision [for the future] diminishes the perfection of
life except when it is done for an imminent, unavoidable famine. But I say
that this is not true, since it is not only laudable to make provision for the
sake of unavoidable famine, it also is laudable to make provision for the
sake of a likely imminent lack of these necessities, ⟨10⟩ where the likely
lack is imminent if nothing is provided for the future. Moreover, when the
Lord had a purse, no famine was imminent. Nor is it valid to say that persecution threatened at the time, for at least when the disciples went into the
city to buy bread,[71] no persecution threatened.

Augustine ⟨15⟩ makes the same point in this text: "The Lord had a
purse. Keeping what had been offered by the faithful, he attended to their
[his and the disciples'] needs and to those of the other poor. This was the
first occasion in which the form of Church finances was instituted so that
we might understand that he directs us not to be concerned about the
morrow, not in the sense that this was a precept that no money should be
kept by the saints, but in the sense that God is not to be served for the sake
of money, and ⟨20⟩ justice is not to be deserted out of a fear of poverty."[72]
Augustine expressly says that when the Lord saved gifts "for their needs
and those of the other poor," the form of ecclesiastical finances was established. But the form of ecclesiastical finances that was instituted by the
Lord did not diminish the perfection of life. Therefore, the perfection of life
is not diminished when the Lord saved donated gifts for the future ⟨25⟩ for
his needs, his apostles' needs, and the needs of other people. Moreover,
Augustine himself says that the saying, "Be not solicitous," does not mean
that money should never be used by holy people. Rather, it means that God
is not to be served for the sake of money and that justice should not be
deserted out of a fear of poverty. This clearly shows that there is no prohibition of every solicitude for the future but only of an excessive prefer-
ence ⟨30⟩ for temporal things over spiritual things by obtaining things in a
way that exceeds a proper measure.

With reference to the same scripture text, Jerome writes that "'the
morrow' in Scripture is to be understood with reference to the future, as
when Jacob says, 'On the morrow my justice will answer for me,' and when,
in the apparition of Samuel, the sorceress said to Saul, 'On the morrow
those present will be with me.'"[73] Therefore, Jerome forbids thinking about

---

[71] Cf. John 4:8.

[72] *In Ioannis evangelium tractatus* 62.5 (*CCSL* 36.485; *PL* 35.1083).

[73] *Commentarii in evangelium Matthaei* I.6 (*CCSL* 77.41; *PL* 26.46). See Gen 30:

the future although he concedes that we ought be solicitous. ⟨⟨265⟩⟩ "It is sufficient for us to think about the present time; let us leave future things, which are uncertain, to God." The phrase "in the present time" does not refer to a present and divisible moment, since thought cannot exist in such a moment. Rather, it refers to the present time ⟨5⟩ which is close at hand and for which it is imperative to make provision for the future. Thus, Jerome says that "Let us leave future things, which are uncertain, to God." The Gloss concurs with this: "There is a superfluous solicitude arising from a defect of people when more fruits and money are reserved than is necessary and, giving up spiritual things, they are intent upon those things as if determined to despair of God's goodness."[74]

There ⟨10⟩ are many authorities who hold the same view which they express in the manner of someone who speaks deeply from the heart, as if someone were to say to his family in distress: "Do not be concerned with eating and sleeping but with gathering goods." While both are needed in times of distress, we should not be dissuaded ⟨15⟩ from obtaining what is primary. Thus, the Lord does not prohibit every solicitude for temporal things, but only the solicitude that impedes us in what we are principally to obtain, namely, spiritual goods.

In opposition to the objections:

1. When it is said that making provision [for temporal things] cannot be accomplished without distraction of the mind and solicitude, etc., then it must be said that this is ⟨20⟩ true, since obtaining such goods, whether for the present hour or the future time, cannot take place without some solicitude and distraction of the mind. But as experience clearly teaches, there is less solicitude and distraction of the mind if one is occupied with obtaining things for a moderate time–so that later one has more time to be engaged with spiritual things–than if one is occupied with doing so on a daily basis.

2. The ⟨25⟩ response is evident from what has been said, since not every sort of solicitude for the future is prohibited but only the superfluous solicitude which puts temporal things above the spiritual. Jerome's authority makes this evident. It also is evident from what we have said, since we are discussing not having solicitude for uncertain future things for which making provision is not imminent, and we are not discussing living without

---

33 for the reference to Jacob and 1 Sam. 28: 6-19 for the reference to Samuel and the sorceress who conjures the appearance of Samuel for Saul.

[74] Text not found in the *Glossa interlinearis* or *Glossa ordinaria* on Matt 6. However, this text is found in Thomas Aquinas, *Catena aurea in quattor evangelia*, *Expositio in Matthaeum* VI.20 on Matt. 6:31-32 (Marietti edition 1.117).

solicitude for any kind of future things.

3. The ⟨30⟩ minor premise is false. To prove this, it must be said that according to Gregory's authority, the holy person retains nothing for himself. Rather, he entrusts himself to divine government either since he retains nothing for himself personally or retains nothing that is superfluous. We say that a person entrusts himself to divine government in the sense that he primarily trusts that ⟨35⟩ God will not abandon him, while for his part he will do whatever is his share, although he will not provide for the future except as it is in his power.

4. Augustine's intention [in what he says] is that it is inimical to true hope to place it principally in things that slip away so that one neglects God. ⟨⟨266⟩⟩ It is significant that he calls this "turning back" a kind of aversion from God, and indicates that it relates principally to temporal things.

5. Augustine's authority should be understood in the sense that if someone does not embrace anything for the sake of God or Christ that turns him ⟨5⟩ away from Christ, then he should be secure in the necessities of life so long as he does what is in his power, as was said above. The person who makes a moderate provision for the necessities of life in the future does not act against this authority.

6. Chrysostom's authority should be understood to mean that a person should place his nourishment in the hands of God as in the hands of the chief ⟨10⟩ provider in whom he ought to trust that nothing will be lacking to him so long as he does what is in his power.

[Question 2B–How the Opposite of Poverty is Related to the Perfection of a State]

Having spoken of the opposite of poverty in relation to the perfection of personal life, we must now discuss the same matter in relation to the ⟨15⟩ perfection of a state. Two things are sought, since the state of perfection is taken in two ways, namely, the religious state and the state of prelacy. The first is whether the perfection of the religious state is diminished by having something in common in regard to ownership and dominion. The second is whether this manner of having things diminishes the state of prelacy.

[Article 1 - Whether Having Things in Common Through Ownership Diminishes the Perfection of the Religious State]

Let ⟨20⟩ us proceed to the first point and argue that to have something in common through ownership and dominion diminishes the perfection of the religious state.

1. The state in which someone retains more for himself and relinquishes less to others is less perfect than the opposite state. But people, who have temporal things in terms of a right to and dominion over them, retain more for themselves and relinquish less to others. ⟨25⟩ Thus, the state of those who have temporal things in this way is less perfect than the opposite state, which is the state of those who have nothing in this way. The major premise is assumed. The minor is easily made evident, since those who have something in common retain something and consequently do not relinquish everything. However, those who have nothing personally or in common relinquish everything ⟨30⟩ and retain nothing for themselves. Consequently, they relinquish more and retain less than the first group.

2. The state in which there is less equality is less perfect than the opposite state. In the state of those who have something in common, there is less equality than in the opposite state, namely, the state of those who have nothing ⟨35⟩ personally or in common. Therefore, etc. The major premise is assumed. The minor is easily proved, since in the state of those who have something in common, everything does not belong equally to an individual and the community, since an individual has nothing but the community has everything. Yet, in the state of those who have nothing in common or personally, everything belongs equally to an individual and to the community, ⟨40⟩ since neither the individual nor the community have anything. Therefore, etc.

3.   The state in which there is less friendship is less perfect. But in the state of those who have something ⟨⟨267⟩⟩ in common, there is less friendship than in the state of those who have nothing. Therefore, etc. The major is assumed. The minor is proved as follows: similitude is the cause of friendship, but there is less similitude in the state of those who have something in common than in the state of those who have nothing. For in the first state, the community and the individual are dissimilar, ⟨5⟩ since the community has everything and the individual has nothing. In the second state, an individual and the community have things to the same degree, since both have nothing.

4.   A state is less perfect which is less assimilated to the state of heaven. But the state of those who have something in common is less ⟨10⟩ assimilated to the heavenly state than the state of those who have nothing. Therefore, etc. The major premise is assumed. The minor is proved, since in the heavenly state the same thing is held by everyone and by each individual. But in the state of those who have something in common, the same thing is not held by everyone and by each one, since each individual has nothing while the community has everything. However, in the state of those who have nothing in common, everything is ⟨15⟩ equally held by everyone and by each one. Therefore, etc.

5.   That state is less perfect which is less assimilated to the state of innocence. But the state of those who have something in common is less assimilated to the state of innocence than the state of those who have nothing. Therefore, etc. The major premise is evident. The proof of the minor is this: in the state of innocence, people had nothing personally or in common ⟨20⟩ in terms of a right to and dominion over things. Thus, those who have something in common–in terms of ownership of and dominion over it–are less assimilated to the state of innocence than those who have nothing. However, in the state of innocence, people had nothing in common or personally in terms of dominion over things, since it is evident that no one ⟨25⟩ could say that "This is mine," "This is yours," or "This is ours."[1]

6.   Whatever diminishes the purity of poverty diminishes perfection. But to have something in common diminishes the purity of poverty. Therefore, etc. The minor premise is self-evident. The major is easily made evident, since what diminishes the purity of something diminishes its value. ⟨30⟩ This is evident when water mixed with wine diminishes the value of the wine. So too, whatever diminishes the purity of poverty diminishes its value and perfection.

---

[1]   See the appendix, pages 137 and 143 below, for related discussions of this argument.

7. Having a right to and dominion over temporal things for what is sufficient for life diminishes the perfection of poverty. But ⟨35⟩ what diminishes the perfection of poverty diminishes the perfection of life. Therefore, etc. The minor premise is assumed. The major is proved, since having wealth diminishes the perfection of poverty, and the first degree of wealth consists in having things for sustaining life. Therefore, etc.

8. Whatever causes the development of poverty not to be serious ⟨40⟩ diminishes its perfection and, consequently, the perfection of life. ⟨⟨268⟩⟩ But to relinquish temporal things personally and have them in common causes the development of poverty not to be serious, since someone relinquishes things in order that he might have them: he puts his hand to the plow[2] in relinquishing what is personal, and he looks back by having things in common. Therefore, etc.

9. What ⟨5⟩ is burdensome to [our] neighbors diminishes the perfection of the state of those who are thus burdened. But to relinquish things personally in order to receive them in common from others is burdensome to the people from whom these things are received. Therefore, etc.

10. When some are said to have something in common, "having" refers to the things possessed either in regard to the use of them in fact or in ⟨10⟩ regard to dominion over them. In the first case, the proposition is proved, since those who exist in the religious state have things in common in regard to the use of them in fact and not in regard to a right to them. In the second case, I ask whether what is held in common is held indivisibly by people who have it or whether it is divided among individuals. If everything is held indivisibly, then what is held in common cannot be divided and, thus, ⟨15⟩ they cannot use it. However, if what is held in common is divided among individuals, then it ought to be divided equally among them, since the individuals in the community have an equal right to it. But this is false according to Augustine, who says in the *Rule* that "Everything should not be given equally to everyone."[3] Thus, the things that are held in common by those who live in common are not held through ownership and dominion ⟨20⟩ but only through use in fact.

11. To be an owner of something diminishes the perfection of the owners. But those who have ownership of things in common are, to that extent, owners just as if any of them had the things personally. Therefore, etc. The major premise is assumed. The minor is proved, since "personal" applies to someone in ⟨25⟩ a community just as it would to this particular person. By similitude, then, those who have ownership of things in common are, to

---

[2] Cf. Luke 9:62.

[3] *Regula ad servos Dei* 1 (*PL* 32.1378).

this extent, the owners of the things just as if any of them had things personally.

12. The wealth of a community pertains to individuals in some manner. However, the perfection of the religious state is diminished if individuals have wealth. ⟨30⟩ Therefore, etc.

13. In the third book of the *Dialogues*,[4] blessed Gregory tells the story of abbot Isaac, whose disciples badgered him to accept the possessions that were offered for the use of the monastery. He refused them, saying that "The monk who seeks earthly possessions is no monk." But ⟨35⟩ these possessions were offered for the common use of the monastery. Therefore, to have something in common in the monastery diminishes the perfection of the monk.

ON ⟨⟨269⟩⟩ THE CONTRARY: Living in common according to the form instituted by Christ does not diminish the perfection of life. But having something in common follows the form instituted by Christ. Therefore, etc. The major premise is self-evident. The minor also is evident through Augustine, as was made evident in ⟨5⟩ the previous question where he said that when Christ had a purse he instituted the form of ecclesiastical finances. However, Christ held the money carried in the purse in common with the disciples. Therefore, etc.

RESPONSE: Three points must be treated in order to clarify this question. The first is to determine what the state of perfection signifies. The second ⟨10⟩ is to apply this discussion to the religious state. The third is to respond to the question.

In regard to the first point, it should be noted as we said above,[5] that charity and the other virtues and their acts that are joined to it pertain essentially to the perfection of a person as that which is itself essentially perfection. However, other things that contribute to this perfection–either for acquiring ⟨15⟩ charity, conserving charity, or increasing charity–pertain to personal perfection as instruments, either positively (e.g., precepts and counsels) or in a privative manner (e.g., rejecting things that impede charity). As we said above,[6] poverty pertains to the perfection of life in this privative manner. ⟨20⟩ Yet, it should be noted that virtuous works not only pertain to the perfection of life essentially, they also pertain to the perfection of life instrumentally or cooperatively. The reason is that virtuous works are certain perfections in themselves, and they advance the increase of the virtues and lead to their conservation. We have already

---

[4] *Dialogi* III.14.5 (*SC* 260.306; *PL* 77.345).

[5] See page 28 above.

[6] See page 35 above.

made this point about personal perfection.

In ⟨25⟩ regard to the perfection of a state, it should be noted that a state is called a manner of living to which someone obligates himself by a solemn vow, as is evident in the case of the profession of the religious state and the ordination of bishops. Thus, since it entails a certain permanence, a state also entails this obligation by its very name. Hence, the perfection of a state or, too, the state of perfection entails an ⟨30⟩ obligation to live in a manner that entails virtuous works and whatever contributes to them, especially works of charity whether they are freely undertaken or commanded. In every case, each state is said to be more perfect so far as its manner of living more completely entails what promotes and conserves love of God and neighbor. In every case, each state is less perfect in so far as it entails less of this sort of thing. ⟨35⟩ This concludes the first point.

As for the second point, it should be noted that some say that the religious state is a state of acquiring perfection, while the state of prelacy is the state of exercising perfection. This matter is treated by the venerable doctor, brother Thomas, in the *Secunda secundae*.[7] However, it seems to me that this claim can be either properly ⟨⟨270⟩⟩ or badly understood. First of all, we can consider the claim in regard to the religious state that is now under investigation. The claim is not true if it means that the religious state is a state of acquiring perfection, but that it is not also a state of exercising perfection in regard to the works of perfection which a person exercises in himself. ⟨5⟩ For, every religious institute, whether dedicated to the contemplative life or the active life, is ordered toward exercising the virtuous works which a person exercises in himself–for example, prayer and the meditation on God that pertain to the contemplative life–or the virtuous works that a person does to help a neighbor and that pertain to the active life.

However, ⟨10⟩ the claim is true if it means the following two things. First, the religious state is one of acquiring but not exercising perfection, so that in such a state a person advances himself toward perfection, conserves it, and avoids what naturally impedes it. Second, in terms of its nature and obligations, the state does not require that someone strengthen[8] perfection in others. ⟨15⟩ The reason is that the religious state is not the state in which one strengthens perfection in others. This activity belongs to those people who are to purge, illuminate, and perfect others[9] by admin-

---

[7]   Thomas Aquinas, *Summa theologiae* II-II.185.1.ad 2.

[8]   "Strengthen" translates *exercendo* which is otherwise translated as "exercising" or "performing."

[9]   Cf. Pseudo-Dionysius the Areopagite, *De ecclesiastica hierarchia* 5 (PG 3.166).

istering the sacraments as well as by correcting and teaching them. This makes the second point evident, since the religious state is the state in which a person is able to promote and conserve personal perfection in himself by performing virtuous works in the active and ⟨20⟩ contemplative life.

In regard to the third point (the response to the question), it should be noted that if one asks whether having temporal things in regard to ownership of and dominion over them diminishes the perfection of a religious institute, then I draw two conclusions. The first conclusion is that having temporal things in common, ⟨25⟩ so far as they are necessary for the end for which each religious institute exists, does not diminish the perfection proper to a religious institute that has things in common in this way. The second conclusion is that, other things being equal, the religious institute that is ordered to an end which has less need of temporal things is more perfect.[10]

Initially, I will prove the first conclusion absolutely: namely, to have temporal things ⟨30⟩ in common, according to the demands of the end to which the religious institute is ordered, does not diminish the perfection proper to the religious institute. The proof is this: the degree of perfection of anything ordered to an end is determined by its proportion to its end. But any religious institute is ordered to some end. Therefore, the degree of ⟨35⟩ perfection proper to any religious institute is understood according to its proportion to its end. Yet, according to the present state of life, the proportion of any religious institute to its end necessarily requires temporal things in a measure necessary in relation to the end. Therefore, etc.

Second, ⟨⟨271⟩⟩ I offer a brief proof that having things in regard to dominion over them does not diminish the perfection of a religious institute, since having things in common in order to use them in fact does not diminish the perfection of a religious institute. Therefore, having these things through dominion and ownership ⟨5⟩ does not diminish this perfection. The antecedent is evident, since no one says that having things in order to use them in fact diminishes the perfection of a religious institute, otherwise religious would necessarily die of hunger and cold. The consequent also is evident from what we have said, since, as was shown above, the use of such things cannot be separated from a right at least to their use. In the case of ⟨10⟩ things consumed in their very use, the use cannot be separated from a right to the things. Moreover, for things whose use can be separated from a right to use them, it has been shown that the lack of a right to something does not bring about greater perfection. For, as was said above,

---

[10]   See the appendix, page 133 below, for a discussion of the distinction between the two religious states and the relation of poverty to them.

the needs of a republic at times require that it be able to transfer such things.[11] If such a transfer is not possible, then in this case there would be more imperfection ⟨15⟩ than perfection.

The second conclusion–namely, that all things being equal, the religious institute that has less need of temporal things is more perfect–is proved as follows. That state in which the mind is less distracted from spiritual things is more perfect. The state which requires fewer temporal things distracts the mind less from ⟨20⟩ spiritual things to the degree that it requires temporal things less. Therefore, etc. The major premise is self-evident. The minor is easily made evident, since as temporal things are more abundant they more naturally distract the mind from spiritual things. Since religious institutes dedicated to the contemplative life require these things less, they are, all things being equal, more perfect than religious institutes dedicated to the active life. Thus, while having ⟨25⟩ an abundance of temporal things does not diminish the perfection required of religious institutes ordered to hospitality and soldiering, since the end of these institutes necessarily requires an abundance of temporal things, nevertheless the necessity of having this abundance causes the state of such an institute to be less perfect than the state of those institutes whose end does not necessarily require such an abundance.

Thus, ⟨30⟩ toward the end of *Ecclesial Property*, Augustine[12] shows it is true that having things in common according to the needs of a religious institute does not diminish its perfection. He writes: "Why should we not consider as holy the things conferred on the Church, which the priests use for necessary purposes, not to serve luxury, as things of the world, but to serve holy ends, as things consecrated to God? Thus, the goods of the Church, collected for this purpose, should serve ⟨35⟩ the needs of all those who place themselves under one person out of love for perfection and do not claim their own for themselves. Whatever profession they make, being freed from all occupation becomes the fruit of him who alone has been occupied on behalf of many. And, consequently, ⟨⟨272⟩⟩ the person who bears responsibility for all who live under him advances in the advancement of his community."

In his *[Retractions on the] Acts of the Apostles*, Bede writes that "Those who live in common in a house are called cenobites. To the extent that this life is happier, then to that extent it imitates ⟨5⟩ the future state of the

---

[11] See above, beginning on page 56, regarding the arguments in this paragraph.

[12] Pomerius, *De vita contemplativa* II.16 (*PL* 59.481). No work of the title *Ecclesial Property* is found among Augustine's works.

world when all things are common, since: 'God is all in all.'"[13]

In opposition to the objections:

1. It must be said that the minor premise is false if it is taken in the proper sense of retaining or relinquishing something, since those people who are in the state of having nothing do not retain or relinquish anything. Moreover, if one is speaking ⟨10⟩ of people who give up things before assuming this state, the minor would be false in regard to those who inordinately retain less for themselves and relinquish more to others. Now, however, retaining nothing personally or in common in regard to the present or future would not be inordinate,[14] just as ⟨15⟩ it would not be licit to have nothing for use in fact at any time, at least, although it could be licit for a brief time.

2. It must be said that there would be neither equality nor inequality in the state of those who have nothing, since both of these notions presuppose some quantity in things that are equal and unequal. Yet, among people who have nothing, there is no quantity. ⟨20⟩ Consequently, in this case there is no equality or inequality in regard to things that are held.

3. The same type of reasoning given above makes the response to this objection evident. Every similitude is founded in something positive. However, to have nothing signifies nothing positive.

4. It must be said that the minor premise is false. To prove this it ⟨25⟩ must be said that among those who have [nothing],[15] nothing is held either equally or unequally, since nothing is held. Yet, in the heavenly state something positive is held, since it is held by everyone and by each individually.

5. It must be said that the minor premise is false. To prove this, it must be said that, in the state of innocence, people had dominion over ⟨30⟩ inferior things, as when it is written, "Have dominion over the fish in the sea"[16] and, further, "of every tree which is in paradise you may eat," etc.[17] Thus, if the time of innocence had endured to the present day, a person would have a right to take the necessities for his life, use them, and exercise dominion over them. The objection, that no one was able to say "This is mine," or ⟨35⟩ "This is yours," does not follow. For, while a person could not have said "This is mine and not yours," and vice versa, those in the state of innocence could have said "This is ours." Thus, truly, they had

---

[13] Bede, *Retractationes in Actibus* 4 (*PL* 92.1010). Also, 1 Cor. 15:28.

[14] In the context of Hervaeus's treatise, one would expect *ordinate*, not *inordinate*: "retaining nothing....would not be ordinate."

[15] Reading *inter nichil habentes* for *inter habentes*.

[16] Gen. 1:28.

[17] Gen. 2:16.

dominion in common over things needed for their use. Accordingly, the state which has dominion over things in common that are necessities of life is, to that extent, similar to the state of innocence.[18]

6. The ⟨⟨273⟩⟩ objection claims that whatever diminishes the purity of poverty [diminishes the perfection of life]. However, if we are speaking about absolute poverty in the sense that greater poverty is better and more nearly brings about the perfection of life, then it must be said that that poverty more nearly brings about the perfection of life so far as it is more nearly proportioned to ⟨5⟩ a moderate sustenance of life without which there can be no life. If one says that it is sufficient to have the use of things in fact, then I say that such use cannot be licit without a right to the things.

7. It must be said that to have necessities for what is sufficient for life [does not][19] diminish the nature of poverty, which is to lack what is superfluous. This sort ⟨10⟩ of poverty is proportioned to the perfection of life.

8. It must be said that the minor premise is false. To give up things personally and to have them in common does not involve giving up things and having them in the same way. Accordingly, it is not the case that such a development[20] is not serious, since it is not a development from the same way of having things to the same way of having them.

9. It must be said that the ⟨15⟩ minor premise is false. A person need not always give up his own things in order to beg from others. For example, consider someone who gives up his personal belongings in order to have things in common with others, which is a better way of having things. Moreover, in this case, the person gives all that he has to the poor and, lacking everything, enters a monastery where, with greater security, he lives from alms. ⟨20⟩ This manner of living is not burdensome to those from whom he receives alms, since they are compensated by spiritual assistance which is more valuable than corporeal assistance. It is true that giving up personal dealings with things in order to live leisurely and in common can be an imperfection. Those mendicants who have nothing, and who must beg on a daily basis, are more burdensome than others who have things in common and ⟨25⟩ do not find it necessary to beg on a daily basis.

10. Consider things held in common by those who live in common. These things are not held indivisibly by everyone in the community in this sense: some part of the common goods are not held by one person in distinction from another part that is held by another person, but each part

---

[18] See the appendix, pages 137 and 143 below, for related discussions of this argument.

[19] Reading *non diminuit* for *diminuit*.

[20] That is, a development from having things personally to having them in common.

is held indivisibly by everyone and each individually. Moreover, ⟨30⟩ it does not follow that what is held in common must remain undivided so that it cannot be divided into parts according to the necessity of individuals. Also, it is not necessary that it be divided equally among individuals according to the equal rights of individuals. Rather, what is held in common ought to be divided so far as the community, as owner, determines it should be divided according to the needs of individuals.

11.[21] It must be said that if ⟨35⟩ having wealth is called having the necessities of life, then such wealth does not diminish the perfection of a state, just as having the necessities of life does not diminish the perfection of a state. Nevertheless, strictly speaking, ⟨⟨274⟩⟩ having the necessities of life does not make someone properly wealthy or poor. Thus, in reference to Luke 12, "I will gather everything which is naturally mine,"[22] Basil says that "If anyone takes what is sufficient for his necessities and gives what is superfluous to those in need, then he is neither wealthy nor ⟨5⟩ poor."[23] However, it is true that abundant and especially excessive wealth naturally diminishes the perfection of a state.

12.[24] It must be said that someone can be called an owner of something in two ways. In one way, what belongs to oneself is distinguished from what is [held in] common. In this sense, to call a person an owner signifies that the person does not have ⟨10⟩ something in common [with another], but only personally. Being an owner of something in this way diminishes the perfection of a state. In the other way, someone can be called an owner of something in the sense that what belongs to oneself is distinguished from what belongs to another. In this sense, those who have something in common are called owners, since what they have does not belong to someone else but to themselves, where "themselves" ⟨15⟩ is taken in common. To have ownership of things in this way does not diminish the perfection of a state. What is adduced in opposition to this–that a person in common is like a person in particular–does not follow, since it contains a double equivocation.

The first equivocation concerns "common," since the community in which a person lives in common with many people is a community ⟨20⟩ in the highest sense. But the community of which we are speaking is a community of possession according to which something is the possession of many. The second equivocation concerns the term "personal" (*proprie*),

---

[21] This response continues the issues raised in objection seven.

[22] Luke 12:18.

[23] *Homilia in illud Lucae "Destruam"* (PG 31.275).

[24] This response corresponds to objection eleven.

since when it is said that a person in common is a personal (*proprie*) individual, "personal" (*proprie*) is understood not as being distinguished from common or other. Rather "personal" (*proprie*) is distinguished from a metaphorical or ⟨25⟩ transferred meaning. Thus, the proposition comes to naught.

13.[25] It must be said that something can be understood to belong to individuals in two ways. First, something may belong to individuals as that to which individuals have a right independently of someone else. In this way, what is held in common does not belong to the individuals in the community. In the other way, something ⟨30⟩ can belong in common to the individuals of a community as to those who have it with others. And in this manner, what is held in common belongs to the individual members. This way of having things does not diminish the perfection of a state.

14.[26] It must be said that the abbot of whom the blessed Gregory spoke did not refuse to receive the necessities of life. Thus, it is not said that he was unwilling to ⟨⟨275⟩⟩ receive some possessions, but that he refused to receive everything that was offered, since it happened that excessive possessions were offered.

[ARTICLE 2–WHETHER HAVING TEMPORAL THINGS
DIMINISHES THE PERFECTION OF PRELATES]

Let us proceed to the second article, where it is argued that having temporal things diminishes the perfection of prelates.

[1.] Whatever diminishes ⟨5⟩ the perfection of a less perfect state diminishes the perfection of a more perfect state. But having temporal things diminishes the perfection of the religious state, which is a state less perfect than the state of prelates. Therefore, etc. The major premise is evident, since a more perfect state contains whatever perfection exists in the less perfect state. Thus, nothing should pertain to ⟨10⟩ perfection in the less perfect state that is not found in the more perfect state. The minor premise is granted by everyone in this sense: the state of prelates is more perfect than the state of religious.

[2.] Further, to have temporal things, at least in abundance, diminishes the perfection of the contemplative life. But the state of the prelates should have the most excellent ⟨15⟩ perfection of the contemplative life. Therefore, etc.

---

[25] This response corresponds to objection twelve.

[26] This response corresponds to objection thirteen.

[3.] Further, to have temporal things diminishes the perfection of the state which requires the greatest degree of study. The state of prelates requires the greatest degree of study. Therefore, etc. The major premise is evident, since care for temporal things quite naturally impedes perfect study. The minor also is evident, since it is the greatest and most prominent duty of the prelate ⟨20⟩ to teach others. This is not possible without a great deal of study. Therefore, etc.

ON THE CONTRARY: Something does not diminish the perfection of some state if the state does not obligate someone to its opposite. The state of prelates does not obligate someone to the opposite of this condition: having temporal things, even in abundance. Therefore, etc. The major premise is evident, since the perfection of any ⟨25⟩ state consists in this: that to which the state obliges someone is brought to completion so that, when completed, it has whatever pertains to the perfection of the state. The minor also is evident, since, the renunciation of temporal things is not contained in the obligation of the state of prelates. This is plain in the case of the most perfect prelates such as blessed Silvester, blessed Gregory, and ⟨30⟩ many others.

RESPONSE: To clarify this question, note that it is one thing to inquire whether personally having temporal things diminishes the perfection required of the state of prelacy so that personally having temporal things removes some perfection to which the state of prelacy obligates someone. It is ⟨35⟩ another thing to ask whether the renunciation of temporal things, especially on a personal basis, makes the state of prelacy more perfect when added to it.

If the question is to be understood in the first manner–namely, whether having temporal things, even personally, diminishes the perfection of the state of prelacy in the specified manner–then ⟨40⟩ the unqualified response is "No." The reason is that something does not diminish the perfection ⟨⟨276⟩⟩ proper to a given state if it does not remove some perfection to which the state obliges someone. But having temporal things, even personally, in terms of a right to and dominion over them does not remove any perfection to which the state of prelacy obliges someone. Therefore, etc. The major premise is evident, since no perfection in the aforementioned sense ⟨5⟩ is due some state unless it is that to which the state obliges someone. The minor is easily made evident, since, in regard to what is due it, the state of prelacy does not obligate the prelate except to do things for subject through which the subject is moved to have perfection: ministering the sacraments, teaching and correcting, and even dying for the defense ⟨10⟩ of perfection in a subject if it cannot otherwise be defended. But none of these activities involve what is contrary to the possession of and dominion over temporal things, since they do not entail the renunciation of temporal things. Therefore, etc.

However, suppose the question is understood in the second sense. That is, suppose one asks whether the renunciation of temporal things added to the state of prelacy makes that state more perfect or makes the person ⟨15⟩ existing in the state more apt for perfection. Then, I say that although the renunciation of temporal things, considered as an exterior effect, is not absolutely necessary for any degree of perfection of human life (as the examples of Abraham and David make clear), nevertheless the renunciation of temporal things, particularly in terms of personal dominion over them, makes one more apt for ⟨20⟩ complete perfection. We said this above in the second article of the first question regarding whether poverty, considered as an exterior effect, contributes instrumentally to perfection.[27]

However, if something is added to a state and it assists instrumentally in making a person more apt to conserve and pursue perfection, then it makes the state ⟨25⟩ considered by itself more perfect. Therefore, the renunciation of temporal things added to the state of prelacy makes the state containing both more perfect than if it included one or the other alone.[28] It should be noted that although the state of prelacy directly and in itself is ordered to bringing about perfection in a subject, it is nevertheless ordered to the ⟨30⟩ advance of perfection in the prelate himself. Otherwise, a prelate would not gain merit through the exercise of his office, which is false.

In opposition to the objections:

1. It must be said that the major premise is true in regard to what naturally diminishes the state of perfection in terms of what pertains to perfection essentially and necessarily. ⟨35⟩ However, to have temporal things does not necessarily of itself diminish what is essentially perfection. Yet, it does remove what contributes instrumentally to perfection, namely, the renunciation of temporal things.

2. It must be said that even though having temporal things might naturally diminish the perfection of the contemplative life, it does not do so necessarily, ⟨⟨277⟩⟩ since to obtain the perfection of the contemplative life it suffices to renounce temporal things through a disposition of the mind: namely, a person is so disposed that for the sake of no temporal thing will he turn away from the things that are God's, whether in the active life or the contemplative life. However, the renunciation of temporal things, ⟨5⟩ considered as an exterior effect, is not necessary for this, although it can be useful.

---

[27] See Question 1, Article 2 beginning on page 31 above.

[28] See the appendix, page 133 below, for a discussion of the distinction between the two religious states and the relation of poverty to them.

3.   It must be said that having temporal things does not necessarily impede the study that is necessary for a prelate, since, for such study, it suffices to renounce temporal things through a disposition of the mind. In this sense, the prelate is thus disposed so that for the sake of no temporal thing would he ⟨10⟩ give up the study which is necessary for his office. Further, it is not necessary that a prelate be occupied with the governance of temporal things, since this can be done by others.

[QUESTION 3–WHETHER IT IS HERETICAL TO ASSERT THAT CHRIST AND THE APOSTLES HAD NO TEMPORAL THINGS IN COMMON IN TERMS OF A RIGHT TO AND DOMINION OVER THEM]

Next we must respond to the principal question of our inquiry: whether the assertion....[1] Two things are sought concerning this question. The first is whether Christ and the apostles had some temporal goods in common ⟨15⟩ in regard to a right to and dominion over them that was at least in common. The second is whether it is heretical to assert the opposite if they did have things in this way.

[ARTICLE 1–WHETHER CHRIST AND THE APOSTLES HAD SOME TEMPORAL THINGS IN COMMON IN TERMS OF A RIGHT TO AND DOMINION OVER THEM]

Let us proceed to the first article, where it is argued that Christ and the apostles did not have something either personally or in common in terms of a right to and dominion over it, so that this proposition–namely, that Christ and the apostles ⟨20⟩ had nothing, personally and in common–is true in an unqualified way. Some argue this point as follows:

1. A proposition is true in an unqualified way when the predicate belongs to[2] the subject to which it belongs in the most eminent way. However, to have nothing personally or in common belongs to Christ and the apostles ⟨25⟩ in the most eminent way. Therefore, etc. The major premise is evident through a simile. Health is said in an unqualified manner to be the health of a person who is well disposed in his bodily perfection. For example, the health of a person who is very healthy is health in an unqual-

---

[1] That is, whether Christ and the apostles, personally or in common, had none of the temporal things which come into use in human life, either in regard to ownership of or dominion over them.

[2] In this objection and its reply, "belongs to" translates *convenio*. Note that *convenio* typically has a stronger sense of "fitting," "appropriate," or "proper," as in the next sentence where "having nothing" belongs to Christ and the apostles as what is fitting or appropriate to them.

ified manner.[3] In the same way, something is unqualifiedly said of all the members of a group without qualification when it is a predicate belonging to a subject according to its complete being.[4]

The minor is proved initially in reference to Christ. ⟨30⟩ As is said in the decretal, *Exiit qui seminat*, etc.:[5] Christ at times assumed the character of those who are weak (e.g., when he had a purse), and at other times he assumed the character of those who are perfect (e.g., when he had nothing personally or in common). Therefore, according to this reasoning, having nothing personally or in common belongs to Christ in so far as he assumed the character of those who are perfect. But whatever belongs to Christ in so far as he assumed ⟨35⟩ the character of those who are perfect, belongs to him according to his own being. Therefore, to have nothing personally or in common belongs to Christ in so far as he is perfect. This proof makes the minor evident in regard to Christ.

The same minor is proved by reference to the apostles by appealing to diverse saintly authorities. ⟨⟨278⟩⟩ One of these authorities is Eusebius, who says that the apostles themselves were bound in their mission to lead a life of extreme poverty in such a way that they had no thought for daily nourishment and did not possess two tunics.[6] Moreover, we have the authority of the decretal, *Exiit*, the chapter beginning with *Porro*, where it is said, ⟨5⟩ "We speak of the renunciation of the ownership of all things," etc., and it continues "How the first founders of the Church militant drank from the vessels of doctrine and life as from the very source, desiring to live perfectly as they drank from them."[7]

2. The virtues that constitute the state ⟨10⟩ of perfection existed most eminently in the apostles. But one finds the poverty of those who have nothing personally or in common among the virtues that constitute the state of perfection. Thus, such poverty was in the apostles. The proof of the major premise is that in each genus a perfection of things is what exists most eminently in the most important members. Yet, the apostles were the chief source of the virtues in the militant ⟨15⟩ Church. Therefore, etc. The minor is made evident by means of Matthew 19, "If you would be perfect, go and sell all that you have and give it to the poor,"[8] since doing this

---

[3] Compare the appendix, page 121 below.

[4] See the argument cited in the appendix at page 121 below.

[5] Nicholas III, *Exiit qui seminat* (*CIC* II.1112).

[6] Cf. Aquinas, *Catena Aurea, Expositio in Lucam* IX.1 on Luke 9:3 (Marietti edition 2.125). Also, cf. Eusebius, *Commentarii in Lucam* (*PG* 24.543).

[7] Nicholas III, *Exiit qui seminat* (*CIC* II.1112).

[8] Matt. 19:21.

involves retaining nothing for oneself, either personally or in common. Therefore, etc.[9]

3. If the apostles had something in common, they had it either from what they reserved for themselves or from alms which came from ⟨20⟩ begging or gifts or from what they acquired through personal labor. However, the apostles did not have something in common in any of these ways. Therefore, etc. The major premise is evident by means of a complete division. The minor is proved initially in regard to the first member of the division, namely, they reserved nothing of what they had for themselves. For, in Matthew it is written: "If you would be perfect, go ⟨25⟩ and sell all,"[10] and "Renouncing everything, he followed him."[11] In regard to the second and third members of the division, the minor is proved by means of Chrysostom, who in his praises of Paul says that "He did not possess money, since he frequently did not have the necessary food."[12] Indeed, Paul says of himself: "Still we go hungry and thirsty."[13] ⟨30⟩ Accordingly, it seems that he did not have the wherewithal to be able to have food or clothing, whether by means of alms or personal labor. Further, in the stories about Simon and Jude, it is said that when the leader wanted to confer priestly property on them, they said that they wanted to possess nothing on earth, since there was possession of these things in heaven.[14]

4. The ⟨⟨279⟩⟩ apostles were bound to adhere to evangelical poverty through precept and vow. But evangelical poverty involves having nothing personally or in common. Therefore, etc. Matthew 19, "Behold we have relinquished everything," makes the major premise evident in regard to a vow.[15] In *The City of God 16*,[16] Augustine explains this text ⟨5⟩ by saying that the apostles vowed then to undertake evangelical poverty. In regard to a precept, the major also is evident in light of what was said to the

---

[9] See the appendix, page 123 below, for a discussion of this argument.

[10] Matt. 19:21.

[11] Matt. 4:20.

[12] *De laudibus Pauli Homilia* 4 (*PG* 50.491).

[13] 1 Cor. 4:11.

[14] See the appendix, page 123 below, for the treatment of this objection. For the story about Simon and Jude, see the appendix, page 124 below. Although, the author refers to Eusebius, *Ecclesiastica historia* I.13 (*PG* 20.130), only the story about Thaddeus is contained in Eusebius' work.

[15] Matt. 19:27.

[16] *De civitate Dei* XVII.4 (*CCSL* 48.559; *PL* 41.530). The Latin text incorrectly refers to Book XVI.

apostles: "Do not ⟨10⟩ possess gold."[17] In commenting on *Acts* 3, "Silver and gold I have none,"[18] Augustine[19] notes that Peter said this in order to follow his teacher's precept which said "Do not possess gold," etc. The minor also is made evident by Eusebius,[20] who says that in their missions, the apostles were bound to adhere to extreme poverty. However, extreme poverty is having nothing personally or in common. Therefore, etc.

5.   Speaking of Peter and Andrew, Gregory says in his Sermon[21] that the apostles gave up everything in so far as it could be desired by them. ⟨15⟩ But they were able to desire temporal things personally and in common; consequently, they gave up temporal things in both forms.[22] The same point is made evident through the authority of Sacred Scripture. First, in Luke 6 it is written: "The foxes have holes, the birds of the air their nests, but the Son of Man has nowhere to lay his head."[23] So too, in Acts 3, Peter says that "Silver and ⟨20⟩ gold I have none,"[24] to which the [Interlinear] Gloss adds "following the precept of his teacher."[25] Also, in Matthew 10, The Lord said to the apostles, "Do not possess gold or silver or money in your wallets, nor a sack for the journey, two tunics, shoes or a staff; for the laborer is worthy of his food."[26]

The same point is proved by many authorities among the saints. For example, in his ⟨25⟩ letter to Eustochius, Jerome says, "It was not possible that the Lord had things he forbade his disciples when he said 'Do not take a bag, or wallet or bread'; accordingly, he had nothing."[27] So too, in his commentary on the *Epistle to the Corinthians*, Ambrose writes that "The women, out of a desire for the Lord's teaching and their love of ⟨⟨280⟩⟩ the virtues, followed the apostles, ministering to them with service and expenses, just as they had followed the Savior and ministered to him out of

---

[17] Matt. 10:9.

[18] Acts 3:6.

[19] Pseudo-Augustine, *De mirabilius scripturae* III.16 (*PL* 35.2201).

[20] Cf. Aquinas, *Catena Aurea, Expositio in Lucam* IX.1 on Luke 9:3 (Marietti edition, 2.125). Also, cf. Eusebius, *Commentarii in Lucam* (*PG* 24.543).

[21] *Homiliae in Evangelium* I.5 (*PL* 76.1095).

[22] See the appendix, pages 131-132 below, for a discussion of this argument.

[23] Luke 9:58.

[24] Acts 3:6.

[25] *Glossa interlinearis* on Acts 3:6 (*Biblia Latina cum glossa ordinaria* IV.459)

[26] Matt. 10:9.

[27] *Epistolae* 22.19 (*CSEL* 54.170; *PL* 22.406).

their property."[28]

From these considerations, it is argued that Christ and the apostles accepted expenses from the women but that they would not have done this if they already had something personally or ⟨5⟩ in common. Therefore, etc. Also, commenting on the word of the Lord, Augustine writes in *Sermon 12*, "Few are those who have given up everything and followed Christ."[29] Again, in his letter to Nebulia, Jerome writes, "Do what the apostles did; sell all that you have and follow the bare and solitary cross."[30] Also, in his commentary on Matthew, Cyril speaks in this way about the apostles: "He [Christ] wants ⟨10⟩ them to lack any mundane solicitude so that they will not show any care for food taken as a necessity or as something that cannot be regained. So, he does not permit them to take anything at all."[31] From this, it is evident that, if the Lord did not allow them to take anything at all, then they had nothing personally or in common.

So, too, in commenting on the Psalms, Augustine writes in the beginning that "The apostles left everything they had for the poor. Having distributed ⟨15⟩ what they had, they remained in the world without wealth."[32] Note that he says that "They gave everything they had." Therefore, they were left with nothing personally or in common.

Also, in his commentary on Mark 6, "he instructed them to take nothing,"[33] Bede says that Christ gave this precept to the apostles "so that with security they would neither possess nor carry the small or minimum necessities of life."[34] Again, in his commentary on Matthew 17, ⟨20⟩ "Open its mouth and you will find a coin,"[35] Jerome says that "Taken without qualification, this story edifies the hearer, since he hears that the Lord was so poor that he did not have the tribute to pay for himself and his disciples.

---

[28] Ambrosiaster, *In I ad Corintheos* 9 (*PL* 17.229). Cf. 1 Cor. 9:4-5.

[29] *Sermo* 113.1 (*PL* 38.648).

[30] *Epistolae* 130.14 (*CSEL* 56.193; *PL* 22.1118).

[31] Presumably, Cyril of Alexandria. Text not found as such. A somewhat similar version of the text is cited in the appendix at page 123 below. However, see Cyril, *Commentarii in Lucam, Homilia* 48 (*CSCO* 140.70.101; *PG* 72.642), which deals with Luke 9:3. The Latin texts in *CSCO* and *PG* differ from one another, although they have the same basic sense. The *CSCO* divides the commentary into separate homilies; the *PG* does not. Also cf. *Commentarii in Matthaeum* 26 (*PG* 72.395) regarding Matt. 10:10.

[32] *Enarrationes in Psalmos* 143.18 (*CCSL* 40.2087; *PL* 38.1868).

[33] Mark 6:8.

[34] *In Marci evangelium expositio* II.6 (*PL* 26.127-8).

[35] Matt. 17:26.

But what if someone chooses to object, since Judas carried money in his purse?"[36] We respond that Jesus thought it ⟨25⟩ sacrilegious to take the goods of the poor for his own use, so that he gave us an example of having a purse with money.[37]

ON THE CONTRARY: In John 12 it is written that "He [Judas] said this, not from any concern for the poor, but because he was a thief. He kept the purse and took what was put into it."[38] From this authority, it is evident that Christ had a purse, and that he saved what was placed in it. ⟨30⟩ Second, at John 13 it is written, "Some thought that since Judas kept the purse, Jesus had said to him: go and buy ⟨⟨281⟩⟩ what we need for the feast, or give something to those in need."[39] From this, it is apparent that Christ had money to buy what was necessary for himself and his followers. But having money in such a way that one can exchange it and give it away means that one has it in terms of a right to and dominion over it. Therefore, etc.

RESPONSE: To ⟨5⟩ clarify this question, it should be noted that there was a twofold nature in Christ: divine and human. Thus, one can ask about the right owed to Christ either in regard to his divine nature or in regard to his human nature only. If one should ask about the right owed to Christ in regard to his divine nature, it is clearly evident that every creature belongs to him ⟨10⟩ in terms of right and the fullest dominion. So, it is said in the Psalms that "The earth is the Lord's and its fullness thereof"[40] as well as "If I am hungry, I will not complain to you, for the earth is mine and all that it contains."[41]

However, if one should inquire about the right owed to Christ in regard to his human nature, then one should make an additional distinction concerning the right owed to him in human things, since this right ⟨15⟩ can pertain to him in two ways: by reason of himself or by reason of other people who gave goods to him. Suppose one takes the first sense and asks whether Christ has a right to such things, that is, according to his human nature. Then I say that the right he is owed to such things in terms of his human nature is greater than the right that would be owed any master in

---

[36] *Commentarii in evangelium Matthaei* III.18 [III.17 in *CCSL*] (*CCSL* 77.155-6; *PL* 26.127-8).

[37] See the appendix, beginning at page 131 below, for a discussion of the basic argument and many of the texts contained in the fourth and fifth objections.

[38] John 12:6.

[39] John 13:29.

[40] Ps. 23:1.

[41] Ps. 49:12.

regard to his slave and the slave's possessions that were ⟨20⟩ justly acquired by the master. Christ is owed this right by reason of redemption. The reason is that anyone who liberates a person justly damned in regard to the death of the body and soul from both of these deaths has a greater right to the person thus liberated than anyone who liberates a person justly damned to bodily death from that death has a right to the person thus liberated. But the person who liberates ⟨25⟩ someone justly damned to bodily death from that death is owed a right to that liberated person as to a slave and to that person's things as to what belongs to a slave. Thus, according to his human nature and by virtue of redeeming the entire human race, Christ is owed a right to all people and all of their goods, as if to his slaves and their goods.

Yet, having ⟨30⟩ a right to these goods does not diminish Christ's perfection in any way, since the possession of goods to any degree of abundance could not move his will to an inordinate love of them or distract his mind from the goods of the soul. Thus, Christ assumed poverty not to assist in living well but ⟨35⟩ to give an example to us who are naturally attracted to temporal wealth in a bad way. It is now evident in what way Christ has a right to human things by reason of himself.

Consider ⟨⟨282⟩⟩ the second major point–namely, both the manner in which Christ had a right to the things that come into use in this life by reason of what others gave to him and the manner in which the apostles also had a right to things through gifts, begging, or what they acquired through personal labor ⟨5⟩ (which is the principal issue of our question). Some say that Christ and the apostles had only a bare use of such things in fact and utterly no right to or dominion over them. Unless one wants to deny Sacred Scripture, no one can deny that Christ and the apostles actually had the things that come into use in human life. This is ⟨10⟩ evident, first of all, in regard to money, since in John 12, it is written about Judas: "He said this, not from any concern for the poor, but because he was a thief. He kept the purse and took what was put into it."[42] Therefore, according to this text, Christ had a purse for his sake and that of his disciples.

Moreover in John 13, when Christ said: "What you do, do quickly. None of them at the table knew for what purpose ⟨15⟩ Jesus said this to him. Indeed some thought that since Judas had the purse, Jesus had said to him, 'Buy what we need for the feast, or to give something to those in need.'"[43] The disciples could not have thought this unless Judas had the

[42] John 12:6.
[43] John 13:27-9.

wherewithal to be able to buy what was needed for the feast day or the wherewithal to give something to the poor. The same point is made in John 4: "The disciples ⟨20⟩ went into the city in order to buy food."[44] Thus, they had the wherewithal to buy food. However, a purchase is commonly made with money. Moreover, it is certain that Christ and the apostles had clothing which they used and a house that they used at various times for habitation or sleeping, unless they always slept under the sky.

I ⟨25⟩ will prove the following assertion, first through reason, then through authorities: Christ and the apostles had a right to use things in regard to the immovable things that they used at times; they also had a right to the use of things as well as a right to the things used with respect to goods that were immediately consumed in their use, such as food and drink, or that were gradually consumed by their use, such as clothing. In regard to the first proof [through reason], I ⟨30⟩ intend to prove the proposition with reference to three considerations: first, Christ's and the apostles' use of such goods; second, the manner in which they had such goods; and third, the explanation of why they were said to renounce ⟨⟨283⟩⟩ the right to such things. Fourth, in light of these considerations, [it will be shown that] the disciples were obligated to transfer the right to such things to others.

First, I argue in relation to the use of things and, initially, in regard to the use of immovable things for which the right to the use of a thing is ⟨5⟩ separated from the right to the thing [itself]. For, no licit use of a thing can be separated from the right to use it. Yet, it is a fact that Christ and the apostles had licit use of some immovable things; therefore, they had the right to use them. The major premise is evident in light of the article in which we inquired whether the right to a thing can be separated from the use,[45] and we showed that it is impossible to separate the licit use of any thing from the right to that very use, whether the thing is movable or immovable. The minor is ⟨10⟩ also evident: namely, that Christ and the apostles had some use of some immovable things, e.g., the houses in which they slept, unless we suppose that they always slept under the sky. Moreover, it is a fact that they did not have the use of things unless the use was licit. It would be sacrilegious to assert the opposite.

Second, I prove that they had a right to the things consumed ⟨15⟩ in use, not just as a right to use the things, but also as a right to the things [themselves] that they used. I prove the assertion in this way: in regard to things that are consumed in their use, the right to a thing cannot be

---

[44] John 4:8.
[45] See Question 2A, Article 1, beginning on page 37 above.

separated from its licit use, or vice versa. For in such cases, the licit use of a thing cannot be separated from the right to its use. Also, the licit use of a thing cannot be separated from the right to the thing [itself] that is used. But it is a fact that Christ and the apostles had licit use of such things, e.g., food, clothing, and the money with which ⟨20⟩ they bought things. Moreover, it is a fact that such things are consumed in their use, e.g., food and clothing, or at least transferred, e.g., money. Thus, Christ and the apostles had a right to the use of such things as well as a right to the things themselves. The major premise is evident in light of what was said in an earlier article which asked whether it is possible to separate the use of a thing from a right to it. The minor ⟨25⟩ also is evident, namely, that Christ and the apostles had the use of such things. It is a fact that they did not have such use unless it was licit.

Next, I prove the same proposition in relation to the manner in which Christ and the apostles had things. I argue as follows, since I ask whether or not they had things which were consumed in their use–which we are now discussing–in a manner that differed from other people. If not, ⟨30⟩ then any other person could take these things and use them just as Christ and the apostles used them. But it is surely irrational that Christ and the apostles would have usurped for themselves what was held in common with anyone else as well as themselves. If, however, they had things in a different way from others, then I ask: how did they have them in a way different from others? For, either they themselves had a right to these things and others did not or ⟨35⟩ they actually kept these things without any right to use or keep them. If the first case is true, then the proposition is proved, namely, that they had a right to the things themselves.

If the second case holds–namely, they actually kept things without a right to keep them–then I ask whether those goods were reckoned among the goods of someone or no one. ⟨40⟩ If these things were reckoned among the goods belonging to no one, then by this very fact, they were granted to the person holding them; ⟨⟨284⟩⟩ and consequently, by this very fact that the apostles held them, they had a right to them. If these things were reckoned among the goods of someone, then Christ and the apostles either kept these goods with that person's permission or they did not. If not, then they took hold of another person's goods without the permission or the will of the other person, namely, the owner of the things. But this is not possible, ⟨5⟩ since it would have been an unjust usurpation of someone else's things. Neither Christ nor the apostles did this. If, however, they had the permission of the owner to keep such things, then it follows that they had a right at least to keep them.

Thus, I ask further whether the owner granted license to Christ and the apostles only to keep these things and do nothing else with them, or whether the owner granted license to keep and use the things and consume them through use. ⟨10⟩ If the first case holds–namely, that things were granted to them to be kept in their hands or where they were, but not for any other purpose–then it follows that they could licitly do nothing else but keep these things. But this is false, since they obviously used these things by consuming them and transferring them in whatever manner was helpful to them to turn the things to their advantage. ⟨15⟩ It is a fact that they licitly used things in this way, unless one supposes that they sinned in this use. But it is false and even laughable that Christ and the apostles busied themselves by keeping other people's things without any use or enjoyment of them.

If the second case holds–namely, that the owner of these things granted them to Christ and the apostles not only to be kept ⟨20⟩ but also to be used and, indeed, to be used at will for their advantage–then it follows that they had a right to these things in all of these ways. The reason is that the various ways in which the owner grants something to another person determines the right that person acquires to any aspect of the thing. But according to the hypothesis, the owner of things ⟨25⟩ granted these things to Christ and the apostles in all of the above mentioned ways. Therefore, etc.

In connection with this point, some say that Christ and the apostles had the things that come into use in human life, especially those things consumed in their use, in terms of every use which the owner enjoyed, namely, consuming and transferring them. However, they say that Christ and the apostles had these things in terms of ⟨30⟩ a bare use in fact, but not in terms of a right to them, since Christ and the apostles were not capable of having such a right. They say this because Christ and the apostles were obligated through a vow and a precept to an opposite condition: namely, not to have such a right. First, they cite Matthew 19, "Behold we have relinquished everything,"[46] and they say that the apostles renounced every right to temporal things through a vow. Second, ⟨35⟩ they cite Matthew 10, "Do not possess gold or money in your wallets, nor a scrip for the journey, nor two tunics, shoes or staff, since the laborer is worthy of his food."[47] They say that ⟨⟨285⟩⟩ the Lord forbade the apostles through a precept from having any right to temporal things.[48]

However, this response seems to me to be quite irrational, namely, that someone would be obligated by a vow or precept to lack a right to things ⟨5⟩ whose use is commanded by a precept. Yet, we are commanded by a precept to use temporal things for the necessities of life. Therefore, it is

---

[46] Matt. 19:27.

[47] Matt. 10:9-10.

[48] See the appendix, beginning at page 137, for discussions of this argument.

clearly irrational to obligate oneself to assume no rights to things or to prescribe that no rights to such things should be held. This is evident for two reasons. First, as was said above,[49] given that the right to such things—whether in regard to the use of a thing or in regard to the ⟨10⟩ very substance of a thing–is nothing other than the power of licitly using them, then it follows that the use of such things without a right to them is illicit. Yet, to prescribe that a person lack that without which the use of such things is illicit is to prescribe that he completely lack the use of temporal things or that he carry out their use illicitly. Both of these alternatives are illicit and contrary to the Lord's precept. ⟨15⟩ Therefore, asserting that someone is prohibited by a divine precept from having a right to such things amounts to saying that God prescribes what is illicit and, by his precept, what is contrary to sustaining life.

Second, according to everyone, a right to temporal things is ordered to their use as to an end, especially in regard to ⟨20⟩ the use of what is necessary for sustaining life. Indeed, people are obligated by a divine precept to do this. Nothing is intrinsically related to an end unless the end cannot be attained without it, or at least cannot be attained very well.[50] Otherwise, it would be related to the end in vain. Thus, that precept which commands someone to lack a right to temporal things ⟨25⟩ thereby prescribes the lack of that without which the use of temporal things cannot be realized in an unqualified way or, at least, very well. However, such a precept seems to be irrational, namely, to prescribe an end and to prescribe the lack of that without which the end cannot be realized in an unqualified way or, at least, very well.

Moreover, the same point follows in respect to a vow: namely, a vow would be ⟨30⟩ irrational and illicit through which someone obligates himself to lack something without which the use of temporal things could not be realized or, at least, realized very well, especially in relation to the use of things that is unqualifiedly contained in a precept. Jesus did not at any time give such a precept, as they say, nor indeed did any apostle take such a vow. The text from Matthew 19, "Behold we ⟨⟨286⟩⟩ relinquished everything,"[51] should be understood in regard to the personal renunciation of

---

[49] See the discussion beginning on page 44 above.

[50] *aeque bene*: literally, "equally well." Cf., for example, St. Thomas Aquinas, *Summa theologiae*, III.1.2.resp. for a similar distinction between what is necessary for an end to exist at all, as food is necessary for the conservation of life, and what is necessary for an end to be attained in a fitting or expeditious manner, as a horse is necessary for a journey.

[51] Matt. 19:27.

temporal things but not, however, in regard to the total renunciation of temporal things both personally and in common.

This meaning is indicated in Acts 4,[52] "Nor did any of them claim ⟨5⟩ that anything he possessed was his own, but everything was common to them,"[53] and in what follows: "Everyone who owned fields or houses sold them. They brought the price of what they sold and laid it at the feet of the apostles; they divided it among everyone according to his need."[54] Note that it is expressly said that everything was common to them and that they had everything in common. ⟨10⟩ Accordingly, in his *Rule*, Augustine says: "Thus, you read in the Acts of the Apostles 'since everything was common [to them].'"[55] Therefore, I ask about this pronoun "them," and whether "to them" refers to the apostles or to some others. "To them" cannot refer to other people, since *ante* ("at") does not allow "to them" to refer to anyone else [than the apostles].[56] Since Augustine writes, "Thus you will read in the Acts of the Apostles ⟨15⟩ since everything was common to them," it follows, according to Augustine's meaning, that everything was common to the apostles and, consequently, that they had something in common. This text, namely, "was common to them," cannot be explained as a reference to the throng of believers and not to the apostles, since Augustine expressly interprets the text as referring to the apostles.[57]

It ⟨20⟩ should be noted that the Gospels give many examples of renouncing temporal things as well as parents and other earthly friends. These examples should be understood in terms of a disposition of the mind by which one prefers God to them. Moreover, these examples should not be understood in regard to renunciation considered as an external effect. For example, in ⟨25⟩ Luke 14, it is written, "If anyone comes to me and does not hate his father and mother and wife and children and brothers and sisters and even his own life, then he cannot be my disciple."[58] But this was not to be understood to mean that we, who are commanded to love our enemies, should hate those who are related to us by blood. According to blessed Ambrose,[59] this text does not mean that we should cease loving

---

[52] The text has "III."

[53] Acts 4:32.

[54] Acts 4:34.

[55] *Regula ad servos Dei* 1 (*PL* 32.1379).

[56] Acts 4:34 says that the proceeds from the goods that were sold were placed "at the feet of the apostles" (*ante pedes apostolorum*).

[57] See page 140 below in the appendix for a discussion of this matter.

[58] Luke 14:26. The Latin text has XIII.

[59] *Expositio evangelii secundum Lucam* VII.201 (*CCSL* 14.284; *PL* 15.1753).

our ⟨⟨287⟩⟩ parents for the sake of God, but that we should prefer God over the love for our earthly parents. Also, in his commentary on Mark 10, "Amen, I say to you that no one who forsakes his father,"[60] Theophylact writes, "This text does not tell us to abandon our fathers and not support them, ⟨5⟩ or to be separated from our wives. But it does instruct us to prefer the honor of God to secular things."[61]

The second point to be adduced from Matthew 10, "Do not possess gold,"[62] is that the text should not be understood as if the Lord unqualifiedly and universally forbade the disciples from having any rights ⟨10⟩ to temporal things. For, he said this when he sent them to preach so that, absolved from every care for temporal things that would impede preaching, they would know that temporal things were owed them by the people to whom they were going to preach. Thus, in his commentary on the text, "Worthy is the laborer of his hire,"[63] blessed Jerome says: "Since the apostles had been sent out to preach in a certain manner naked and unencumbered ⟨15⟩ and since the condition of teachers will seem to be harsh, he tempered the severity of his precept with the following opinion, 'The laborer is worthy of his food' as if to say: 'accept as much food and clothing as is necessary for you.' Thus the Apostle says, 'With food and clothing let us be content,'[64] and elsewhere 'Let the catechumen ⟨20⟩ share all his goods with his teacher.'[65] Accordingly, those to whom the disciples sow spiritual goods should make them sharers in their earthly goods not out of avarice, but out of necessity."[66]

Chrysostom also comments on the same text saying: "Next, so that the apostles do not speak as beggars, 'Thus you command us to live, and in this way be ashamed,' he shows the indebtedness owed to them by calling them workers and by calling what ⟨25⟩ is given to them wages."[67]

So too, in his commentary on the text "Do not possess," Augustine says: "For when the Lord said, 'Do not possess gold...' etc., he added without interruption, 'The laborer is worthy of ⟨⟨288⟩⟩ his food.' By means of this remark, he made it sufficiently obvious that he did not want them to possess or carry these things. His reason was not that these things are not

---

[60] Mark 10:29.

[61] *Enarrationes in evangelium Marci* X (PG 123.603).

[62] Matt. 10:9-10.

[63] Luke 10:7.

[64] 1 Tim. 6:8.

[65] Gal. 6:6.

[66] *Commentarii in evangelium Matthaei* I.10 (CCSL 77.66-7; PL 26.65).

[67] *Homilia 32 in Matthaeum* 5 (PG 57.382-3).

necessary for sustaining life; rather, he sent them in order to demonstrate that these things were owed to them by the believers to whom they proclaim the Gospel as wages are due to soldiers. ⟨5⟩ However, it is apparent that, by these instructions, the Lord did not mean that the evangelists should not live only on those to whom they proclaimed the Gospel (otherwise Paul acted contrary to this precept when he acquired food by the work of his own hand),[68] but that he gave the apostles the power to know that these things were their due. ⟨10⟩ When something is commanded by the Lord, there is the guilt of disobedience, if it is not observed. However, it is licit for someone not to use a power and as it were to recede from his right. Therefore, the Lord ordained that those who proclaim the Gospel should live by the Gospel, saying to the apostles that all things were owed to his own ministers, who required nothing superfluous."[69]

It might be said that the debt about which Chrysostom ⟨15⟩ and Augustine speak is understood in terms of a debt of gratitude and not a debt of right. But this does not follow, since Chrysostom says that the necessities are owed to the apostles as a wage is owed to workers, and Augustine says that the necessities are owed to the apostles as pay is owed to soldiers. Moreover, he says that the Lord gave the apostles the power to ⟨20⟩ know that this was owed to them. However, this sort of debt is not called so much a debt of gratitude, as a debt of right. Augustine's subsequent comment shows this more expressly: in not using such a power, the Apostle surrendered his right. Thus, such a power is a power of a right and not only a debt of gratitude.

However, ⟨25⟩ it should be noted that the Lord prohibited the apostles from having gold and silver, or such things, not by denying them altogether any right to temporal things but for other reasons, and especially, for two. The first reason is that they were owed temporal goods from another source, namely, from those whom they taught. The second reason is that they should not have things in a superfluous manner as blessed Jerome explains in connection with the text, "neither two tunics."[70] Jerome says ⟨30⟩ "Two tunics seems to me to indicate two sets of clothing. ⟨⟨289⟩⟩ He does not mean that we ought be content with one tunic in the region of Sichyon[71] frozen with icy snow. Rather, since tunics refers to clothing, we should be clothed with one set but not reserve another for ourselves out of a fear for the future." It is clear that Jerome understands "two tunics" to

---

[68] 1 Thess. 2:9.

[69] *De consensu evangelistarum* II.30 (*CSEL* 43.177f.; *PL* 34.1113-4).

[70] *Commentarii in evangelium Matthaei* I.10 (*CCSL* 77.66; *PL* 26.65).

[71] Perhaps Sicyon in the Peloponnesian province of Achaia.

refer to two sets ⟨5⟩ of clothing, of which only one is necessary for the present.

Third, the same point[72] will be proved from the reasons for saying that the apostles did not have a right to temporal things. The reason is that some people argue that the apostles did not have such a right because the lack of such a right pertains to evangelical perfection. But this is false, since ⟨10⟩ to have something in common, as was shown above,[73] does not diminish the perfection of a person or a state. Therefore, etc. In light of these remarks, moreover, what was said in that question[74] applies to the present question: not only is the perfection of a person or state not diminished by having such a right but, indeed, the opposite seems ⟨15⟩ to diminish the perfection of life in regard to a person or a state. For in lacking such a right one would lack what is ordered to the use of temporal things with respect to its end, so that the end could not be attained either in an unqualified way or very well. Nevertheless, to achieve such an end, let us be bound by a divine precept to use temporal things for the necessities of life.

Fourth, the same point is proved in regard to transactions made by Christ and the ⟨20⟩ apostles, since it is a fact that they sold some things: e.g., fish that they caught, and things that they made with their hands. At times they even bought some things with money as is evident in John 4[75] and intimated in John 13.[76] Thus, I ask whether or not the money they gave to the sellers when they bought things transferred in right to the sellers. ⟨25⟩ If not, the sellers had no right to the money. This is inappropriate because, at that point, the sellers were cheated, since they intended to have a right to the money that was given to them. Thus the apostles were deceivers, since, at that point, some other group of people besides the apostles strove after evangelical perfection in regard to having a bare use of things in fact ⟨30⟩ without a right to them. For those sellers actually used the money that was given to them and yet, as is supposed, they had no right to it.

If, however, one should suppose that the right to the money was transferred to those who sold something to Christ and the apostles, then I ask:

---

[72] That is, the proposition asserted on page 98 above: Christ and the apostles had a right to use things in regard to the immovable things which they used at times; they also had a right to the use of things as well as a right to the things [themselves] when considering goods that were immediately consumed in their use, such as food and drink, or that were consumed over a period of time, such as clothing.

[73] See pages 57 and 82 above.

[74] That is, Question 2B, Article 1.

[75] John 4:8.

[76] John 13:29.

who transferred the right to that money to the sellers? Either that right was transferred to the sellers by the apostles themselves, ⟨35⟩ or by someone else in their name, or by a different person but not in their name. The apostles or someone else in their name could not transfer the right to that money to anyone at all, for someone who does not have a right to something cannot ⟨⟨290⟩⟩ transfer the right to that thing to anyone at all, nor can another do it in his name. But it is stipulated that the apostles had no right to the money or to any other temporal thing. Therefore, etc.

However, if someone else transferred the right to the money, then it was either the one who gave [the money] to the apostles or it was God. It was not the person who gave the money to the ⟨5⟩ apostles, since in giving [the money] to the apostles, the person intended to strip himself of all right which he had to the money. It was not God, since if God had transferred that right to the sellers over and above what was contained in any other contract [with them], then God would have done something special in the purchases made by the apostles that he does not do in other purchases. But neither experience nor authority would indicate this ⟨10⟩ unless someone has dreamt it. Therefore, etc.

The same conclusion can be drawn in reference to occasions when the apostles sold fish or things made with their own hands to other people. For, we can ask whether things that were sold to others transferred to the right of others or whether the right to the things sold was transferred to the buyers. If it was transferred, who transferred it? Unless ⟨15⟩ one should wish to fantasize, it is certain that no one else transferred the right to these things to the buyers unless it was the apostles or someone acting in their name. They could not transfer the right unless they had it beforehand, since no one can transfer a right to someone else that he does not have. ⟨20⟩ Thus, I do not see that someone can show or even appear to imagine that the apostles did not have a right to the things that they exchanged. Therefore, in my judgement it seems to me that it has been efficaciously proved by rational arguments that Christ and the apostles had a right to temporal things, so that in regard to all of the temporal things that they used they had a right at least to the very use of the things. Moreover, in regard to consumable things that they used, they had the right to their very use and to the things that they used.

This ⟨25⟩ same point, which has been proved in this way by rational arguments, can also be proved from authorities, the first of which are the authorities of Sacred Scripture. In 1 Corinthians 9, the Apostle writes, "Do we not have the power to eat and drink,"[77] and in a following verse he writes, "What soldier ever fought at his own expense? Who plants a vine-

---

[77] 1 Cor. 9:4.

yard and does not live off its fruits? Who tends a flock and ⟨30⟩ does not live on its milk?"[78] Thus, according to the Apostle, expenses were owed to an apostle by those to whom he preached, just as a wage is owed to a soldier, the fruits of the vineyard to him who plants the vines, and the milk of the flock to him who tends it. Therefore, etc.

Saintly authorities have expressly made this point, as we saw above. ⟨35⟩ In addition to those authorities, one finds also the authority of Augustine, who in his commentary on ⟨⟨291⟩⟩ Luke 9, "Take nothing with you for your journey,"[79] writes: "The Lord did not want the disciples to possess or even carry these things, not because these things are not necessary to sustain this life, but he sent them in order to show them that they were owed these things by those believers to whom they proclaimed the Gospel, and also that they might, with security, neither ⟨5⟩ possess nor carry what is necessary for this life, whether much or very little."[80] From this authority, it is evident that the necessities of life were owed to the disciples by those believers to whom they proclaimed the Gospel. But this debt could not otherwise be called a debt unless it is the type of debt by which some compensation is owed the laborer for his labor, at least in regard to those things which are necessary ⟨10⟩ to the laborer. But the laborer has a right to what is owed him by reason of his work. Therefore, etc.

From other texts of this authority, it is evident that the necessities of life were owed to the apostles as something to which they had a right. For, Augustine says that "he sent them in order to show them that they were owed these things," and then he says, "so that with security they would neither ⟨15⟩ possess nor carry what is necessary for this life."[81] Thus, according to blessed Augustine, Christ sent the apostles as if secure in the necessities of life, since they were owed to them. Yet, the disciples would not have been secure in the necessities of life as if these things were owed them unless they already had some right to receive them. Therefore, etc. Further, concerning ⟨20⟩ the text, "Do not be solicitous for the morrow,"[82] Augustine makes the same point: "Here we must be careful, when we see a servant of God taking care so that he does not lack what is necessary either for himself or for those in his care, lest we judge him to be acting against God's precept not to be solicitous for the morrow, for even the Lord, to whom the angels ministered, deemed it worthy ⟨25⟩ to have a

[78] 1 Cor. 9:7.

[79] Luke 9:3.

[80] *De consensu evangelistarum* II.30 (*CSEL* 43.177f.; *PL* 34.1113-4).

[81] Ibid.

[82] Matt. 6:34.

purse as an example."[83]

Augustine expressly chooses to say in this text that Christ had a purse, although he did not have it for the sake of personal necessity, since he could obtain the necessities of life through the ministry of the angels. Rather, Christ had a purse in order to give an example to future prelates that just as he, who had no necessity, carried a purse and accepted the necessities of life from those to whom ⟨30⟩ he preached, so, too, prelates should accept the necessities of life from those to whom they ministered. They are the successors to the apostles, and it is incumbent on them by virtue of their office to minister to spiritual things. Yet prelates, the successors of the apostles, have a right to such things, at least in common. Therefore, etc.

It seems ⟨⟨292⟩⟩ moderately clear to me that it is factually untrue to assert that Christ and the apostles did not have at least the necessities of life. The reason is that every authority (whether from Sacred Scripture or the saints), which seems to suggest either that ⟨5⟩ Christ forbade such things, or that the apostles renounced them, should be understood either in regard to a manner of having these things, namely, not personally but in common, or in regard to making provision for them with superfluous care. If there were a hundred thousand authorities, one could not conclude more from them.

In opposition to the objections, it must be stated that:

1. Taken ⟨10⟩ universally, the major premise is false, since just as a person who lacks sight in an unqualified manner can be said to be unqualifiedly blind, so, too, the person with sight can be said to see in an unqualified manner. After all, it is not because a predicate belongs to a subject in which it is found in a preeminent manner that the predicate belongs unqualifiedly to the subject. Rather, the predicate is said of the subject in an unqualified manner because of the nature of the predicate, or ⟨15⟩ because what is predicated is found in the subject according to its proper nature. Moreover, the minor is unqualifiedly false, namely that Christ and the apostles, in their own perfection or when they displayed the character of those who are perfect, had nothing personally or in common.[84]

In reference to Basil's[85] authority which is brought forward against this view, it must be said that the extreme poverty to which the disciples adhered ⟨20⟩ (and of which Basil speaks) did not consist in having absolutely nothing but in not having anything beyond the necessities of life. Otherwise, they ought to have had nothing both with respect to the use of things

---

[83] *De sermone Domini in monte* II.17 (*CCSL* 35.150; *PL* 34.1294-5).

[84] Compare the appendix, page 121 below.

[85] Eusebius, not Basil. See objection one, page 92 above.

in fact and with respect to a right to things. For poverty is greater when things are lacked in both of these respects and not just in one only.

If it also is said that they ought not to care even for nourishment, ⟨25⟩ this should not be understood to mean that they should show absolutely no care for nourishment as if they wanted to die of hunger. Rather, it should be understood in the sense that they should not neglect preaching or divine things in order to care for nourishment beyond what is necessary. This is evident in light of subsequent remarks in Basil's text, namely, that they should not possess two tunics. This text should not be ⟨30⟩ understood absolutely (as the saints explain); but, as was said above, it should be understood to refer to the impediment which comes of possessing things beyond what is necessary.

In regard to the text in that decretal, *Exiit*, the chapter beginning with *Porro*, that treats the renunciation of all things, and so forth, it can be said that ownership there refers to what belongs to oneself in distinction from what is held in common. In this sense, the personal renunciation of all things ⟨35⟩ pertains to those who are perfect. Yet, in this context, what belongs to oneself is not understood in distinction from what belongs to another. Religious have ownership of things in common, since they hold what belongs to them in common, and they do not have what belongs to another. Moreover, that decretal does not say that Christ and the apostles had absolutely nothing, personally or ⟨⟨293⟩⟩ in common, but it does say that the renunciation of things personally and in common is a holy and meritorious poverty. What is said in the decretal about the personal renunciation of things is sufficiently evident. What is said about the renunciation of things in common can be understood to mean that neither Christ nor the apostles laid claim to these common things for themselves ⟨5⟩ as if they were their own in an unqualified manner.[86]

2. It must be said that the minor premise is false, since poverty is neither formally a perfection nor a part of perfection. By way of proof, it must be said that the text, "If you would be perfect,"[87] does not mean that poverty, considered as an exterior effect, is formally a perfection or a part ⟨10⟩ of perfection. Rather, poverty disposes us to perfection in the manner established in the second article of the first question.[88]

3. It must be said that the minor premise is false. This is proved with reference to the first part of the minor premise, where it cites the text, "Go and sell all," etc. This text does not mean that to gain perfection ⟨15⟩ a per-

---

[86] See the appendix, page 133 below.

[87] Matt. 19:21.

[88] See the appendix, page 123 below, for a discussion of this argument.

son is required to sell his things and give the proceeds to the poor. It suffices either that he sell things or that, without selling things, he give them to the poor. When he does this, he gives most perfectly when he gives himself and his things to a community of poor people with whom he lives in common to the same degree that he gives them to others. The text from Matthew, "having relinquished everything,"[89] should be understood in terms of forsaking what had been inordinately acquired or in terms of ⟨20⟩ forsaking everything held personally.

However, consider what is said in the second and third parts of the minor premise, i.e., what Chrysostom says in his praises of Paul: namely, that Paul did not possess money, since he often did not have the necessary food. If this means that he never had money, then ⟨25⟩ it is false, since Paul says that he labored with his own hands so that he and those who followed him would have the wherewithal to live. Chrysostom's remark means either that Paul did not aim principally at the possession of money or that at times he was without money and food. Further, when it is said that Simon and Jude did not want to possess earthly things, ⟨30⟩ this should be understood in regard to their principal intention and not in the sense that they did not accept the necessities of life.[90]

4.   The minor premise is false. To prove this, it must be said that Eusebius does not understand extreme poverty as having nothing at all, but as not having anything beyond the necessities. The text, ⟨35⟩ "Behold we have relinquished everything,"[91] should be understood in regard to personal renunciation. Concerning what is written in Acts 3, "Silver and gold I do not have,"[92] it must be said that this is understood according to the Interlinear ⟨⟨294⟩⟩ Gloss:[93] either they did not carry silver and gold or, that at the time, they did not have any on hand. Augustine's remark, "Following the precept of the teacher," should not count against this exposition, since the Master's precept was not that they should never carry [gold or silver]. Rather, the precept was given for a specific occasion, namely, ⟨5⟩ when he initially sent them to preach and to show them that the necessities of life were owed to them by others.

5.   Gregory's words are understood in regard to a disposition of the mind, since, properly speaking, no one gives away what he has never had

---

[89] Matt. 4:20.

[90] See the appendix, page 124 below, for the treatment of this objection.

[91] Matt. 19:27.

[92] Acts. 3:6.

[93] *Glossa interlinearis* on Acts 3:6 (*Biblia Latina cum glossa ordinaria* IV.459). The gloss reads "following the precept of his teacher."

except as a disposition of the mind. ⟨10⟩ Moreover, in this sense, one need not give away the necessities of life, since one cannot have perfection in the present life without these things.[94]

In regard to Jerome's authority, it must be said that the text he repeated was spoken to the disciples when they were sent to preach, and they were shown that the necessities of life were owed to them by those to whom they preached. ⟨15⟩ Consequently, it was not necessary that they be solicitous about these things.

In reference to the second authority, which is Ambrose's, it must be said that at those times when the women ministered to the apostles, they did not have things in common except for what the women supplied. It does not follow from this that they never had anything, but rather that the others did not have [them].[95] Nor does it follow that ⟨20⟩ at these times they did not have a right to what the women gave them, since the owner of a thing can turn it over to another.

In reference to the third authority, it must be said that Augustine understood that those whom he calls the least had given up everything either in regard to what is held personally or in regard to what exceeds necessities.

In ⟨25⟩ reference to the fourth authority, which is Jerome's, it must be said that nudity in that sense should be understood as lacking whatever exceeds necessities or as lacking things personally. It is not necessary for someone to sell what belongs to him. Rather, it suffices that he give himself and what belongs to him.

In reference to the fifth authority, which is Cyril's, it must be said that Christ ⟨30⟩ forbade the apostles worldly concern. Yet, it is not worldly, but divine and holy, to care for the necessities of life in order to serve God. When it is said that the apostles should not be concerned with food, it must be said either that this was spoken to assure them that they would obtain things from what others owed them, or that what is meant should be understood to refer to superfluous concern.

In ⟨35⟩ reference to the sixth authority, which is Augustine's, it must be said that the apostles are understood to have given up everything that belonged to them, or to have given all their possessions to the poor in so far as they gave themselves and what belonged to them to Christ and his community. However, it does not follow that they had nothing in common, but only that they had nothing personally.[96]

---

[94] See the appendix, page 131 below, for a discussion of this argument.

[95] The meaning is not clear; perhaps the text is corrupt.

[96] See the appendix, beginning at page 131 below, for a discussion of the basic

[ARTICLE 2–WHETHER IT IS HERETICAL TO ASSERT THAT CHRIST
AND THE APOSTLES HAD NOTHING PERSONALLY OR IN COMMON]

Let us proceed to the second article which argues that it is not heretical to
assert that Christ and the ⟨40⟩ apostles had nothing personally or in common. The reason is that nothing is called heretical unless it is contrary to
the ⟨⟨295⟩⟩ articles of faith, Sacred Scripture, or the teachings of the Church.
But this assertion is contrary to none of them. Therefore, etc.[97] The major
premise is evident. The proof of the minor is that the opposite of this assertion is not contained in the articles of faith or in Sacred Scripture. It has not
been established by the Church. Indeed, just the opposite is the case, ⟨5⟩ as
is seen in the decretal, *Exiit*.[98] Therefore, etc.

ON THE CONTRARY: An assertion which is contrary to what is contained
in Sacred Scripture is heretical. But the assertion under consideration is
something of this sort. Therefore, etc. The major premise is evident. The
minor is proved through Sacred Scripture, since it is a fact that Christ and
the apostles had the use of immovable as well as movable things. They
would not have had use of them ⟨10⟩ unless it was licit. Yet, as has already
been proved, there is no licit use of things without a right to them. Therefore, etc.

RESPONSE: To clarify this question, it should be noted that in regard to
what pertains to faith and morals–the knowledge of which is necessary for
salvation–these three things are related: rashness, error, and heresy. ⟨15⟩
It seems rash to assert as certain something [in matters of faith and morals]
which cannot be efficaciously proved through reason or authority, as for
example, one might assert that the world will end in one or two hundred
years. I say that this assertion might be true, but to assert it with certainty
would be a rash, since there is no efficacious authority or reason for it.

However, error exceeds the ⟨20⟩ rashness of a false assertion, since to
err is to depart from the right way, and since to have truth in matters of
faith and morals pertains to the path which leads to blessedness. Every
false assertion strays from the rectitude of truth; therefore, a false assertion
in these matters is called error. Heresy exceeds simple error when the
falsehood is notorious and ⟨25⟩ is adhered to tenaciously. Not every error

---

argument and many of the texts contained in the responses to the fourth and fifth
objections.

[97] See the appendix, page 133 below.

[98] See the appendix, page 133 below.

is a heresy, otherwise Augustine would not have written: "I can err, but I will not be a heretic."[99]

Applying these distinctions to the proposition in question, I say that the assertion that Christ and the apostles ⟨30⟩ had nothing in the way of temporal goods is, absolutely speaking, rash, erroneous, and heretical. It is rash to say that they had no temporal things in terms of a right to use the things that they used. In regard to the consumable things that they used, it also is rash to add that they had no right to use those things and that they had no right to the things [themselves]. The reason is that this claim cannot be proved by reason or authority. Also, it is erroneous because false, since, as has been said, it is not possible to use things licitly without a right to use them in the ⟨35⟩ manner we have specified: namely, in terms of a right to use the things, or in terms of a right to the things themselves, or in terms of both of these rights. However, it is a fact that Christ and the apostles did not have these things except through the licit use of them. Therefore, ⟨⟨296⟩⟩ etc.

However, if one rejoins that they had use of these things as if they were administrators and not the owners of them, then we maintain at least that, first of all, they had a right to administer such things. This is a particular right. A second point can be made against this rejoinder, since I ask for whom were they administrators: ⟨5⟩ namely, were they administrators for the community of Christ and the apostles or for someone else? If it is said that they were administrators for the community of Christ and the apostles, we maintain that this community had a right to these things. If they were administrators for another, then I ask "For whom?" For it is not possible to imagine for which person or community, other than themselves, that Christ ⟨10⟩ and the apostles were administrators.

Third, no one is said to administer a thing or to use it as an administrator if it is converted to personal advantage and it is not used in another person's name. But Christ and the apostles converted at least the movable things they used to personal advantage, namely, in eating and drinking, as well as in clothing themselves. ⟨15⟩ In fact, we do not find that Christ and the apostles dispensed these things in the name of someone other than themselves. Therefore, etc.

An objection cannot be raised if one finds a saint who says that Christ did not have temporal goods for himself but for others, since the sentence, "Christ did not have these things for himself," can be understood in two ways. The first sense, which refers to the use of things, is that Christ did not have these things ⟨20⟩ as if to use them. But this is false and contrary to Scripture, since Christ used such goods in eating, drinking, and clothing

---

[99] Text not found.

himself. The second sense, which can be understood with reference to the necessity of having things, is that Christ did not find it necessary for his sustenance to have such things in a purse or in other places of keeping. The sentence is true in this sense: namely, he did not have ⟨25⟩ such necessity, since he was the creator of everything and he could have things in other ways.

Thus, in deference to a superior judgment, especially that of the Holy See, as well in showing a healthy reverence for each person and state, it seems to me that the previously mentioned assertion is heretical: namely, the assertion that Christ and the apostles did not have temporal goods in terms of a right to and ownership of them.

Nevertheless, ⟨30⟩ it should be noted that an assertion can be called heretical in two ways. It can be called heretical in one sense in that it expressly contains what is contrary to the articles of faith, the contents of Sacred Scripture, or the teachings of the Church. In another sense, an assertion can be deemed heretical in that it contains what is contrary to a conclusion which clearly follows from the contents of the articles of faith, ⟨35⟩ Sacred Scripture, or the determination of ecclesiastical teaching.[100]

In the first sense, the assertion does not appear to be expressly heretical, since, in its proper form, the opposite assertion is not contained in Sacred Scripture or in the articles of faith. In other words, the assertion that Christ and the apostles had temporal goods in regard to dominion over and ownership of them is not ⟨⟨297⟩⟩ expressly contained in these words in these sources. Moreover, this assertion has not been expressly established by the Church.

In the second sense, however, it seems to me that the assertion is heretical, since it is opposed in a contradictory manner to a conclusion which clearly follows from the content of Sacred Scripture. For one clearly finds in the contents of ⟨5⟩ Sacred Scripture the fact that Christ and the apostles used such things. Yet, from the nature of the case, it is manifest that their use of these things was licit and that the licit use of things cannot exist without a right to their use or a right to the thing [itself] that someone uses. That is, in both cases no licit use of things is possible without some right to them.

In light of these considerations, it infallibly follows that Christ ⟨10⟩ and the apostles had a right to temporal things. The assertion which we are considering contains the contradiction of this implication. From this, it follows that the assertion we are considering contains what is opposed to something contained in Sacred Scripture, since what is opposed to the consequent is necessarily opposed to the antecedent.

---

[100] See the appendix, page 133 below.

In reply to the objection, it must be said about the minor premise that, ⟨15⟩ although the assertion under consideration does not literally and explicitly contain what is opposed to the contents of Sacred Scripture, nevertheless, in fact and implicitly, it contains what is opposed to something contained in Sacred Scripture in the manner that has been shown.

These are the words of brother Hervaeus, a humble teacher of the ⟨20⟩ Order of Preachers, who submits them to the correction of your Holiness, publicly bearing witness before God that he speaks not out of irreverence to any person or state but simply to declare the truth which he believes.

Appendix
A Summary of Franciscan Positions Concerning
the Poverty of Christ and the Apostles

This appendix contains a scribe's summary of the responses of several Franciscans to the question about the nature of the poverty of Christ and the apostles. The summary and some of the original responses were submitted along with Hervaeus Natalis's treatise and the writings of other Dominicans to Pope John XXII to serve as expert opinions for his bull *Cum inter nonnullos*. The text of the summary was published in Felice Tocco's *La quistione della povertà*, pages 51-87. As noted in the introduction (page 18 above), the summary comprises the second part of a much longer manuscript.

Eight Franciscans are represented in the summary. The most prominent are Cardinal Vital du Four (see pages 121-126 and 140-145 below), Cardinal Bertrand de la Tour (see pages 130-137 and 145-146 below) and Arnauld Royard, the archbishop of Salerno (see pages 138-140, 143 and 146 below). The summaries of their work are drawn from longer treatises contained in the first part of the manuscript. The original contributions of the remaining Franciscans–the bishops of Capha, Badajoz, Lisbon, and Riga (Latvia) as well as a teacher of the Franciscans[1]–are not contained in the manuscript. Douie speculates that the scribe may have summarized speeches given in consistory.[2] Tocco offers no speculation as to the nature of the original contributions.

Like Hervaeus, Vital du Four (†1327), Bertrand de la Tour (†1332) and Arnauld Royard (†1334) were masters in theology at the University of Paris.[3] Each man belonged to the conventual group of the Franciscans, and

---

[1] Their remarks are contained on pages 126-130 below.

[2] Douie, 279.

[3] Cf. Tocco, 22-4 and 29 and Spiers, "Four Evangelical Manuscripts on Evangelical Poverty," 330-332 for brief biographical notes about each of the Franciscans found in this appendix. There are brief biographies and bibliographies for Vital, Bertrand, and Arnauld in P. Glorieux, *Répertoire des maîtres en théologie de Paris au XIIIe siècle*, II.137-40 (Vital du Four), II.238-242 (Bertrand de la Tour) and II.242-243 (Arnauld Royard). The article on Vital in the *New Catholic Encyclopedia* (New York: McGraw

each had a lengthy career of service in the Church. Vital du Four (otherwise known as Vitalis de Furno or Vidal de Furno) was the Provincial of Aquitaine from 1307 to 1312, was elevated to the cardinalate in 1312, and was consecrated bishop of Albano in 1321. He was appointed by Clement V to a committee that investigated the writings of Peter John Olivi. With the other Franciscan provincials, he drafted the official response of the Order to the accusations leveled against it by the Spirituals in 1310. He was the most prolific author of the Franciscans represented in the summary.

Bertrand de la Tour (otherwise known as Bertrand de Turre) succeeded Vital as the provincial of Aquitaine. He was named archbishop of Salerno (1320), cardinal-priest of the church of Saint Vitalis (1323), and cardinal-bishop of Frascati (1323). He was involved in the suppression of the Spirituals of Provence in 1315 and, in 1318, was appointed to a papal commission that investigated the apocalyptic writings of Olivi. Arnauld Royard succeeded Bertrand de la Tour as the archbishop of Salerno. As Tocco notes,[4] he was "no less hostile" to the Spirituals than were Vital and Bertrand.

Despite their common opposition to the Spirituals, each man sided with the Spirituals against the pope on the matter of the poverty of Christ and the apostles, although each apparently hastened to submit to the pope after *Cum inter nonnullos*. It is worth noting that Vital's presentation in consistory so angered John XXII that he frequently and furiously interrupted Vital, charging Vital with implying that the pope was a heretic for countering the teachings of Nicholas III's *Exiit qui seminat*.[5] Royard also was severely chastised by John XXII and, later, was forced to exchange his post at Salerno for a less important bishopric. Bertrand, however, retained the favor of the pope, and in 1228, when the pope deposed Michael Cesena as Minister General of the Franciscans and excommunicated him, Bertrand was appointed as temporary Minister General. Eventually, after having ousted various provincials of the order, Bertrand was elected its Minister General.[6]

Hill, 1967), XIV.723-34 lists additional biographical sources. Also, one can consult Patrick Gauchat, *Cardinal Bertrand de Turre: His Participation in the Theoretical Controversy Concerning the Poverty of Christ and the Apostles under Pope John XXII* (Vatican City, 1930) for an extensive and highly sympathetic account of Bertrand and the pope.

[4] Tocco, 23.

[5] Cf. Stephanus Baluze, *Vitae paparum Avenionensium*, II.163. See also, Tocco, 29 and Gauchat, 28-30.

[6] For more details concerning the complex events surrounding Michael's rebellion against the pope, see Douie, 165-196 and Gauchat, 97-111.

A brief word about the Franciscan bishops named in the summary: The bishop of Capha was a certain Brother Jerome. He was named bishop for the regions of Tartaria by Clement V in 1301 and promoted as bishop of Capha by John XXII in 1320. Brother Stephan, the confessor to the king of Portugal, was appointed bishop of Porto in 1310 by Clement V and, in 1313, moved to the more important bishopric of Lisbon. He was chastised by John XXII for his part in the controversy over the poverty of Christ and, later, was transferred to the diocese of Cuença. The bishop of Riga was named Brother Frederico; the bishop of Badajoz was named Brother Simon.[7]

One final note: the identity of "teacher (*magister*) of the Franciscan order" seems unknown. Glorieux thinks the teacher is Michael Cesena, the Minister General of the Franciscan Order and, thus, Hervaeus Natalis's Franciscan counterpart.[8] Tocco, however, thinks the author is unknown. Tocco considers the suggestion that this teacher might be a certain Brother Alfredo, whose treatise is contained in the first part of the manuscript. However, as Tocco notes, the summary of the discussion or treatise attributed to the "teacher" does not correspond to Alfredo's treatise.

Although the summary translated in this appendix does not offer a comprehensive treatment of the views of Franciscan thinkers, it does give a good representation of the sorts of arguments and authorities that Franciscans used to support their interpretation of the nature of the poverty of Christ and the apostles and, thus, of the poverty they sought to imitate within the order. In particular, these summaries present many of the particular positions that Hervaeus himself discusses and critiques. I have noted them in footnotes and cross-referenced them to Hervaeus's treatise.

Bonagratia of Bergamo's *Tractatus de Christi et apostolorum paupertate* offers a detailed Franciscan response to the question that is contemporary with the text translated here. One can also consult the works of Peter John Olivi, listed in the bibliography, which had a particular influence on the Spirituals in the order. Unfortunately, there are no English translations of any of this material. Perhaps the most important source for the Franciscan position is Bonaventure's *Apologia pauperum*. Written a little more than fifty years before the papal investigation into the poverty of Christ and the apostles, it provided the doctrinal basis, as well as the key collection of Fran-

---

[7] Apart from their names and ecclesiastical appointments, little seems known about these men. The information presented here is found in Tocco, 19-20. Tocco's principal source is Luke Wadding, *Annales Minorum* (Florence: Quarachi), 1931.

[8] Glorieux, 235. It is odd, though, that Cesena would not have made some contribution to the examination of this question.

ciscan scriptural and Patristic authorities, that was used by subsequent Franciscan thinkers and apologists, whether Spiritual or Conventual. This work is available in English translation.

As a critical edition, Tocco's volume is not comparable to Sikes's edition of Hervaeus. While there are various misprints and misspellings, none of them seem critically to distort the meaning of text. I have noted more significant misprints or misquotations in the notes. Page numbers from Tocco's volume are indicated in double braces: ⟨⟨ ⟩⟩. Tocco uses both roman and arabic numerals in the Latin text (e.g., in citing chapters for citations from the Bible). I have preserved this distinction in the translation. However, I have moved all references to Bible verses in the text to footnotes, as such references clearly would not have been in the original manuscripts.

⟨⟨51⟩⟩ A Brief Summary of the Remarks of
Cardinal Vital, Bishop of Albano

In every art and science, that proposition seems to be unqualifiedly true, and its opposite is judged to be unqualifiedly false, when the predicate is said of a subject in which it exists in the most perfect and eminent way. To have nothing personally or in common is said of Christ and the apostles in regard to their most perfect and eminent being.[1] Therefore, this proposition is unqualifiedly true: Christ and the apostles did not have something in common through dominion and ownership, although they had simple use of it in fact. Consequently, the opposite of this statement–namely, Christ and the apostles had something in common as owners or as those who exercise dominion over things–is unqualifiedly false, although it can be made true through some qualification or change in circumstances.

The proof of the major premise lies in the following response: consider that what is unqualifiedly healthy is healthy in reference to a healthy person, although with a change of circumstances it can be called unhealthy as, for example, wine is for someone who is feverish.[2] The proof of the minor: although Christ was most perfect ⟨⟨52⟩⟩ in every state in regard to the habit of charity, nevertheless in regard to an extrinsic act he occasionally assumed the character of those who are weak and imperfect. However, at times he did not assume this character, but showed himself to be the exemplar of the highest perfection of the perfect by retaining for himself no ownership of or dominion over anything.

The decretal, Exiit,[3] makes this clear as well as Hugh [of St. Victor]. Commenting on Psalm XCI, "It is good to confess the Lord,"[4] Hugh[5] says that Christ had a purse, conforming himself to the imperfect.[6] Thus, if one says that Paul and Joseph Barnabas accomplished something more than

---

[1]   Compare pages 91 and 108 above in Hervaeus's text.

[2]   Compare page 91 above in Hervaeus's text.

[3]   Nicholas III, Exiit qui seminat (CIC II.1112).

[4]   Ps. 91:2.

[5]   Hugh of St. Victor, Miscellanea lib2: Adnotationes elucidariae in quosdam psalmos David, 91, 64 (PL 177, 626).

[6]   Compare pages 53 and 62 above in Hervaeus's text.

Christ,[7] this is understood in regard to an extrinsic act. However, in regard to an intrinsic act of charity, which constitutes unqualified perfection, no one accomplishes more [than Christ]. The reason is that Christ eats and drinks out of greater charity than those who abstain [from these things], as Augustine says in regard to the verse from the Psalm, "bringing forth hay":[8] "Christ had a purse, since many of the weak would have sought it, he assumed the character of those who are weak by having a purse."[9]

Yet even in regard to an exterior act, he assumed the state of those who are perfect in which he had nothing personally or in common in terms of ownership or dominion. The decretal, *Exiit*, [the chapter beginning with] *Porro*, etc., makes this point evident: ⟨⟨53⟩⟩ "He established [having nothing] by example and, at that time, he was the exemplar of the perfect life."[10] This text concurs with Exodus 25, "Observe and work according to the example that was shown to you."[11] So, too, Jerome writes to Eustochius: "the Lord could not have what he forbade the disciples to whom he said, 'Do not carry a satchel, staff or bread.'"[12] In commenting on Corinthians, Ambrose writes: "Out of a desire for the teaching of the master and a love of the virtues, the women followed the apostles, providing for them as they provided for Christ."[13] Because of this, it is evident that at this time they [Christ and the apostles] did not have a purse.

The *Gloss* on Mark XV, "Silver and gold," etc. [14]says: "Be mindful of his precept, Do not possess gold," etc. "Indeed, this was true of the apostles."[15] Commenting on Matthew, Eusebius says, "He prohibited the possession of gold and money." A bit further, he says, "he thought it necessary that the previously mentioned oxen of the kingdom of God draw the plow. They

---

[7] At this point, Tocco supplies the following text of Hugh from a folio of the manuscript: "Christ had a purse, being conformed to the imperfect. However, Paul did not want to receive assistance. So it happened that Paul accomplished something more than Christ."

[8] Ps. 103:14.

[9] *De opere monachorum* V.6 (*CSEL* 41.539; *PL* 40.552).

[10] Nicholas III, *Exiit qui seminat* (*CIC* II.1112).

[11] Exod. 25:40.

[12] *Epistolae* 22.19 (*CSEL* 54.170; *PL* 22.406).

[13] Ambrosiaster, *In I ad Corintheos* 9 (*PL* 17.229). Cf. 1 Cor. 9:4-5.

[14] Acts 3:6, not Mark 15.

[15] *Glossa ordinaria* on Acts 3:6 (*Biblia Latina cum glossa ordinaria* IV.459). Although emphasized in Tocco's edition, the sentence–"Indeed, this was true of the apostles"– does not appear in the *Glossa ordinaria*.

ought not estimate as valuable any of the things appreciated by monks[16] when heavenly works had been given to them."[17] Also, commenting on Matthew, Cyril makes the same point: "He commands them to be without a belt, since he wants them to lack any sort of worldly solicitude."[18] Jerome also makes the same point to Demetriades, "The apostolic summit lies in selling everything and giving it to the poor."[19]

2. In every speculative science and in every natural science, the first principles are greater, more certain, more evident, and they have a more perfect power than those which follow. Yet after Christ, ⟨⟨54⟩⟩ the apostles are the first exemplars of the virtues and the first founders of the Church. Thus, the perfections–which are, were, and indeed will be in the Church and in any of the saints–were in the apostles in a more perfect manner. The exuberant outpouring of the Holy Spirit in them manifests every sort of perfection: understanding of Scripture, knowledge of tongues, etc. Similarly, evangelical poverty coincides with the perfection of virtue according to Matthew 18, "If you would be perfect, go," etc.[20] But such poverty consists in having nothing in common. Therefore, etc.[21]

3. If the apostles had something in common, the reason was that in following Christ either they did not relinquish everything but retained something; or, they kept what they humbly begged, or was liberally given [to them], or acquired through manual labor. There are no additional cases that fall outside any of the previously mentioned cases.[22] The first case is

---

[16] The word *monachales* makes no sense here. This quote is a very loose paraphrase of what is found in Eusebius. Aquinas has a version of the text (see *Contra retrahentes* 15 (*Opera Omnia* (Leonine) XLI.C70)) to which the last sentence of the present text more closely corresponds. The version in Aquinas's work has *mortales* rather than *monchales*, which clearly makes more sense.

[17] *Commentaria in Lucam* (PG 24.544-5).

[18] Presumably, Cyril of Alexandria. Text not found as such. A somewhat similar version of the text is cited in Hervaeus at page 95 above. However, see Cyril's *Commentarii in Lucam, Homilia* 48 (*CSCO* 140.70.101; *PG* 72.642), which deals with Luke 9:3. The Latin texts in *CSCO* and *PG* differ from one another, although they have the same basic sense. The *CSCO* divides the commentary into separate homilies; the *PG* does not. Also cf. *Commentarii in Matthaeum* 26 (*PG* 72.395) regarding Matt. 10:10.

[19] *Epistolae* 130.14 (*CSEL* 56.193; *PL* 22.1118).

[20] Matt. 19:21, not Matt. 18.

[21] See Hervaeus, pages 92 and 109 above, for a discussion of this argument.

[22] "Non enim est dare partes plures sed nullo praedictorum modorum." This rather convoluted sentence seems to express the author's conviction that he has given all the

ruled out, since the Lord says, "If you would be perfect," etc. This text cannot mean that they[23] gave to the poor, i.e., the apostles, for in *The City of God* 17 chap. 7 Augustine says, "The apostles vowed the highest poverty,"[24] as is evident from what has been said. Also, in the Gospel it is written that "They relinquished everything, and followed the Lord Christ."[25] The other cases are ruled out, since in his praises of Paul, Chrysostom says that "Paul did not possess money as he himself testified, 'Even to this day we hunger and thirst.'"[26] The same is true of the other apostles, as is evident form the story about Simon and Jude "who refused the property of the profane priests, and also from [the story] about the apostle Thaddeus."[27]

4. ⟨⟨55⟩⟩ It seems erroneous to judge that some state is more perfect than the state of the apostles, since if this is true, that state, consequently, would have greater merit and, consequently, reward. But in the Church, as the decretal, *Exiit*[28], makes evident, there is a state which renounces everything both personally as well as in common. This state is most perfect. Therefore, the state of the apostles was such a state.

5. As is evident from the text of Augustine[29] cited above, the apostles vowed evangelical [poverty]. The renunciation which they vowed was more perfect than[30] it would have been without a vow. Therefore, since they were the principal exemplar, etc, as was said above, perfect renunciation was in them. This is confirmed, since, if what is simple[31] is related to what is simple, then what is greater is related to what is greater and what is greatest is related to what is greatest. Therefore, since simple renunciation is perfection, greatest renunciation is greatest perfection.

6. Glory and punishment are the opposed ends of the cities of God and the devil. Good citizens and bad citizens are opposed to one another. Charity and cupidity are fundamentally opposed to one another. Thus, so far as someone is more drawn to one member of a pair of opposites, he is more withdrawn from the other member of the pair. It is granted that the

---

cases for a complete proof by division.

[23] Presumably they would seek to be perfect and give everything to the poor.

[24] *De civitate Dei* XVII.4 (*CCSL* 48.559; *PL* 41.530).

[25] Luke 5:11.

[26] *De laudibus Pauli, Homilia 4* (*PG* 50.491). Also, 1 Cor. 4:11.

[27] Eusebius, *Ecclesiastica historia* 1.13 (*PG* 20.130). See Hervaeus, pp. 93 and 109-110 above, for the treatment of this objection.

[28] Nicholas III, *Exiit qui seminat* (*CIC* II.1112).

[29] *De civitate Dei* XVII.4 (*CCSL* 48.559; *PL* 41.530).

[30] Reading *quam* for *quia*.

[31] In this case, *simpliciter* is better translated by "simple" than "unqualified."

apostles were drawn to charity in the utmost way and withdrawn from cupidity in the utmost way. Thus, it is evident that the apostles renounced temporal things in the utmost way.[32] This is confirmed by Augustine: "The flesh of spiritual wings is the love of temporal things."[33] So, in regard to [the apostle] Matthew, Bede says, "He was led by such an intense desire ⟨⟨56⟩⟩ to follow the Lord that he kept nothing of this life because of care or thought for himself. However, it is certain that those who have things in common are forced to do this."[34]

7. The three counsels of poverty, chastity, and obedience are like a three-stranded rope which it is difficult to unravel. Thus, since chastity and obedience are perfections which retain nothing for themselves, poverty also must be understood in the same way.[35]

8. The path between two points is more perfect and straighter to the degree that the mid-point is more like the extremes. But the extremes of the beginning and end of human life involve total nakedness. Thus, the mid-point [of human life] is more perfect so far as it involves greater nakedness.[36]

9. [The same conclusion] is drawn from a sign,[37] since Bonaventure, a doctor in theology and a cardinal, has declared such in a book which treats this matter. The same is true for [the bishop of] Lincoln.[38]

---

[32] See Hervaeus, pages 29, 50 and 57 above, for a treatment of this argument.

[33] *Sermo* 112.6 (*PL* 38.646).

[34] *In Marci evangelium expositio* I.2 (*CCSL* 120.48; *PL* 92.155). Although placed in quotes in the Latin text, the last sentence, "However, it is ...," does not appear in Bede's text.

[35] See Hervaeus, pages 25 and 30 above, for a treatment of this argument. At this point, Tocco provided the following text from the manuscript: "so far as obedience is more universal and, as subject to authority, retains nothing for itself of personal will, then so far is that obedience greater and more perfect."

[36] See Hervaeus, pages 50 and 57 above, for a discussion of this argument.

[37] Cf. Aquinas *De veritate* 7.1.ad 11 where the distinction is made between the knowledge of things from their causes and the knowledge of things from books which is from a sign (*a signo*).

[38] Presumably this refers to Robert Grosseteste, who was the bishop of Lincoln c. 1253 (Tocco, p. 25). Tocco supplied the following text from one of the folios he consulted: "I have another sign, since brother John Pecham, of the Friars Minor, was an excellent doctor who for some time taught in the Roman curia and, after a time, was made the archbishop of Canterbury by the Roman Curia. It is said that brother John solemnly disputed this same question and wrote a great treatise concerning it: the book on evangelical perfection. In light of many of the original saints, economic rights,

10. ⟨⟨57⟩⟩ It seems possible to draw the same conclusion from the teaching of our most holy Father and Reverend, John 22 who says: "As the odor of religion itself draws, knowledge shines forth, charity attracts, and prayer gains worth, then prayer not only makes progress from virtue to virtue but, remaining in them, is itself made better day by day and ascends higher, as it were by means of the stages of the virtues that lead to perfection, despising earthy things and embracing heavenly things."[39]

⟨⟨58⟩⟩ A BRIEF SUMMARY OF THE FELICITOUS REMARKS OF THE BISHOP OF CAPHA

Is it heretical to assert that Christ and the apostles did [not] have something in common? The response is "No," as is evident from the words and deeds of Christ, the authority of the saints, and the determinations of the Church, all of which have already been cited. In response to the question properly sought–whether it is heretical to assert that it is clearer in Scripture that Christ [had] something in common than that he was God and human–the response is "Yes." For, it is clearly contained in Scripture that Christ is true God and true man, but nowhere is it expressly found that Christ had something in common. Thus, it is evident that this sort of assertion is the greatest heresy.

A BRIEF SUMMARY OF THE REMARKS OF THE BISHOP OF LISBON

The response to the question–whether it is heretical to assert that Christ and the apostles did [not][40] have something in common–is "No," since having something in common pertains to the natural law which does not touch upon the nature of personal or common ownership. Thus, however much everything may have been held in common in the apostolic life

---

as well as many arguments, he came to the conclusion that Christ and the apostles did not have something in common in terms ownership or dominion. However, I have never heard that his determination or conclusion has been reputed erroneous, since his book can still be obtained nearly everywhere. The same conclusion can be drawn, since [the bishop of] Lincoln, who was a great doctor, disputed the same question, wrote a great book about it and held the same conclusion as was held by the two previously mentioned doctors. Nevertheless, so far as I have heard, his teaching was never reputed false or erroneous." [The texts of Grosseteste and Pecham are not indicated.]

[39] *Quorumdam exigit (Bullarium Franciscanum*, V.128)

[40] It seems necessary to supply "not" (*non*) here, as did Tocco at the beginning of the immediately preceding section.

according to the natural law, this life was not thereby impeded, since the apostles renounced ⟨⟨59⟩⟩ the common and personal ownership of things introduced by the law of constitution and custom. Therefore, a threefold principle can be formulated about this matter.

First, nothing is held in an unqualified way unless it is held according to positive law. But the apostles held nothing according to positive law. Second, something is not held in an unqualified way if it is not possessed in an unqualified way, because every possession is something positive. But the apostles possessed nothing as is written in Luke 9: "Everyone who does not renounce what he possesses."[41] Third, if something is relinquished in an unqualified way, then it is not held in an unqualified way. Yet, speaking on behalf of himself and the apostles, Peter said, "Behold we have relinquished everything."[42] Accordingly, it evidently is true to assert that Christ and the apostles had nothing in common according to positive law. However, it also is true that they had something in common according to natural law. But whether it[43] is heretical I leave to the Holy See.

It seems to me that the use of a thing which terminates in its consumption pertains to a particular act of consumption both in regard to natural law as well as positive law. However, consider use in regard to something possessed which pertains to the nature of using something according to the right to what is advantageous. I say that, according to both laws, this use is common and personal so far as the thing is [held in] common or personally.

⟨⟨60⟩⟩ A BRIEF SUMMARY OF THE REMARKS OF THE BISHOP OF RIGA

In regard to the previously stated question, I respond that it is not heretical to assert that Christ and the apostles had nothing in common. The reason is that Christ had every perfection in the greatest degree. However, the greatest degree of poverty is not to have anything personally or in common. Therefore, etc. This is what Bernard says, commenting on Luke 2, "When Jesus was twelve years old":[44] "And you, Lord, conformed to all of our poverty. As one of the poor multitude, you begged for a small offering by the door."[45] The same point is made evident by other authorities among the

---

[41] Luke 14:33 for Luke 9 in the text.

[42] Matt. 19:27.

[43] The referent here is, presumably, the claim that Christ and the apostles held something in common according to positive law.

[44] Luke 2:42.

[45] Aelred of Rivaulx, *Tractatus de Iesu puero duodenni* I.6 (*CCCM* 1.254; *PL*

saints, all of whom have been previously cited.

Further, it is not heretical to assert that from its inception the Church has maintained and maintains, and also has taught and teaches [this point]. Moreover, it was clear to the apostles and their successors up to the present time that Christ taught in word, and confirmed by example, the renunciation of temporal things personally as well as in common. This is evident in light of the teachings of the Church and the first book of the stories of the history of the Church (the last chapter) where it is told that the apostle Thaddeus rejected King Abagari's gold.[46] This matter also is made evident by blessed Francis who was marked by the stigmata of Christ himself because he followed Christ in such renunciation. On account of this, our ⟨⟨61⟩⟩ holy predecessors determined Francis's entire rule to be evangelical. The decretal, *Exiit*,[47] makes this evident. He [the bishop] refers to other authorities that were cited earlier.

A Brief Summary of the Remarks of a Teacher of the Franciscan Order

In connection with the question of whether it is heretical to assert that Christ and the apostles did not have anything in common, I respond that if the question is understood in regard to dominion over things and not in regard to the simple use of them in fact, then it is not heretical, since its opposite cannot clearly be proved through the teaching of the precepts of the saints and the Church. Moreover, probable, apparent, or sophistic proofs do not suffice to judge something heretical. The determination of the precepts of the saints or the Church do not clearly prove that Christ had something in common. Indeed, the opposite is the case as is made evident by the authorities cited above, the decretal, *Exiit*,[48] and the declaration of the most holy father and Lord, Pope John XXII.[49] Therefore, etc.

This point is confirmed through the following argument. Christ had nothing in common if he did not want it, since no one can be the owner of anything involuntarily. But it cannot clearly be proved that Christ wanted to have dominion over any temporal thing. Therefore, it is not heretical to

---

184.853).

[46] Eusebius, *Ecclesiastica historia* 1.13 (*PG* 20.130).

[47] Nicholas III, *Exiit qui seminat* (*CIC* II.1110).

[48] Ibid.

[49] No work of John XXII is indicated at this point in the manuscript. It is not clear whether the author is appealing to the text of John XXII cited above (see page 126) or some other text.

assert that he had nothing in common. Further, it is not heretical to assert that an exemplar, rule, and measure are not exceeded ⟨⟨62⟩⟩ in perfection by a copy, what is ruled, or what is measured. But blessed Francis was voluntarily poor in the sense that he did not have anything personally or in common. Therefore, it is not heretical to assert that blessed Francis did not exceed Christ in poverty, who is the exemplar, rule, and measure of all perfection. Further, the same point is evident because of the stigmata impressed on Francis on account of his singular manner of following Christ in poverty in the manner that has been previously set forth. So too, it is not heretical to assert what is taught in the decretal, *Exiit*, which was cited earlier. Also, authorities were cited [by the author] that had been previously cited.

A Brief Summary of the Remarks of the Bishop of Badajoz

In regard to the question that has been posed, I say that it is not heretical to assert that Christ did not have anything in common in regard to ownership and dominion, as the decretal, *Exiit*,[50] makes clear. However, Christ did have things in regard to use. The bishop establishes this point in the same way as above. In responding to the question, he draws five conclusions. First, according to [Gratian's *Decretum*] 24, q.3, some understand Sacred Scripture in a manner different than the Holy Spirit who created[51] it.[52] Second, one should accept as the true sense of the Holy Spirit in Sacred Scripture what the Roman Church defines to be true. Accordingly, the bishop also says: I would not believe in the Gospel if the authority of the Church did not instruct me.

⟨⟨63⟩⟩ Third, it is not permissible to call into question what has been once defined by the Church. As Pope Gelasius says (24 q.1), "Our ancestors who discerned all things by inspiration necessarily took precautions so that once a synod had promulgated what was binding concerning every single heresy for the common and true Catholic and apostolic faith, then after these corrections what has been promulgated may not be disturbed by anything new."[53] Fourth, the decretal, *Exiit*, makes it clear that Christ renounced all ownership of things not only individually but also in common,[54] that the apostles were taught this, and that this matter was declared

---

[50] Nicholas III, *Exiit qui seminat* (*CIC* II.1112).

[51] Reading *condidit* for the apparent misprint *condidit*.

[52] *Decretum magistri Gratiani* C 24,q 3,c 27: *Haeresis* (*CIC* I.997-98).

[53] *Decretum magistri Gratiani* C 24,q 1,c 2: *Maiores nostri* (*CIC* I.966).

[54] Nicholas III, *Exiit qui seminat* (*CIC* II.1112).

and settled by the Holy See once and for all. Fifth, the words of the Gospel about the renunciation of ownership that was accomplished and observed by Christ and the apostles should be understood according to what the previously mentioned decretal says about ownership of things personally and in common. It is not permissible to depart from that understanding.

Accordingly, it is evident that the proposition, "Christ and the apostles had nothing personally or in common," is unqualifiedly true. The opposite– that Christ had something in common–is unqualifiedly false, since it is contrary to the sense the Roman Church, taught by the Holy Spirit, gives to the gospel words. Consequently, it is heretical, since, as was said, the heretic is one who understands Sacred Scripture in a manner other than that which is demanded by the Holy Spirit. In light of these suppositions, the bishop responds to the authorities as have the others.

⟨⟨64⟩⟩ A BRIEF SUMMARY OF THE REMARKS OF
CARDINAL B[ERTRAND] DE LA TOUR

That Christ and the apostles had nothing personally nor in common is proved as follows. First, Christ, who was compelled to beg during the entire course of his life, had nothing personally or in common. It is evident that Christ lived in such a condition, since, in the first place, he was born in another person's dwelling, and he was born of a poor mother who barely had one tunic to cover her nakedness, as Chrysostom says in his commentary on Matthew.[55] Moreover, in the course of his life, he ate someone else's food that was provided by the women who followed him. Further, as Bernard says, he begged in the temple when he was twelve years old and remained in Jerusalem.[56]

Again, he begged when he said to a person who had not invited him, "Zachaeus, make haste and descend, since today I must tarry in your house" (Luke 19).[57] The *Gloss* says the same thing.[58] Further, there is the *Gloss*[59] on the Psalm text "A poor and needy person was persecuted";[60] that is, Judas persecuted Christ toward the end of his life. Therefore, etc. In addition, during the entire course of his life he did not have a personal

---

[55] Pseudo-Chrysostom, *Homilia 2 in Matthaeum* 11 (*PG* 56,642).

[56] Aelred of Rivaulx, *Tractatus de Iesu puero duodenni* I.6 (*CCCM* 1.254; *PL* 184. 853).

[57] Luke 19:5

[58] *Glossa interlinearis* on Luke 19:5 (*Biblia Latina cum glossa ordinaria* IV.205).

[59] *Glossa interlinearis* on Ps. 108:17 (*Biblia Latina cum glossa ordinaria* II,597).

[60] Ps. 108:17.

dwelling: "The wolves have dens," etc., "but the Son of Man has nowhere to lay his head" (Matthew 8).[61] Jerome's gloss testifies to the same point.[62] Further, Christ did not have the wherewithal to pay the tribute (Matt. 17).[63] When he died he did not have the means to cover his nakedness. Further, as is evident in the Gospel, his corpse was wrapped in another person's shroud, and he was buried in a sepulchre that belonged to someone else.[64]

Moreover, the same point[65] is evident for two reasons. The first is that Christ did not have what he forbade the apostles and other perfect people. Yet, consider Matthew X, "Do not possess gold or silver," etc.;[66] Matthew 19, "If you would be perfect," etc.;[67] as well as Mark 6 and Luke 9, "Take nothing for the journey."[68] Therefore, it follows that he had nothing as its owner.

Second, the same point is proved in regard to the apostles. The first proof is drawn from the texts cited immediately above from Matthew, Mark, and Luke which give Christ's precept about having nothing personally or in common. The glosses according to Chrysostom[69] and Jerome[70] give two reasons for this precept. The precept was given lest the apostles appear to preach for the sake of lucre and not for the sake of the salvation of people. It was also given, so that in order to be freed from all care and solicitude in this life, they would provide for every care and contemplative quiet by the ministry of the word of God.

Third, speaking in his own name and in that of the other apostles, Peter says, "Behold we have relinquished everything and followed you."[71] Concerning this text, Augustine says, in book 17 of the *City of God*, "These powerful men, i.e., the apostles, vowed this vow in a most powerful manner. Whence this [vow]," he continues, "except from him of whom it is said, granting fulfillment to one who made a vow?"[72] In his homily, Gregory says

---

[61] Matt. 8:20.

[62] *Glossa ordinaria* on Matt. 8:20 (*Biblia Latina cum glossa ordinaria* IV.33).

[63] Matt. 17:23.

[64] Matt. 27:59-60.

[65] Namely, that Christ had nothing personally or in common.

[66] Matt. 10:9.

[67] Matt. 19:21.

[68] Mark 6:8 and Luke 9:3.

[69] *Homilia 32 in Matthaeum* 5 (*PG* 57.382-3).

[70] *Commentarii in evangelium Matthaei* I.10 (*CCSL* 77.66; *PL* 26.65).

[71] Matt. 19:27.

[72] *De civitate Dei* XVII.4 (*CCSL* 48.559; *PL* 41.530).

that "The apostles not ⟨⟨66⟩⟩ only relinquished things they possessed, but they even relinquished having a will."[73] He also said that those who followed Christ gave up all things to the extent that they could be desired by those who did not follow him.[74] Consequently, they gave up all things that they could desire, in common as well as personally, and personally as well as in common.[75]

Also, the *Gloss* on the text, "Silver and gold I have none,"[76] comments that "Peter said this in order to remember the divine precept."[77] Augustine makes the same point in his book on the wonders of Sacred Scripture.[78] Commenting on the text above, Bernard says in book 2 of his treatise to Pope Eugene: "There is no time for leisure when every solicitude for the Church flourishes with zeal. He does not give something to you, either gold or silver, since he says to you: 'Gold and silver I have none.' If you happen to have them, use them not at will but as the occasion demands, and you will use them as if not using them."[79] And in the first book, he writes that "It may be that you will claim this for yourself by some other reason but not by apostolic right. For, I could not give to you what I did not have."[80]

Writing to Hitruncia, Jerome makes the same point: "Wandering over the entire earth, the disciples of Christ did not have money in their belts or sandals on their feet."[81] Again, Jerome writes to Egbidia: "If you would be perfect and in the first rank at the height of dignity, then do what the apostles did: 'Go and sell all,' etc; thus you will follow the Savior and by a naked power you will follow the naked cross alone."[82] Again, commenting on Matthew 6, "He commands them not to take things on their journey,"[83] Bede says that in order to be free of care, Christ commanded the apostles not to possess or ⟨⟨67⟩⟩ to carry the small or minimum necessities of this life.[84]

---

[73] *XL Homiliarum in Evangelium* I.5 (*PL* 76.1093).

[74] Ibid. I.5 (*PL* 76.1095).

[75] See Hervaeus, pages 94 and 110 above, for a discussion of this argument.

[76] Acts 3:6.

[77] *Glossa interlinearis* on Acts 3:6 (*Biblia Latina cum glossa ordinaria* IV.459).

[78] Pseudo-Augustine, *De mirabilibus sacrae scripturae* III.16 (*PL* 35.2201).

[79] *De consideratione ad Eugenium papam* II.6.10 (*Opera* [Rome, 1957-] III.417; *PL* 182.748).

[80] Ibid.

[81] *Epistolae* 123.15 [section 14 in *CSEL*] (*CSEL* 56.90; *PL* 22.1057).

[82] *Epistolae* 120.1 (*CSEL* 55.477-8; *PL* 22.985).

[83] Mark 6:8. See also, Matt. 10:9. The Latin text mistakenly refers to Matthew 6.

[84] *In Marci evangelium expositio* II.2 (*CCSL* 120.505; *PL* 92.505). See Hervaeus, beginning at pages 93 and 110 above, for discussions of the basic argument and many

Therefore, the clarification of the question about this matter can be made in light of three presuppositions. First, the state of Christ and the apostles was most perfect, containing supereminently in itself whatever could pertain to the perfection of any other state.

Second, there are two states of perfection in the Church, neither of which has the nature of the other. On the one hand, there is the religious state which is the state of acquiring perfection. Poverty, or the renunciation of things, pertains to the intrinsic nature of this state, not indeed essentially but instrumentally, since, as has been said, poverty does not pertain to nature of perfection but to the nature of acquiring perfection. On the other hand, there is the state of exercising perfection, namely, the state of prelates. Poverty, or the renunciation of things personally and in common, does not pertain to the nature of this state. Indeed, prelates can possess things personally or in common without any detriment to perfection. Rather, according to Dionysius, purgation, illumination, and bringing about perfection pertain to the nature of this state.[85]

[Third], no proposition is called heretical unless its opposite is an article of faith, or a conclusion immediately drawn from such an article, or something clearly proved through Sacred Scripture or determined by the Church.[86]

Thus, in light of these considerations, it must be said in response to the question ⟨⟨68⟩⟩ that the proposition properly seems heretical if "nothing" is taken in the widest sense, excluding in the most general way everything that can pertain to the sustenance of human nature in terms of use alone, ownership and dominion. For, it can be proved through Sacred Scripture that Christ exercised dispensation of some things. There also is the ecclesiastical determination contained in the decretal, *Exiit*, where it is indicated that Christ had a purse.[87]

However, if the word "nothing" is taken in a stricter sense that excludes ownership of and dominion over things which is repugnant to the state whose nature is to have nothing personally or in common, then the proposition is not heretical. For, it is not [contained] in an article of faith, nor has it been determined by the Church. Indeed, just the opposite is the case as is made evident in the decretal, *Exiit*, where it is said that "The renuncia-

---

of the texts contained in this third point.

[85] Cf. Pseudo-Dionysius the Areopagite, *De ecclesiastica hierarchia* 5 (PG 3.166). See Hervaeus, page 81 and beginning at page 88 above, for a discussion of the distinction between the two religious states and the relation of poverty to them.

[86] See Hervaeus, pages 112 and 114 above.

[87] Nicholas III, *Exiit qui seminat* (CIC II.1112).

tion of all things, both personally as well as in common, for the sake of God–which Christ shows as the way of perfection–is meritorious and holy," etc.[88]

This same point is made evident through a fourfold argument. First, the state of acquiring perfection is more perfect to the degree that it excludes solicitude for temporal things. For, according to Gregory in Book 1 of the *Moralia in Job*: "Temporal things are all the more harmful to the degree that they have care and solicitude joined to them."[89] The state of renouncing ⟨⟨69⟩⟩ all things personally as well as in common is something of this sort. Therefore, etc.[90] This point is confirmed, since, in *On Christian Doctrine*, Book 3, Augustine says that "The greater is the destruction of the kingdom of desire, the greater is the increase of the kingdom of charity."[91]

Confirmation also is found in the *Collections of the Fathers*, *Collatio* X: "There is no greater or holier poverty than that which, having nothing for defense and knowing nothing of rights, has begged daily assistance from the liberality of others."[92] Also, it is written in the decretal, *Exiit*, that "Such a state is the more perfect as its members are withdrawn from temporal things to a greater extent."[93] It does not matter that the apostles acted to obtain funds, since they did not do this for themselves but to be solicitous for others.

Second, the apostles were not more perfect in the first mission than they were later. Indeed their perfection continually grew until their final reception by the Holy Spirit. Yet, in their first mission for Christ, Peter, Andrew, James, and John relinquished whatever they had in common, namely, ship and nets as is evident in Matthew 4[94] and Luke 6.[95] Therefore, etc. And, as we said above, this is confirmed through what Gregory says in the homily cited above in reference to Matthew 19, "Behold we have relinquished everything."[96]

Third, the apostles had gold and silver either in the manner that Christ

---

[88]   Ibid. See Hervaeus, pages 109 and 112 above.

[89]   The text, as such, was not found. However, cf. Gregory the Great, *Moralia in Job* XXII.2 (*CCSL* 143A.1094; *PL* 76.214).

[90]   See Hervaeus, beginning at page 66 above.

[91]   *De doctrina Christiana* III.10 (*SL* 32.88; *PL* 34.72).

[92]   John Cassian, *XIV Collationes patrum*, collatio X.11 (*CSEL* 13.303; *PL* 49.837).

[93]   Nicholas III, *Exiit qui seminat* (*CIC* II.1114).

[94]   Matt. 4:20.

[95]   Luke 6:14.

[96]   *XL Homiliarum in evangelium* I.5 (*PL* 76.1093). Cf. Matt. 19:27. See above, p. 131.

had a dwelling or in some other manner. If [they had it] in the same manner [the conclusion holds], since Christ had a dwelling to the extent of using it. If [they had it] in another manner, then there is a contradiction with what Chrysostom says when he comments on the text from Matthew, "Wolves have dens":[97] "This text confirms that Christ did not have a dwelling, and ⟨⟨70⟩⟩ it reflected the more potent law that was enjoined on the apostles not to have gold or silver."[98]

Fourth, considered in itself, the most perfect state always shows the way of perfection even if at times it accidentally displays some weakness or imperfection. In the same way, the sun intrinsically illuminates, although when it is blocked then in an accidental manner it does not always illuminate. So too, a habit always elicits a perfect act, although it might happen that it does not. The state of Christ and the apostles was most perfect. Therefore, this state in itself always displays the way of perfection, although accidentally and for the sake of those who are weak it may exhibit something imperfect. However, what happens accidentally neither falls under the category of skill nor does it falsify a general rule. Therefore, when showing the way of perfection, Christ verbally taught the renunciation of all things personally and in common, and he confirmed it by example as is evident in the decretal, *Exiit*. Thus, what has been proposed is clear.

However, it should be noted that having dominion over and ownership of temporal things in common is a weak and imperfect work, since, as Augustine writes in a certain letter, "Things possessed ⟨⟨71⟩⟩ are loved more strongly than things desired constrain [us]. The former are cutoff just like certain members; the latter are repudiated just like something extraneous."[99] Further, it should be noted that there are two ways one can understand the reservation of things in order to use them for future necessity, which is given the name of a wallet, a purse, and money.

In one sense, reserving things in this way occurs when someone cannot be supplied through another person's liberality. However, this is not a weak or imperfect work but it is granted to perfect men. The decretal, *Exiit*, makes this evident.[100] Christ dispensed things for himself and the apostles in this sense, since he went among the Samaritans who were inhospitable (Luke X)[101] and, since he said as he approached his death, "Now whoever

---

[97] Matt. 8:20.

[98] *Homilia 22 in Matthaeum* 4 (*PL* 57.304).

[99] *Epistolae* 31.5 (*CSEL* 34(pt.1).5; *PL* 33.124). See, Hervaeus, page 35 above, for a more accurate and clearer version of this text.

[100] Nicholas III, *Exiit qui seminat* (*CIC* II.1113).

[101] Luke 9:52.

has a purse should take it as well as a wallet" (Luke 22).[102] Concerning this text, Bede says: "The same rule did not guide the disciples in the time of persecution as in the time of peace. When he sent the disciples to preach, Christ commanded the disciples not to take anything on the journey. Yet as the moment of death drew nigh, he gave a rule appropriate to the circumstances, permitting them to take all of the necessities of life as soon the Jewish race persecuted the shepherd and his flock."[103] In light of this, it should be understood that for urgent reasons we can set aside something pertaining rigorously to our undertaking or state.

Reserving things in order to use them for future necessity can be understood in another sense when it is assumed ⟨⟨72⟩⟩ that one can be supplied through another's liberality. This is a weak and imperfect work in which Christ, who is worshipped by the perfect and the imperfect, dispensed things. As Augustine says in his book *On the Work of Monks*: "With his customary mercy, the Lord had a purse, thereby sympathizing with the weaker."[104] Similarly, I say that neither Christ nor the apostles ever dispensed[105] themselves or others from the precept, "Do not possess gold," etc. But Christ dispensed from the precept, "Do not carry a purse or wallet," just as those who are perfect: namely, when future assistance was not assumed. However, when it could be assumed, he dispensed things, thereby condescending to those who are weak.

The second point to be noted is that the power of dispensing something gives no ownership of or dominion over the thing to the person who dispenses it. Thus, by law, prelates do not have ownership of or dominion over the goods of the Church which, nevertheless, they are obligated to dispense. Accordingly, dispensing temporal things is not repugnant to the state whose nature lies in having nothing personally or in common. Christ and the apostles dispensed temporal things in this way. So, in *Homily 60* on [the gospel of] John, Augustine says: "He had a purse. Keeping the gifts of the faithful, he apportioned them according to needs of himself, the apostles, and the other poor. The form of ecclesiastical finances was established for the first time."[106] Also, in *Homily 71* on John, Chrysostom writes that "Christ did not permit taking a sack or coins, and nevertheless he car-

---

[102] Luke 22:36.

[103] *In Lucam evangelium expositio* VI.22 (*CCSL* 120.383ff; *PL* 92.601).

[104] *De opere monachorum* V.6 (*CSEL* 41.539; *PL* 40.552).

[105] This is one of the few occurrences in this work where *dispenso* is used in the intransitive sense of dispensing from something, e.g., a precept. Most often it is used in the transitive sense of dispensing things.

[106] *In Ioannis evangelium tractatus* 62.4 (*CCSL* 36.485; *PL* 35.1083).

ried a purse to provide for the poor."[107]

[Third],[108] as is evident in the decretal, *Exiit*, the chapter beginning with *non autem* ⟨⟨73⟩⟩ *talem abdicationem*, simple use in fact can be separated from ownership, usufruct, and the right to use something even in regard to those things that are consumed in use.[109] Otherwise the slave, dependent child, and the monk would have dominion over and ownership of the goods which they use, which is contrary to law.[110] And what is more, Christ and the apostles would have dominion over things they used not only in common but also personally, thereby contradicting the decretal, *Exiit*, the chapter beginning with *Porro*.

If you say that the dominion is pointless without use, then it must be said that this is not true of those things that are given to the poor for the sake of God, since this is meritorious in regard to eternal life. Therefore, since Christ and the apostles were not capable of exercising dominion over the things that were given to them, dominion over such things was not transferred to them but to those from whom they bought necessities for themselves.[111]

[Fourth],[112] it is not inappropriate to say that Christ and the apostles had use of some things over which God alone and not people held dominion. The reason is that Christ's life restored the world as far as possible to the state of innocence and the natural law in which all things are common to all. Nor could someone [in that state] say "This is mine" or "This is yours," as these sorts of statements derive from the law of nations and human custom which arise contrary to natural justice. Rather, ⟨⟨74⟩⟩ as is written in [Gratian's *Decretum*] 8 dist. c. *Differt*, as well as c. *Quo jure*, and 12 Q.I c. *Dilectissimis*,[113] all things belong to God alone in regard to dominion and ownership. Thus, if, in terms of use, Christ and the apostles had use of something which belonged to no one, as the coin taken from the mouth of the fish, then they had use of it while the ownership of it was held by God alone.[114]

---

[107] *Homilia 72 in Ioannem* 2 (*PG* 59.392).

[108] The Latin text has *quarto*.

[109] Nicholas III, *Exiit qui seminat* (*CIC* II.1113).

[110] See Hervaeus, page 37 above, for the discussion of this argument.

[111] See Hervaeus, beginning at page 100 above, for a discussion of this argument.

[112] The Latin text has *quinto*.

[113] *Decretum magistri Gratiani* C 12, q 1, c 2: *Dilectissimis* (*CIC* I.676-77); Dist. 8, I. Pars: *Differt* (*CIC* I.12); Dist. 8, c. 1: *Quo iure* (*CIC* I.12-13).

[114] See Hervaeus–pages 38, 49, 78, and 84 above–for discussions related to this argument.

A BRIEF SUMMARY OF THE REMARKS OF THE ARCHBISHOP OF SALERNO

Is it heretical to assert that Christ and the apostles did not have something in common? To understand the truth of the matter, I make three points. The first is that the apostles vowed the most perfect evangelical poverty according to Augustine in *The City of God* Book 17,[115] a text very often cited as evidence. The second is that they fulfilled this vow according to the text "Let vows be made and fulfilled."[116] Third, having something in common can exist in two ways: in one way, perfectly–namely, in regard to right and ownership; in the other way, imperfectly and relatively–namely, in regard to simple use in fact, as the decretal, *Exiit*, makes evident.[117]

In reference to the truth of the matter, it must be said that after they assumed the state of evangelical perfection, Christ and the apostles ⟨⟨75⟩⟩ had nothing personally or in common in regard to right and ownership. However, they had a simple use of things in fact. This point is proved as follows. First, consider the decretal, *Exiit*, which says that Christ taught this matter and confirmed it by example.[118] Second, consider "Do not possess gold," etc.[119] in which the previously mentioned renunciation is commanded. Also, the aforementioned decretal sets forth the purpose for the precept, since the Gospel adds, "Worthy is the laborer for his food."[120] In this way, Christ removed [their doubt and lack of confidence about not having these necessities], which he need not have removed if the apostles could take something in common.

It does not matter that Augustine says in *The Harmony of the Gospels*, Book 2,[121] *The Work of Monks*,[122] and *Against Adimantus*,[123] that ["Do not possess gold"] was only a permission and not a precept, since it is evident from the text of Matthew[124] and Mark[125] that it was a precept. The same point is made by Ambrose who, commenting on Luke,[126] says that "Peter

---

[115] *De civitate Dei* XVII.4 (*CCSL* 48.559; *PL* 41.530).

[116] Ps. 75:12.

[117] Nicholas III, *Exiit qui seminat* (*CIC* II.1110).

[118] Ibid.

[119] Matt. 10:9.

[120] Matt. 10:10.

[121] *De consensu evangelistarum* II.30 (*CSEL* 43.177-8; *PL* 34.1113-4).

[122] *De opere monachorum* VI.7 (*CSEL* 41.541; *PL* 40.553).

[123] *Contra Adimantum* 20 (*CSEL* 25.177; *PL* 42.164).

[124] Matt. 10:9.

[125] Mark 6:8.

[126] Luke 9:3.

did not boast, since he did not have silver or gold, for in so doing, he obeyed the mandate of the Lord who commands, 'Do not possess,'" etc.[127] In regard to Acts 3,[128] the *Gloss* also makes the same point, "Remember his precept, 'Do not possess.'"[129] Again, Jerome writes to Demedriades: "When the clothes of Jesus were divided, the soldiers did not find leather shoes they could take. For the Lord could not have what he prohibited to his disciples."[130] Augustine's words can be explained: they are understood in regard to the second point: namely, one is allowed to receive food but commanded not to possess it. Thus, in *Against Adimantus*, Augustine writes, ⟨⟨76⟩⟩ "These things must be examined spiritually, lest to impious people the Lord appears to have gone against his own precept when he had a purse."[131]

Third, it is evident from what has been said that the apostles vowed the most perfect poverty. Consequently, Christ preserved this poverty most perfectly. Yet, renouncing all things not only personally but also in common is most perfect. Therefore, etc.

Fourth, Christ and the apostles did not have their own room. This is evident, since they celebrated the passover in another person's room.[132] Yet, the first thing that people who gather together seek out is a room. Therefore, if they denied themselves the right to a room, then it is even more apparent that they would have denied themselves the right to any other things. Nor does it matter that Christ is said to have entered into the house of Simon Peter,[133] for it happens that this was said because the house belonged to his wife or because the incident took place before Peter was chosen as an apostle. Thus, it is evident how the question should be resolved in regard to the truth of the matter.

So, in terms of the accuracy of the words, I say it is evident that to assert "Christ and the apostles did not have something is common" is not heretical, speaking about the meaning of the words. Suppose something is said of one thing in a primary way and, if extended, of a second thing in a less primary way. It follows that, because of the meaning of the words, what is said must be understood to refer in an unqualified way to the first thing about which it is said in a primary way and in relation to which the

---

[127] *Expositio evangelii secundum Lucam* VII.55 (*CCSL* 14.232; *PL* 15.1801-2).

[128] Acts 3:6.

[129] *Glossa ordinaria* on Acts. 3:6 (*Biblia Latina cum glossa ordinaria* IV.459).

[130] *Epistolae* 22.19 (*CSEL* 54.170; *PL* 22.406). The letter is to Eustochius.

[131] *Contra Adimantum* 20.1 (*CSEL* 25.117; *PL* 42.164).

[132] Matt. 26:28.

[133] Cf. Matt. 8:14 and Mark 1:29.

proposition is made true. But "having something" is said in a primary way when the thing is held in regard to right and ownership. Accordingly, neither a monk nor a slave are said to have something in a primary way, ⟨⟨77⟩⟩ since neither have ownership of a thing or a right to it. Thus, in regard to meaning of the words, the simple proposition is not heretical.

THE OPPOSITE STANCE ARGUED THROUGH AUTHORITIES AND ARGUMENTS

However, the opposite view is argued by means of authorities and arguments. It is argued by means of certain authorities such as Luke 22, "Now he who has a satchel" in which he may carry money should see that there is something in it. "Similarly, he should take a pack" in which he may carry other necessities and see that there is something in it.[134] This according to the *Gloss*.[135]

RESPONSE OF THE LORD CARDINAL VITAL TO THE OBJECTION

I say that this [utterance] was not a precept but a dispensation given on the eve of the most grave persecution of the apostles after the death of Christ, as Bede says in his comment on the same text.[136] The Lord Cardinal Bertrand concurs with this response.

SECOND OBJECTION

According to Acts 4, "The multitude of believers were of one heart and everything was common to them."[137]

⟨⟨78⟩⟩ RESPONSE OF THE LORD CARDINAL VITAL TO THE OBJECTION

I say that it was not the apostles who were called believers but rather the crowd who followed the apostles. The apostles were called teachers and miracle workers. Accordingly, the text, "With a great power they con-

---

[134] Luke 22:36.

[135] Text not found in the *Glossa ordinaria* or *Glossa interlinearis*. However, cf. Thomas Aquinas, *Catena aurea in quattor evangelia, Expositio in Lucam* XXII.10 on Luke 22:36 (Marietti edition 2.290) where Aquinas cites a text attributed to Chrysostom which reads in part: "'Dixit ergo eis: sed nunc qui habet sacculum,' quo scilicet portatur pecunia, 'tollat similiter et peram,' qua scilicet portantur cibaria."

[136] *In Lucam evangelium expositio* VI.22 (*CCSL* 120.383ff; *PL* 92.601).

[137] Acts 4:32. See Hervaeus, page 102 above, for a discussion of this text.

fessed," etc.[138] refers to the apostles, while the text, "Everything was common to them," refers to the crowd. In the same vein, Cardinal Vital says it is true that the proceeds of the possessions that were sold "were placed at the feet of the apostles" in so far as they were placed at the feet of stewards and administrators. But it is not true if they were placed at the feet of those who exercised dominion over and ownership of things they held. The Lord Cardinal Bertrand makes the same point, citing what was said above by Bede.

THIRD OBJECTION

The third objection is drawn from the text Acts 11, "The disciples decided that each, according to his means, should send what he had to the brothers in Judea. And they did so."[139] From this text, it seems that the apostles not only had things in common but also that they had things personally.

⟨⟨79⟩⟩ RESPONSE OF THE LORD CARDINAL VITAL TO THE OBJECTION

In response to this, I say that "disciples" in this context does not refer to the apostles. The apostles did not send anything. However, it is said that blessed Saul and Barnabas carried money and had the duty of dispensing things, although they did not own things or have dominion over them.

OTHER OBJECTIONS

Objection 4: "And the disciples said, 'We will buy bread with two hundred denaries and give it to them to eat'" (Matt. 6).[140]

Objection 5: "The disciples went into the city in order to buy food" (John 4).[141]

Objection 6: "He sent Peter and John into the city so that they might prepare the Pasch" (Luke 22).[142]

Objection 7: The prophet spoke in the person of Christ: "They divided my clothes among them."[143]

Objection 8: "Having food and clothing wherewith to cover ourselves,

---

[138] Acts 4:33.
[139] Acts 11:20.
[140] Mark 6:37.
[141] John 4:8.
[142] Luke 22:8.
[143] Ps. 21:8.

let us be content" (1 Tim 6).[144]

Objection 9: "I have everything and I abound" (Phil. 4).[145]

Objection 10: "When you come, bring the cloak which I left at Troas in Carpus' hands, as well as the books and, most especially, the rolls of parchment." (2 Tim. 4)[146]

In light of all of these texts, it is evident that Christ and the apostles had dominion over some things.

⟨⟨80⟩⟩ RESPONSE OF THE LORD VITAL, [BISHOP OF] ALBANO, TO ALL OF THE FOREGOING OBJECTIONS

In regard to all of the foregoing objections and others like them, I say that one reads that Christ had a purse, albeit very rarely, yet so that every scripture might be fulfilled concerning his neediness. He had a purse to sustain himself and the poor in order to condemn future heretics who would say that the Church could not have temporal goods just as, according to Augustine, Christ wanted to attend the wedding with his mother.[147] [Also, he had a purse] on the condition that they[148] were merely distributors of the previously mentioned money, purses, clothes or other goods which have been cited, and on the condition that they did not have dominion over them but a simple use of them in fact.

By having a purse, they did not contradict taking a vow to have nothing personally or in common, since it is likely that someone who borrows a room to celebrate the Passover also will borrow the rest of the necessities. Moreover, just as the Lord said that my teaching, which belongs to me in a primary way by virtue of divinity, does not pertain to me in a primary way by virtue of my humanity but only in the manner befitting a servant, so he could say that my clothes [are mine] in regard to a simple use of them in fact but they are not mine in regard to dominion over them. In regard to all the other things they are said to have held, it must be said that, since "to have" does not have just one sense but many, it should be understood that things were held in regard to simple use in fact.

The Lord Reverend Bertrand, previously mentioned, ⟨⟨81⟩⟩ resolves all of these texts and those similar to them in the same way. He adds that

---

[144] 1 Tim. 6:8.

[145] Phil. 4:18.

[146] 2 Tim. 4:13.

[147] Cf. *Sermo* 123.2 (*PL* 38.684-5).

[148] The pronoun presumably refers to Christ and the apostles, and not to Christ and his mother.

Christ appropriately granted things in the way mentioned, because he and the apostles went among the Samaritans, because extreme necessity [was experienced] at other times, and since there was a time of persecution. Thus, it is evident according to Lord Vital, that we have proceeded from many cases of the truth to one when it is said that because Christ and the apostles had things, they therefore had dominion over them. The reason is that this statement is made true for something held in terms of use in fact alone.

The Lord [archbishop of] Salerno responds in the same way. He adds that if Christ had a purse in the sense of owning it, this did not happen regularly, since, as the decretal, [*Exiit*], says, Christ confirmed by example that perfection [consists in] the renunciation of all ownership of things. Or, it can be said that although Christ is said in an unqualified way to have had a purse, this is not understood in an unqualified way but in a qualified and relative manner regarding the use of something. In the same way, the statement "I said that you are gods and sons of first rank in every way" is said in an unqualified way but it is understood relatively and not in an unqualified way.

NEW OPPOSITION

Against this response, it is objected that the simple use of something in fact is not some entity but only the consumption of a thing in certain ways such that this use does not endure but only exists at the time when the thing is actually consumed. Accordingly, the use of a thing cannot be separated from dominion over it. On account of this, the proposition "that person has simple use of this thing in fact" is not true in many cases but ⟨⟨82⟩⟩ in only one, since in such cases use and dominion are inseparable. Thus, when it is said that this person had such simple use of things in fact, therefore he had dominion over them, the fallacy of [affirming the] consequence is not committed.

THE RESPONSE OF THE LORD VITAL TO THE OBJECTION

In response to the objection, it must be said that the use of things and dominion over them are separable even in regard to things that are consumed in use. For, it is a fact when the natural law held sway no one could say about something that "This is mine" and "This is yours." These two pronouns ["mine" and "yours"] were introduced as a result of the wickedness and cupidity of the race, as Clement says in [Gratian's *Decretum*]

Q12, I c *Dilectissimis*.[149]

Yet, it is a fact that a precept was given to use things consumed in use: namely, "eat of every tree in paradise."[150] Since things were used without dominion and ownership when there was no mine or yours, it is evident by a ⟨⟨83⟩⟩ clear light that the use of things which are consumed in use can exist without ownership or dominion. So, Adam was able not to sin.[151] In this way, both Adam as well as his successors had usufruct [of things] in paradise without having dominion over them. If one asks who owned the goods that Adam used at the time of the natural law, then it must be said that they were God's and that they did not belong to anyone else. The reason is that "This is mine" and "This is yours" could not be said at that time.[152] Accordingly, because of his desire that the community of the apostles be brought back as far as possible to the state in which nature was established, Christ permitted them the use of necessities, but he did not permit them the possession of or dominion over them. The Lord Cardinal Bertrand gives the same sort of response.

OTHER OBJECTIONS

If it is insisted that having possession of temporal things does not impede perfection except because of the solicitude joined to it, and it also is insisted that those who say they have nothing in common do not have less solicitude for food, clothing, and buildings than those who say they have things in common, then it does not follow that those who have nothing in common are in a greater state of perfection than those who have something in common.

⟨⟨84⟩⟩ RESPONSE OF THE LORD CARDINAL VITAL TO THE OBJECTION

The objection is not true. Indeed, those who have nothing in this way are in a state of greater perfection, since evangelical or apostolic poverty pertains to this state only. This is evident for two reasons. The first reason is drawn from Christ and the apostles who undertook this poverty. The decretal, *Exiit*, makes this evident.[153] The second reason is drawn from solicitude.

---

[149] *Decretum magistri Gratiani* C 12,q 1,c 2: *Dilectissimis* (*CIC* I.676-77).

[150] Gen. 2:16.

[151] "Unde potuit Adam non peccare."

[152] See Hervaeus–pages 38, 49, 78, and 84 above–for discussions related to this argument.

[153] Nicholas III, *Exiit qui seminat* (*CIC* II.1112).

It is not the solicitude which arises from the weakness of the one who is solicitous nor is it joined to the state of poverty, but indeed, it is repugnant to this state, since this solicitude cannot exist with the highest and most perfect grade of Christ's poverty. However, [the second reason is drawn from] the solicitude that arises accidentally and from something extrinsic, since, of course, the customary charity of people to sustain the poor grew cold. And in such a case, those who are solicitous have necessities not only for the moment but for the period of time in which they believe with probability that they cannot find necessities. In the third case,[154] it must be supposed that solicitude is not repugnant to the perfection of evangelical poverty.

ANOTHER OBJECTION

It is insisted that the Apostle worked with his hands and that, therefore, he at least had dominion over the compensation [for his work].

⟨⟨85⟩⟩ RESPONSE OF THE LORD CARDINAL BERTRAND DE LA TOUR

In response to the objection, it must be said that just as Christ and the apostles only used things they bought and sold, so in relation to the compensation, the full dominion was transferred to him from whom the apostle was able to attain it.

OTHER OPPOSITION

It might be said that a community does not use things but, nevertheless, that it can have dominion over them. Therefore, the community of the apostles had dominion over things but not the use of them.

RESPONSE OF THE LORD CARDINAL BERTRAND DE LA TOUR

In response to this objection, it must be said that "community" can be taken in two ways: community as a community and community as comprised of individuals. In the first sense, a community does not use things nor does man run in the sense that a man runs to the house. However, in the second sense a community uses things as man, in the sense of an individual [man], runs. In response to everything that has been taken from the decretal, [Exiit], the Lord Cardinal Bertrand responds that it must be understood

---

[154] That is, the solicitude of those who have things for the period of time in which they believe with probability that they cannot find necessities.

that the apostles had such things only in terms of [their] administration and dispensation. However, the dominion over these things was held by God or the community of other faithful people. If ⟨⟨86⟩⟩ it is insisted that use of things in fact cannot be common to many, the response is that it can, both with reference to a diversity of things as well as the same thing until the time that the thing is completely consumed.

ANOTHER OBJECTION

In regard to the claim that Christ had a purse but no dominion over it, some nevertheless insist that, since he had dominion over it in regard to its use, it must then be maintained that he had a purse otherwise than in regard to use alone.

RESPONSE OF THE LORD CARDINAL BERTRAND

First of all, this objection commits a fallacy of affirming the consequence. The argument–Christ had a purse, therefore he had it in terms of dominion –moves from many cases of truth to one. Perhaps we might even say that Christ had a purse in regard to its use and dominion. Yet, against this view, we read that Christ ate another's food which he did not have except in terms of its use. To counter this view, moreover, we read that, "Do not possess gold or silver,"[155] was said to the apostles, yet they used these things just as Christ used a house. Further, in Acts 3, Peter said, "Silver and gold I have none."[156] Yet at times, he had these things in terms of their use.

⟨⟨87⟩⟩ RESPONSE OF THE ARCHBISHOP OF SALERNO[157]

In the first place, it is urged in this matter that, according to Augustine, Christ had a purse which established the form of Church finances. But the Church has money and not just in regard to its use. Therefore, etc. [Second,] if Christ did not have dominion [over the purse], then Judas was not a thief. [Third,] if the use of money can be separated from dominion over it, then usury does not involve money. [Fourth,] a community does not have use of things. Thus, it exercises dominion over the things that it has.

To the first objection, I say that the form of ecclesiastical finances was established in regard to having [money] but not in regard to the mode of

---

[155] Matt. 10:9.

[156] Acts 3:6.

[157] This final section combines objections with the archbishop's replies.

having it. Moreover, the prelates in the first period were not only prelates but also perfect religious.

To the second, the objection does not follow. For someone is a thief not only by acquiring another person's things against the will of the owner but also because he takes another's things without the owner's knowledge or because he takes the place of the owner. To the third, it must be said that usury is not illicit, because use cannot be separated from dominion–for it can be separated–but because usury does not yield usufruct. To the [fourth],[158] I respond as others have responded above.

---

[158] The Latin has *quinto*.

Bibliography

PRIMARY SOURCES

Biblia Latina cum glossa ordinaria: facsimile reprint of the editio princeps Adolph Rusch of Strassburg 1480/81. Introduction by Karlfried Froehlich and Margaret T. Gibson. 4 vols. Turnhout: Brepols, 1992.

Bonagratia of Bergamo. *Tractatus de Christi et apostolorum paupertate.* Edited by L. Oliger. *Archivum Franciscanum Historicum* 22 (1929): 323-35, 487-511.

Bonaventura. *Apologia pauperum contra calumniatorem.* Vol. 8 of *Opera Omnia.* Quaracchi, 1882-1902. Translated by J. de Vinck under the title *Defense of the Mendicants,* Vol. 4 of *The Works of Bonaventure* (Paterson, NJ, 1966).

——. *De perfectione evangelica.* Vol. 5 of *Opera Omnia.* Quaracchi, 1882-1902.

——. *Expositio super regulam fratrum minorum,* Vol. 8 of *Opera Omnia.* Quaracchi, 1882-1902.

Bullarium Franciscanum. Edited by J.H. Sbaralea. Vols. I-III. Rome, 1759-65; edited by C. Eubel. Vol. V. Rome, 1898.

Corpus juris civilis. Edited by T. Mommsen, revised by P. Krueger. 15th ed., Vol. 1. Berlin: Weidmann, 1928.

Douie, D. "Three Treatises on Evangelical Poverty by Fr. Richard Conyngton, Fr. Walter Chatton and an Anonymous." *Archivum Franciscanum Historicum* 24 (1931): 341-69, 25 (1932): 36-58, 210-40.

Esser, Kajetan. *Opuscula Sancti Patris Francisci Assisiensis.* Grottaferrata, 1976.

Gerard of Abbeville. *Contra adversarium perfectionis christiane.* Edited by S. Clasen. *Archivum Franciscanum Historicum* 31 (1938): 276-329, 32 (1939): 89-202.

——. *Quodlibet XVI, qq. 1 and 2. Quatre questions inédites de Gérard d'Abbeville pour la défence de la superiorité du clergé séculier.* Edited by A Teetart. *Archivio italiano per la storia della pietà* 1 (1951): 168-178.

Habig, M., ed. *St. Francis of Assisi, Writings and Early Biographies: English*

Omnibus of the Sources for the Life of St. Francis. Chicago: Franciscan Herald Press, 1983.

Hervaeus Natalis. *Liber de paupertate Christi et apostoloroum.* Edited by J.G. Sikes. *Archives d'histoire doctrinale et littéraire du moyen âge.* 11 (1937-8): 209-97.

Hugh of Digne. *Hugh of Digne's Rule Commentary.* Edited by D. Flood. Grottaferrata, 1979.

Imperatoris Iustiniani Institutionum libri quattor. Introductions, commentary, and excusus by J.B. Moyle. 5th ed. Oxford: Clarendon Press, 1923.

Pecham, John. *Fratris Johannis Pecham; tractatus tres de paupertate.* Edited by C.L. Kingsford, A.G. Little, and F. Tocco. Farnborough: Gregg International Publishers, 1969.

Peter John Olivi. *An status altissime paupertatis sit simpliciter melior omni statu divitiarum.* In *Das Heil der Armen und das Verderben der Reichen.* Edited by J. Schlageter. Werl/Westfalen: Dietrich-Coelde-Verlag, 1989.

——. *Expositio regulae fratrum minorum.* In *Peter Olivi's Rule Commentary,* edited by D. Flood. Wiesbaden, 1972.

——. *An usus pauper includatur in consilio seu in voto paupertatis evangelicae, ita quod sit de eius substantia et integritate.* Edited by David Burr, *De Usu Paupere: The Quaestio and the Tractatus* (Perth: University of West Australia Press, 1992).

Thomas Aquinas. *Catena aurea in quattuor evangelia.* 2 vols. Edited by P. Guarienti. Marietti, 1953. Translated by John Henry Cardinal Newman under the title *Catena aurea: Commentary on the Four Gospels Collected out of the Works of the Fathers* (Southampton: Saint Austin Press, 1997).

——. *Contra impugnantes Dei religionem et cultum.* Vol. 41 of *Opera Omnia.* (Leonine Edition) Rome, 1882-. Translated by J. Proctor under the title *Against Those who Attack the Religious Profession.* In *An Apology for the Religious Orders,* Pt. 1 (St. Louis: Sands and Co., 1902): 43-373.

——. *Contra pestiferam doctrinam retrahentium homines a religionis ingressu.* Vol. 41 of *Opera Omnia.* (Leonine Edition) Rome, 1882-. Translated by J. Proctor under the title *Against Those who Would Deter Men from Entering Religion.* In *An Apology for the Religious Orders,* Pt. 2 (St. Louis: Sands and Co., 1902): 375-483.

——. *De perfectione spiritualis vitae.* Vol. 41 of *Opera Omnia.* (Leonine Edition) Rome, 1882-. Translated by J. Proctor under the title *The Religious State, the Episcopate, and the Religious Office (The Perfection of Spiritual Life)* (Westminster, MD, 1950).

——. *Summa contra gentiles*. Vols. 13-15 of *Opera Omnia*. (Leonine Edition) Rome, 1882-. Various translations.

——. *Summa theologiae*. Vols. 4-12 of *Opera Omnia*. (Leonine Edition) Rome, 1882-. Various translations.

Tocco, F. *La quistione della povertà nel secolo XIV*. Naples, 1910.

Wadding, Luke. *Annales Minorum seu trium ordinum a S. Francisco institutorum, auctore a.r.p. Luca Waddingo Hiberno*. 30 vols. Florence: Quaracchi, 1931-.

William of Ockham, *Opus nonaginta dierum*. In *Guillelmi de Ockham: Opera Politica*, 2 Vols., edited by J. G. Sikes, R.F Bennet, and H.S. Offler. Manchester: Manchester University Press, 1940 and 1962.

SECONDARY SOURCES

Baluze, Stephanus. *Vitae paparum Avenionensium*. Edited by G. Mollat. Paris: Letouzey et Ané, 1914-27.

Bennett, R.F. *The Early Dominicans*. Cambridge: The University Press, 1937.

Bulsano, P. Alberto. *Expositio regulae fratrum minorum*. Rome, 1932.

Burr, D. *Olivi and Franciscan Poverty: The Origins of the Usus Pauper Controversy*. Philadelphia, 1989.

Damiata, M. *Guglielmo d'Ockham: Povertà e potere*. 2 vols. Florence: Studi francescani, 1978-79.

Douie, D. *The Nature and the Effect of the Heresy of the Fraticelli*. Manchester: Manchester University Press, 1932.

——. *The Conflict between the Seculars and the Mendicants at the University of Paris in the Thirteenth Century*. Aquinas Society of London, Aquinas Paper no. 23. London, 1954.

Eijnden, Jan G. J. van den. *Poverty on the Way to God: Thomas Aquinas on Evangelical Poverty*. Leuven: Peeters, 1994.

Felder, Hilarin. *The Ideals of St. Francis of Assisi*. Chicago: Franciscan Herald Press, 1982.

Gauchat, Patrick. *Cardinal Bertrand de Turre: His Participation in the Theoretical Controversy Concerning the Poverty of Christ and the Apostles under Pope John XXII*. Tipografia Poliglotta Vaticana, 1930.

Glorieux, P. *Répertoire des maîtres en théologie de Paris au XIIIe siècle*. Paris: J. Vrin, 1933.

Guimarães, A. de. "Hervé Noël (†1323). Étude biographique." *Archivum Fratrum Praedicatorum* 8 (1938): 5-81.

Hauréau, B. "Hervé Nédlec Général des Frères Prêcheurs." *Histoire littéraire de la France* 24 (1914): 308-351.

Hinnebusch, W.A. *The History of the Dominican Order.* 2 vols. Staten Island, N.Y.: Alba House, 1966 and 1973.

Horst, Ulrich. *Evangelische Armut und Kirche: Thomas von Aquin und die Armutskontroversen des 13. und beginnenden 14. Jahrunderts.* Berlin: Academie, 1992.

——. *Evangelische Armut und papstliches Lehramt: Minoritentheologen im Konflikt mit Papst Johannes XXII. (1316-34).* Stuttgart: W. Kohlhammer, 1996.

Huber, Raphael M. *A Documented History of the Franciscan Order: 1182-1517.* Washington; Catholic University Press, 1944.

Jones, John D. "The Concept of Poverty in St. Thomas Aquinas's *Contra impugnantes Dei religionem et cultum.*" *The Thomist* 59, 3 (July, 1995): 109-139.

——. "Poverty and Subsistence: St. Thomas Aquinas and the Definition of Poverty." *Gregorianum,* 75 (1994): 135-49.

——. "St Thomas Aquinas and the Defense of Mendicant Poverty." *Proceedings of the American Catholic Philosophical Association* 70 (1996): 179-192.

Kaeppeli, Thomas. *Scriptores ordinis praedicatorum medii aevi.* Rome: Ad S. Sabinae, 1970-.

Lambermond, H.C. *Der Armutsgedanke des heiligen Dominikus und seines Ordens.* Zwolle, 1926.

Lambert, M.-D. "The Franciscan Crisis under John XXII." *Franciscan Studies* (1972): 123-143.

——. *Franciscan Poverty: The Doctrine of the Absolute Poverty of Christ and the Apostles in the Franciscan Order 1210-1323.* London: S. P. C. K., 1961.

Lapanski, D. *Evangelical Perfection: An Historical Examination of the Concept in the Early Franciscan Sources.* St. Bonaventure, N.Y.: Franciscan Institute, St. Bonaventure University, 1977.

Leff, Gordon. *Heresy in the Later Middle Ages.* 2 Vols. Manchester: Manchester University Press, 1967

Little, A.G. *Religious Poverty and the Profit Economy in Medieval Europe.* London: Cornell University Press, 1978.

Langholm, O. *Economics in the Medieval Schools: Wealth, Exchange, Value, Money and Usury according to the Paris Theological Tradition, 1200-1350.* Leiden: E. J. Brill, 1992.

Maier, Annaliese. "Annotazioni autografe di Giovanni XXII in codici Vaticani." *Rivista di storia della Chiesa in Italia* 6 (1952): 317-333.

Mollat, Michel. *Les pauvres au moyen âge.* Hachette, 1978. Translated by Arthur Goldhammer under the title *The Poor in the Middle Ages: An Essay in Social History* (New Haven: Yale University Press, 1986).

Moorman, John. A History of the Franciscan Order. Oxford: Clarendon Press, 1968.

Mulhern, Philip. *Dedicated Poverty.* Staten Island, NY: Alba House, 1972.

Roensch, Frederick. *Early Thomistic School.* Dubuque, IA: Priory Press, 1964.

Schalück, H.F. *Armut und Heil: Eine Untersuchung über den Armutsgedanken in der Theologie Bonaventuras.* Munich: F. Schoningh, 1971.

Spiers, Kerry E. "Four Medieval Manuscripts on Evangelical Poverty: *Vaticanus Latinus 3740* and Its Copies." *Collectanea Franciscana.* 59, 3-4 (1989): 323-349.

——. "A Significant Manuscript of Poverty Treatises by Hervaeus Natalis, O.P. and Pierre Roger, O.S.B., (Pope Clement VI)" *Manuscripta* (Forthcoming).

Tabarroni, A. *Paupertas Christi et Apostolorum: L'ideale francescano in discussione (1322-1324).* Rome, 1990.

Tóth, Lazlo. *Tanulmanyok a szegénységu vita forasainak töténetéhez XXII Jano papa koraban.* Budapest, 1934.

Vollert, Cyril. *The Doctrine of Hervaeus Natalis on Primitive Justice and Original Sin.* Rome: Apud Aedes Universitatis Gregorianae, 1947.

Published too recently to be referenced in this volume:

William of Ockham. *The Work of Ninety Days* [computer file]. Trans. John Kilcullen and John Scott. Pittsboro, NC: InteLex Corp, 1998. [See above, William of Ockham, *Opus nonaginta dierum.*]

Index of Persons

Abraham, 26, 34, 61, 62, 89
Adam, 144
Aelred of Rivaulx: *Tractatus de Iesu puero duodenni*, 127, 130
Alfredo, Brother, 119
Ambrose, 94, 102, 122, 138; *Epistolae*, 94; *Expositio evangelii secundum Lucam*, 102, 138-139. *See also* Ambrosiaster
Ambrosiaster: *In I ad Corintheos*, 94-95, 122
Andrew, 94, 134
Aristotle: *Nicomachean Ethics*, 27
Augustine, 80, 83, 94, 102, 111, 113, 132, 146; *Confessiones*, 52; *Contra Adimantum*, 138, 139; *De civitate Dei*, 93, 124, 131, 138; *De consensu evangelistarum*, 103-104, 107, 138; *De doctrina Christiana*, 134; *De gratia et libero arbitrio*, 71; *De libero arbitrio*, 27; *De opere monachorum*, 53, 122, 136, 138; *De sermone Domini in monte*, 62, 73, 107-108; *Enarrationes in Psalmos*, 95; *Epistolae*, 35, 52, 135; *In Ioannis evangelium tractatus*, 74, 136; *Regula ad servos Dei*, 79, 102; *Sermones*, 63, 95, 125, 142. *See also* Pomerius; Pseudo-Augustine

Barnabas, 121, 141
Basil: *Homilia in illud Lucae "Destruam,"* 34, 86, 108
Bede, 141; *In Lucam evangelium expositio*, 136, 140; *In Marci evangelium expositio*, 95, 125, 132; *Retractationes in Actibus*, 83-84
Berengar Toloni, 5

Bernard of Clairvaux, 127, 130; *De consideratione ad Eugenum papam*, 132. (*See* Aelred of Rivaulx)
Bertrand de la Tour, 117, 118, 130-137, 140, 141, 142, 144-146, 151
Bonagratia of Bergamo, 6; *De paupertate Christi et apostolorum*, 13, 119, 149
Bonaventure, 1, 2, 4, 19, 125; *Apologia pauperum*, 3; *Expositio super regulam fratrum minorum*, 15; *Quaestio de paupertate*, 17

Cassian, John: *XIV Collationes patrum*, 134
Cesena, Michael, 118, 119
Chrysostom, John, 64, 93, 104, 110, 124, 130, 131, 140; *De laudibus Pauli*, 93, 110, 124; *Homiliae in Matthaeum*, 35, 103, 131, 135; *Homiliae in Ioannem*, 136-137. *See also* Pseudo-Chrysostom
Clement of Alexandria, 143
Clement V, 118, 119
Cyril of Alexandria: *Commentarii in Lucam*, 92, 94, 95, 123; *Commentarii in Matthaeum*, 123

David, 4, 26, 34, 61, 89, 121, 150
Dominic, Saint, 7

Elijah, 71, 73
Eusebius, 108, 110; *Commentarii in Lucam*, 92, 94, 95, 122-123; *Ecclesiastica historia*, 93, 124, 128

Francis of Assisi, 1, 2, 7, 9, 128, 129
Frederico, Brother (bishop of Riga), 117, 119, 127

Gelasius, 129

Gerard of Abbeville: *Contra adversarium perfectionis Christianae*, 3

Gratian: *Decretum magistri Gratiani*, 129, 137, 143-144

Gregory the Great, 34; *Dialogi*, 80, 87; *Homiliae in Evangelium*, 94; *Homiliae in Hiezechihelem prophetam*, 63; *Moralia in Job*, 134; *XL Homiliarum in evangelium*, 52, 132, 134

Gregory IX, 1, 3

Hervaeus Natalis: biography, 7-8; John XXII and, 1, 5, 8; poverty defined, 8; relation of use and ownership, 11-12; simple use, analysis of, 11, 12, 15; Thomas Aquinas and, 16, 18; wealth defined, 10

Huber, Raphael, 1, 12, 13, 14, 152

Hugh of St. Victor: *Miscellanea*, 121

Innocent IV, 3

Jacob, 74

James, Saint, 134

Jerome, Brother (bishop of Capha), 117, 119, 126

Jerome, Saint: *Commentarii in evangelium Matthaei*, 63, 74-75, 96, 103, 104, 131; *Epistolae*, 52, 62, 94, 95, 122, 123, 132, 139; *In Marci evangelium expositio*, 95, 125, 132

John of Belna, 5

John XXII, 8, 13-14, 117, 118-119, 128; *Cum inter nonullos*, 1, 6, 117, 118; *Ad conditorem*, 6; *Quorumdam exigit*, 126; *Quia nonnumquam*, 5; *Quia vir reprobus*, 14

Judas, 96, 97, 130, 146

Jude, 93, 110, 124

Kilwardby, Robert, 7

Lambert, M.-D., 1, 2, 6, 8, 12, 14, 19, 152

Lazarus, 61, 72

Leff, Gordon, 1, 12, 152

Matthew, Saint, 125

Moorman, John, 12, 117, 118, 149, 151

Nicholas III: *Exiit qui seminat*, 4, 5, 6, 12, 13, 51, 92, 109, 112, 118, 121, 122, 124, 128, 129, 133, 134, 135, 137, 138, 144

Olivi, Peter John, 4, 19, 118, 119

Paul, Saint, 28, 56, 93, 103, 104, 106, 107, 110, 121, 122, 124, 145

Pecham, John, 7, 126

Peter, Saint, 4, 94, 118, 119, 127, 131, 134, 139, 141, 146

Peter of Poitiers: *Sententiarum*, 27

Pomerius: *De vita contemplativa*, 83

Pseudo-Augustine: *De conflictu virtutum et vitiorum*, 63. *See also* Augustine

Pseudo-Chrysostom: *Homiliae in Matthaeum*, 130; *Opus imperfectum in Matthaeum*, 64. *See also* Chrysostom, John

Pseudo-Dionysius Areopagite: *De ecclesiastica hierarchia*, 81, 133

Royard, Arnauld (archbishop of Salerno), 117, 118, 138, 143, 146

Samuel, 74, 75

Saul, 74, 75, 141

Seneca, Lucius Annaeus: *De moribus*, 51

Sikes, J.G., 1, 5, 6, 18, 19, 25, 43, 73,

Simon, Brother (bishop of Badajoz), 5, 117, 119, 129

Simon, 93, 110, 124

Stephan, Brother (bishop of Lisbon), 117, 119, 126

Thaddeus, 93, 124, 128

Theophylact, 103; *Enarrationes in evangelium Marci*, 103

Thomas Aquinas, 7- 8, 16-18, 19, 27, 75, 81, 101, 140; *Catena Aurea*, 19, 75, 92, 94, 140; *Contra impugnantes Dei*, 17; *Contra retrahentes*, 17, 18, 123; *de Veritate*, 125; *Summa theologiae*, 9, 16-18, 27, 81, 101

Tocco, F., 1, 18, 19, 117-120, 122, 125, 126

Vital du Four, 117-118, 121-126, 140-145

William of Ockham. 12-14
William of St. Amour, 7, 17

Index of Citations to Scripture
and Scriptural Glosses

Gen. 1:28, 84
Gen. 2:16, 49, 84, 144
Gen. 13:2, 26
Gen. 30:33, 74

Exod. 16:11, 69
Exod. 25:40, 122

1 Sam. 6-19, 74

2 Sam. 8:4, 26

1 Kings 17:4, 71

Ps. 21:8, 141
Ps. 23:1, 96
Ps. 48:7, 35, 66
Ps. 49:12, 96
Ps. 75:12, 138
Ps. 91:2, 121
Ps. 103:14, 53, 122
Ps. 108:17, 130

Prov. 6:6-7, 64

Matt. 4:7, 69
Matt. 4:20, 93, 110, 134
Matt. 5:3, 26
Matt. 5:39-40, 57
Matt. 6:31-32. 75
Matt. 6:34, 62, 63, 73, 107
Matt. 8:14, 139
Matt. 8:20, 131, 135
Matt. 10:9, 94, 100, 103, 131, 132, 138, 146
Matt. 10:9-10, 100, 103
Matt. 10:10, 95, 123, 138
Matt. 16:24, 52
Matt. 17:23, 131
Matt. 17:26, 95

Matt. 19:21, 32, 92, 93, 109, 123, 131
Matt. 19:27, 93, 100, 101, 110, 127, 131, 134
Matt. 26:28, 139
Matt. 27:59-60, 131

Mark 1:29, 139
Mark 6:8, 95, 131, 132, 138
Mark 6:37, 141
Mark 10:29, 103

Luke 2:42, 127
Luke 5:11, 124
Luke 6:14, 134
Luke 9:3, 2, 92, 94, 95, 107, 123, 131, 138
Luke 9:52, 135
Luke 9:58, 94
Luke 9:62, 79
Luke 10:7, 103
Luke 12:18, 34, 86
Luke 14:26, 25, 102
Luke 14:33, 25, 127
Luke 16:20-21, 35
Luke 19:5, 130
Luke 22:8, 141
Luke 22:36, 136, 140
John 4:8, 23, 74, 98, 105, 141
John 12:6, 96, 97
John 13:27-29, 97
John 13:29, 23, 96, 105
John 18:23, 58

Acts 3:6, 94, 110, 122, 132, 139, 146
Acts 4:32, 3, 102, 140
Acts 4:33, 141
Acts 4:34, 102
Acts 11:20, 141

Acts 11:27-30, 73

Rom. 13:10, 28

1 Cor. 4:11, 93, 124
1 Cor. 9:4, 106, 122
1 Cor. 9:4-5, 95
1 Cor. 9:7, 107

Gal. 6:6, 103

Phil. 4:18, 142

1 Thess. 2:9, 104

1 Tim. 4:3, 56
1 Tim. 6:8, 103, 141-142

2 Tim. 4:13, 142

Glossa interlinearis, 75, 94, 110, 130, 132, 140
Glossa ordinaria, 75, 94, 110, 122, 130-132, 139, 140, 149

Subject Index

(Terms marked with an "*" have special significance in this volume. All entries for these terms are provided after the main listing of the term. The corresponding Latin term or phrase is given when appropriate.)

active life, 66, 68, 81, 83, 89. *See also* contemplative life
alms, 31, 38, 59, 71, 85, 93; predial alms, 48
angels, minister to Christ: 94, 95, 123, 130
apostles*, 1, 2, 4, 5, 6, 8, 11, 16, 18, 21, 23, 28, 56, 73, 74, 83, 91, 92, 93, 94, 95, 97, 98, 99, 100, 101, 102, 103, 104, 105, 106, 107, 108, 109, 111, 112, 113, 114, 117, 118, 119, 121, 122, 123, 124, 125, 126, 127, 128, 129, 130, 131, 132, 133, 134, 135, 136, 137, 138, 139, 140, 141, 142, 143, 144, 145, 146, 151, 152; as administrators of goods, 6, 113-114, 141-142, 146; dominion/ ownership/rights and, 1, 5, 6, 11-12, 23-24, 97-111, 113-114, 121-123, 127-133, 139, 141-145; having nothing and, 1, 23-24, 91-96, 108-113, 122-123, 127-33, 136, 138, 142, 144; having things in common and, 102, 111, 123, 127, 141-142; making provision for the future and, 73-74, 136; ministered to by women, 94-95, 111, 122; necessities of life and, 73, 95, 103-4, 107-108, 110, 111, 132, 136-138, 140, 142, 144; owed support by faithful, 103-104, 107-108, 111; perfection [evangelical] of, 5, 23, 92-93, 108, 121, 123, 124, 131, 132, 133, 134, 135, 138; poverty [evangelical] of, 4, 5, 11, 16, 92, 93, 95, 100, 108, 109, 118, 119, 124, 131-132, 138-139, 144; renunciation of things and, 3, 4, 5, 91-96, 100, 101, 103-104, 108, 109, 123-124, 126-127, 128, 129-130, 131, 146; rights to things consumed in use, 11-12, 98-99, 106, 113; rights to things not consumed in use, 11-12, 98; simple use and, 6, 12, 24, 100, 105, 121, 128, 137, 138, 142, 143; as source of virtues in Church, 92, 123; state of, 124, 133, 135; state of perfection and, 92; "to take nothing for their journey," 1, 94, 95, 100, 103, 107, 111, 134 (*see also* Mark 6:8; Luke 9:3); use and, 6, 11-12, 23-24, 97-101, 105, 112, 113, 121, 128, 133, 135, 137, 138, 142, 143, 145, 146. *See also* dominion, whether heretical to attribute to Christ/apostles

baptism, 27
begging: by Christ/apostles, 93, 97, 103, 123, 127, 130, 134; as means of support, 69, 71, 85, 130
birth, 51, 57
books (as objects of use), 3, 19, 68, 125, 142. *See also* things, not consumed in use

cenobites, 83
charity* (*caritas*), 9, 27, 28, 29, 31, 32, 33, 34, 35, 36, 50, 51, 53, 54, 55, 57, 66, 67, 68, 70, 80, 81, 121, 122, 124, 125, 126, 134, 145; of

apostles, 125; of Christ, 121-122, 124; dominion / ownership / rights and, 34, 36, 56; earthly vs. heavenly, 54-55; impediments to, 28, 35, 51, 54-56, 57, 66-68, 70, 80; lack of and imperfection, 54-55; love of God and, 27-28, 51; love of neighbor and, 27-28; love of temporal things and, 29, 31, 35-36, 50, 57, 66, 70, 124-125, 134; making provision for the future and, 67, 68; means to, 32-35; opposed to cupidity, 124; perfection and, 28, 34, 50, 57, 67, 80, 122, 126; perfection of a state and, 81; personal perfection and, 53-55, 80; personal rights and, 56-57; poverty and, 28, 29, 31-36; as preeminent virtue, 27-28; renunciation of things and, 28, 33; sustaining life and, 57; to sustain the poor, 145; wealth and, 34, 36, 53, 55

chastity (vow of), 25, 30, 31, 125

children of Israel, 38, 49, 71, 73

Christ*, 1, 2, 4, 5, 6, 8, 11, 15, 16, 18, 21, 23, 25, 30, 52, 62, 63, 64, 76, 80, 91, 92, 95, 96, 97, 98, 99, 100, 105, 106, 107, 108, 109, 111, 112, 113, 114, 117, 118, 119, 121, 122, 123, 124, 126, 127, 128, 129, 130, 131, 132, 133, 134, 135, 136, 137, 138, 139, 140, 141, 142, 143, 144, 145, 146, 151, 152; as administrator of goods, 6, 113-114, 142; as beggar, 127; charity of, 121-122, 124; condescends to weakness, 53, 92, 121, 122; dominion over humans and, 96; dominion/ownership/rights and, 1, 5, 6, 11-12, 23-24, 97-111, 113-114, 121-123, 127-133, 139, 141-145; economic transactions of, 105-106; having nothing and, 1, 23-24, 91-96, 108-113, 122-123, 127-133, 136, 138, 142, 144; having things in common (see Christ, having nothing and); making provision

for the future and, 73, 136; ministered to by angels, 53, 62, 73, 107, 108; ministered to by women, 94, 95, 122, 130; moral teaching of, 25, 30; nature of, 96, 126; necessities of life and, 62, 73, 95, 108, 109, 142; perfection of, 5, 23, 80, 92, 97, 108, 121, 122, 127, 129, 133, 135, 138; poverty [evangelical] of, 2, 4, 5, 8, 11, 92, 95, 97, 100, 109, 118, 119, 127, 129, 130-131, 139, 144, 145; purse of, (see purse, Christ's); renunciation of things and, 3, 4, 5, 91-96, 98, 100, 101, 103-104, 108, 109, 123-124, 126-127, 128, 129-130, 131, 135, 138, 139, 146; resisting evil and, 57; rights to things consumed in use and, 11-12, 98-99, 106, 113; rights to things not consumed in use and, 11-12, 98; simple use and, 6, 12, 24, 100, 105, 121, 128, 137, 138, 142, 143; state of, 133; state of innocence and, 137, 144; use and, 6, 11-12, 23-24, 97-101, 105, 112, 113, 121, 128, 133, 135, 137, 138, 142, 143, 145, 146. See also dominion, whether heretical to attribute to Christ/apostles

clothing* (as object of use), 14, 15, 35, 37, 55, 62, 68, 69, 93, 98, 99, 103, 104, 105, 113, 139, 141, 142, 144. See also things consumed in use; things, not consumed in use

common* (commune), 3, 4, 5, 6, 7, 10, 11, 17, 18, 23, 33, 34, 35, 40, 41, 43, 46, 49, 50, 51, 52, 53, 55, 56, 57, 58, 59, 60, 62, 65, 67, 69, 71, 72, 73, 77, 78, 79, 80, 82, 83, 84, 85, 86, 87, 91, 92, 93, 94, 95, 99, 102, 105, 108, 109, 110, 111, 112, 118, 121, 122, 123, 124, 125, 126, 127, 128, 129, 130, 131, 132, 133, 134, 135, 136, 137, 138, 139, 140, 141, 142, 144, 146; course of nature /events, 55, 62, 69, 71, 72, 73; desire for things in, 94, 132; dominion, 3, 4, 6, 23, 33, 43, 49, 50, 58, 72, 77, 78, 85, 91, 121, 122, 135, 137; goods, 85; having nothing in, 60, 77, 91, 92, 111, 112, 121, 123, 126, 127, 128, 129, 130, 132, 133-134; 136, 138, 142, 144; having things in, 6, 34, 50, 51, 52, 56, 57, 58, 65, 77, 78, 79, 80, 82, 83, 85, 89, 93, 94, 95, 96, 102, 105, 108, 125, 128, 130, 137, 138, 140, 141, 144; living in, 69, 80, 83, 85, 110; meaning of, 86-87; money held in, 80; necessities of life held in, 58, 67; ownership, 3, 5, 6, 10, 11, 23, 41, 77, 78, 79, 85, 109, 121, 122, 126, 127, 129, 130, 135, 138; possession(s), 6, 7, 17, 18, 56; renunciation, 4, 51, 62, 84, 93, 102, 109, 123, 128, 129, 133, 139; right(s), 11, 33, 49, 42, 50, 51, 56, 78, 79, 87, 91, 138; subsistence, 43; use, 18, 79, 80, 92, 127, 144; wealth, 35. *See also* expressions of ownership: what is held in common

community: of Christ/apostles, 111, 113, 144; contrasted with members, 42-43, 77, 78-79, 80, 85-86; dominion/ownership/rights and, 42-44, 77, 78-79, 80, 85-86, 87; early Christian in Jerusalem, 3, 102, 104 (*See also* Acts 4:32, 33, 34); meaning of, 86, 145; of possession, 86; poverty of, 33-34; use of goods by, 145-146

conditional gift, 43, 46

contemplative life* (*vita contemplativa*), 35, 65, 66, 67, 68, 69, 70, 81, 82, 83, 87, 89; ends of, 81; having temporal things and, 89; impediments to 35, 65-68, 89; making provision for the future and, 67-68, 70; necessities of life and, 69, 83; perfection and, 68; state of prelacy and, 87. *See also* active life

Conventuals, 4, 5. *See* Franciscans, Conventuals

counsels, 32, 80, 54, 125

cupidity, 124, 125, 143

death, 7, 51, 57, 97, 135, 136, 140

dependent child* (*filiusfamilius*), 37, 43, 44, 46, 48, 137

desire* (*desiderio/volo*), 33, 50, 52, 57, 59, 60, 61, 70, 71, 72, 92, 94, 122, 125, 132, 134, 135, 144; for Christ's teaching by women who followed him, 94, 122; for evil, 33; for necessities of life, 59, 71; for perfect life, 92; for temporal things, 35, 50, 52, 57, 70, 71, 94, 132, 135 (*see also* love, of temporal things); kingdom of, 134; sensuous, 61; to follow Christ by Matthew, 125; virtuous works and, 60-61. *See also* love

diminish* (*diminuo*), 37, 50, 51, 52, 53, 55, 56, 57, 58, 61, 62, 63, 64, 65, 66, 67, 68, 69, 70, 73, 74, 77, 78, 79, 80, 82, 83, 85, 86, 87, 88, 89, 97, 105. *See* charity, impediments to; perfection, diminished by having temporal things

disposition of the mind* (*praeparatio animi*), 9, 28, 29, 30, 31, 58, 89, 102, 110, 111. *See also* poverty, as disposition of the mind

Dominican order, 5, 7, 16

dominion* (*dominium*), 1, 2, 3, 4, 6, 7, 8, 10, 11, 12, 15, 18, 23, 24, 28, 33, 34, 35, 36, 37, 38, 39, 40, 41, 42, 43, 44, 46, 47, 48, 49, 50, 51, 52, 53, 55, 56, 57, 58, 59, 61, 72, 77, 78, 79, 82, 84, 85, 88, 89, 91, 96, 97, 114, 121, 122, 126, 128, 129, 133, 135, 136, 137, 141, 142, 143, 144, 145, 146; charity and, 34, 36; common, 3, 4, 6, 23, 33, 43, 49, 50, 58, 72, 77, 78, 85, 91, 121, 122, 135, 137; common and perfection of a state, 77-90; contrasted with right and ownership, 11n. 42, 40; discord and, 57; dispensation of things and, 136; exchange and, 96; excluded by having nothing, 77, 133; granting of things and, 38-39, 47; held by administrator, 43; held by child, 43-44, 48; held by a community, 42-43, 146; held by Dominicans, 7; held by Franciscans, 2-4, 6; held by God, 137; held by monk, 43-44, 48, 137; held by prelate, 43, 136; held by slave, 43-44, 48; kinds of, 41-42; licit use and, 39, 40-41, 42; love of things and, 51, 52, 59; meaning of, 40; in paradise, 144; perfection and, 23, 50-62, 77, 135; personal, 23, 33, 35, 36, 50, 58, 72, 88, 89; poverty and, 28, 29, 33-34, 35, 37, 61, 72, 78, 79; religious institutes and, 82; renunciation and, 89; separability from use and, 6, 8, 10, 11, 15, 18, 37-62, 79, 97, 137, 143, 144, 146, 147; in state of innocence, 49, 78, 84-85; state of prelates and, 87-90; taking hold of things and, 49; unqualified, 33, 41, 42, 44, 48; whether heretical to attribute to Christ/apostles, 1, 5-6, 23, 91, 112-115, 126-130, 133, 139-140. See also apostles, dominion/ownership/rights over things; Christ, dominion/ownership/rights over things

error, nature of, 112
evangelical* (evangelicum), 1, 18, 93, 105, 117, 123, 124, 125, 128, 138, 144, 145
expressions of ownership: mine*, 34, 78, 84, 86, 96, 142, 144; ours*, 37, 49, 78, 84; yours*, 3, 38, 49, 78, 84, 137, 143, 144; "what belongs to another"* (alienum), 38, 39, 41, 48, 58, 59, 86, 109; "what belongs to oneself"* (proprium), 41, 58, 86, 109; "what is held in common" (commune)*, 58, 79, 86, 87, 109
exterior effect* (exterior effectus). See poverty, as exterior effect

faith, 60, 112, 114, 129, 133
fatherland, 54, 55

food (as use object), 3, 11, 14, 15, 35, 40, 55, 56, 57, 64, 93, 94, 95, 98, 99, 100, 101, 103, 104, 105, 110, 111, 130, 138, 139, 141, 144, 146. See also, things consumed in use
Franciscan order: Conventuals, 4, 5, 118; dominion / ownership / rights held by, 2-4, 6; poverty of, 1-7, 16, 119; Spirituals, 2, 4-6, 118, 119; use of goods and, 2-4, 6

God*, 4, 11, 27, 28, 31, 32, 35, 36, 38, 45, 48, 49, 51, 52, 54, 56, 58, 59, 62, 63, 64, 65, 66, 69, 70, 71, 72, 73, 74, 75, 76, 81, 83, 89, 93, 101, 102, 103, 106, 107, 111, 115, 122, 124, 126, 131, 137, 138, 144, 146; city of, 124; commands humans to sustain life, 100-101, 144; grants things for human use, 38, 45, 48, 56; having things in common and, 84; infused virtue and, 27; love for by humans, 27, 28, 32, 35-36, 51, 52, 58, 59, 65, 81, 89; love for in making provision for the future, 63-64, 76; moves humans to render assistance to others, 71, 72; precept not to be solicitous for tomorrow and, 63, 73-74, 107-108 (see also Matt 6:34); providential source of things, 62, 64-66, 71-72; tempting of by humans, 62, 69, 70-71; things renounced for sake of and, 4, 102-103; trust in by humans, 63-64; whether intervenes in economic transactions, 106. See also things, reckoned as God's
gold, 94, 100, 103, 104, 110, 122, 128, 131, 132, 134, 135, 136, 138, 139, 146. See also money; silver
goods, temporal* (bona temporalia), 5, 9, 23, 28, 29, 30, 31, 32, 33, 34, 35, 36, 37, 40, 44, 50, 51, 52, 55, 56, 57, 58, 59, 61, 62, 64, 65, 66, 67, 68, 70, 72, 73, 74, 75, 76, 77, 79, 82, 83, 87, 88, 89, 90, 91, 94, 100, 101, 102, 103, 104, 105, 106, 113,

114, 125, 128, 134, 135, 136, 142, 144. See also things, temporal
granting (concedo) of things*, 38, 39, 40, 42, 43, 44, 47, 48, 49, 71, 72, 95, 99, 100, 135, 136, 143, 144; to administrator, 143; as conditional gifts, 43, 44; gives dominion/owner-ship/rights to things, 39-40, 42, 43, 49, 47, 100; by God, 38-39, 45, 48-49; right to retain things granted and, 44, 47; for use, 38-39, 42, 43, 44, 47, 48-49, 72, 95, 99-100. (Note that concedo is occasionally trans-lated as "permit.")

having nothing* (habeo nihil), 17, 23, 51, 60, 67, 69, 70, 77, 78, 84, 85, 91, 92, 93, 94, 95, 108, 110, 111, 112, 113, 121, 122, 123, 127, 128, 129, 130, 131, 133, 134, 136, 138, 142, 144; as burdensome to others, 85; by Christ/apostles, 1, 23-24, 91-96, 108-113, 122-123, 127-133, 136, 138, 142, 144; difficulty of, 60; for dominion/ownership/rights, 23, 77, 133; equality and, 77, 78, 84; evangelical poverty and, 93; ex-treme poverty and, 94; friendship and, 78; heavenly state and, 78, 84; love of God and, 51; makes living impossible, 17; making provision for the future and, 67-71, 84; meaning of, 133; perfection [of a state] and, 77-78, 144; personally or in com-mon, 51, 60, 77-78, 84, 91-95, 108-113, 122-123, 127-134, 136, 138, 142, 144; poverty [evangelical] and, 92, 93, 94, 123, 125, 127; state of innocence and, 78, 84; use and, 79, 84, 108, 113; whether erroneous to assert of Christ/apostles, 113; whe-ther heretical to assert of Christ/apostles (see dominion, whether her-etical to assert of Christ/apostles); whether rash to assert of Christ/apo-stles, 113

having things* (habeo res)10, 12, 23,

34, 42, 50, 51, 52, 53, 56, 57, 58, 65, 66, 67, 73, 77, 78, 79, 80, 82, 83, 85, 86, 87, 91, 93, 94, 95, 99, 102, 104, 105, 111, 114, 121, 123, 125, 126, 127, 128, 129, 130, 138, 139, 140, 141, 143, 144, 145; mean-ing, 23n. 1. See also common, hav-ing things in; dominion; having nothing; ownership; personal(ly), having things; right(s); things, tem-poral; use
head of the family* (paterfamilius), 43, 44
heavenly state, 78, 84
heresy*, nature of, 112, 114, 129, 130, 133. See also dominion, whether heretical to assert of Christ/apostles
hope, 19, 63, 71, 72, 76
house (as use object), 11, 41, 42, 43, 46, 56, 68, 69, 83, 98, 102, 139, 145, 146, 152, 153. See also things, not consumed in use

illicit* (illicit), 40, 45, 46, 56, 59, 60, 68, 101, 147; actions, 60, 68; love of temporal things, 59; ownership, 60; use, 40, 45, 56, 101; usury as, 147. See also licit, just/unjust
impatience, and what moves us to, 70-72
impede* (impedio), 31, 32, 33, 35, 36, 46, 57, 65, 66, 67, 68, 70, 75, 80, 81, 88, 90, 103, 127, 144. See also charity, impediments to
impediment* (impedimentum), 9, 28, 29, 31, 32, 35, 36, 65, 109. See also charity, impediments to
imperfect* (imperfectus), 54, 62, 121, 122, 135, 136. See also imperfection
imperfection* (imperfectio), 32, 36, 52, 53, 54, 55, 62, 83, 85, 135; charity and, 54-55; condescension to weakness and, 53, 121, 135, 136; human compared with Christ, 62; in wayfaring state, 54-55; meanings of, 52; negative mode of, 54-55; pover-ty can coexist with, 32, 36; privative

mode, 54, 62; state of perfection and, 135; unqualified, 54. *See also* perfection

instrument(ally)* (*instrument-um/-aliter*), 25, 31, 32, 33, 34, 35, 53, 80, 89, 133. *See also* perfection, instrumental contribution to; poverty, instrumentally contributes to perfection

just/unjust* (*iustus/iniustus*), 8, 10, 39, 45, 48, 50, 57, 60, 63, 64, 74, 97, 99. *See also* licit; illicit

law* (*ius*), 2, 6, 10, 13, 15, 28, 39, 126, 127, 135, 136, 137, 143, 144; canon, 136; civil, 2, 6, 10, 13, 15, 137; of constitutions, 127; of custom, 127, 138; divine, 28, 135; Roman, 38n. 3; natural, 126, 127, 137, 143, 144; of nations, 137

licit* (*licet*), 10, 11, 12, 13, 14, 15, 16, 18, 39, 40, 41, 42, 45, 46, 47, 49, 50, 53, 55, 56, 60, 61, 69, 71, 84, 85, 98, 99, 100, 101, 104, 112, 113, 114; action, 40, 61; possession, 60; power, 10, 11, 39, 40, 41, 42, 45, 56; use, 10, 11, 12, 13, 14, 15, 16, 18, 39, 41, 47, 49, 50, 53, 55, 56, 98, 99, 100, 101, 104, 112, 113, 114. *See also* illicit; just / unjust; right, as power of licit use

love* (*amor/amo*), 27, 28, 29, 30, 31, 32, 35, 36, 51, 52, 57, 59, 65, 66, 67, 70, 81, 83, 94, 97, 102, 103, 122, 125, 135; of enemies, 102-103; of God, 27, 28, 29, 32, 35, 36, 52, 65, 81; of neighbor, 27, 28, 23, 26, 65, 81; for perfection, 83; of self, 35; sexual, 30-31; of temporal things, 29, 35, 51, 52, 57, 59, 66, 70, 97, 125, 135; of virtue, 94, 122

making provision for the future* (*facere provisionem pro futuro*), 37, 62, 63, 64, 65, 66, 67, 68, 69, 70, 71, 72, 73, 74, 75, 76, 108; in active life, 68-69; by Christ/apostles, 73-74; charity and, 68; in contemplative life, 65-70; divine providence and, 70; fortune and, 70; hope and, 63; in case of imminent necessity, 37, 71, 73, 74; licit, 37, 65; love of God and, 65; love of neighbor and, 65; love of temporal things and, 67; for necessities of life, 64, 66; necessity for, 69-70; as obligation, 71; poverty and, 37; as temptation of God, 63, 69-73; for things consumed in use, 69-70; for things not consumed in use, 68-69; perfection and, 37, 62, 63-65, 70, 73; solicitude and, 62, 65, 67, 73-75, 108; virtue and, 66, 68. *See also* reserve things for use; solicitude

master (of a slave)*, 7, 15, 43, 44, 96, 97, 122

means/end relation: examples of (A necessary for B), 10, 59, 62, 64, 67, 68, 71, 82, 89, 90, 96, 101, 103, 104, 105, 107, 111, 112, 114; nature of, 101. *See also* necessities [of life]/needs

mine. *See* expressions of ownership: mine

monastery*, 42, 43, 44, 48, 80, 85, obligations to monks, 43; rights held by, 42

money*, 2, 11, 13, 46, 68, 73, 74, 75, 80, 93, 94, 96, 97, 98, 99, 100, 105, 106, 110, 122, 124, 132, 135, 140, 141, 142, 146, 152; Christ's/apostles' use of, 73, 80, 96, 97, 98, 99-100, 105-106, 132, 142; Church's use of, 146; as consumable good, 11, 46, 68, 99; early Franciscans refusal of, 2; economic exchange and, 105-106; God not to be served for sake of, 74; Judas's use of, 96; Paul's use of, 93, 110, 124; precept forbidding use of, 74, 94, 100, 122, 140 (*see also* Matt. 6:34, 10:9; Mark 6:8; Luke 9:3). *See also* gold; purse, Christ's; silver

monk*, 37, 38, 43, 44, 46, 48, 52, 53, 80, 123, 136, 137, 138, 140; dominion held by, 43-44, 48, 137; necessities of life and, 43-44; ownership held by, 37, 48, 137, 140; perfection of, 80; rights held by, 37, 43-44, 46, 48, 140; use by, 37-38, 43-44, 80

moral life, 26, 27

nakedness/nudity*, 53, 62, 111, 125, 130, 131

necessities [of life]/needs* (necessaria vitae), 2, 10, 18, 34, 43, 50, 53, 56, 57, 58, 59, 61, 64, 65, 66, 67, 68, 69, 70, 71, 72, 73, 74, 76, 83, 84, 85, 86, 87, 95, 100, 104, 105, 107, 108, 110, 111, 132, 136, 137, 140, 142, 144, 145; apostles and, 73, 95, 104-105, 107-108, 110, 111, 132, 136-178, 140, 142, 144; charity and, 57, 59, 66; Christ and, 63, 73, 95, 104-105, 108, 132, 136-138, 142, 144; contemplative life and, 65, 69; daily only accepted by early Franciscans, 2; extreme poverty and, 110; making provision for the future and, 64-65, 66, 67, 71-72, 73-74, 76; nudity and, 111; owed to a dependent child, monk and slave, 43-44; perfection and, 53, 55-57, 58, 83, 111; poverty and, 10, 34, 58, 72, 85, 86, 110; prelates and, 108; provided by God, 64, 71, 73; religious institutes and, 18, 82, 83; renounced through disposition of the mind, 111; right to use of, 50; solicitude for, 67, 69-70, 145; in state of innocence, 84; use of to sustain life, 53, 59, 87, 100, 104, 107; vary according to state, 61; wealth and, 78, 86

neighbor, love of. See love, of neighbor

obedience (vow of), 25, 30, 125

occupy* (occupo). See take hold of

ours. See expressions of ownership: ours

owner* (proprietarios), 39, 40, 42, 43, 44, 45, 46, 47, 79, 86, 99, 100, 111, 128, 131, 147; community as, 80; grants rights to things, 40, 46, 111; grants things to administrator, 43; grants use of things, 39-40, 44, 46; holds unqualified dominion over things, 44; things used against will of, 39, 45, 49, 147; transfers rights to things, 44; ways of granting things, 42-44. See also ownership

ownership* (proprietas), 1, 2, 3, 4, 5, 6, 9, 10, 11, 12, 14, 16, 18, 23, 24, 37, 40, 41, 42, 46, 48, 52, 53, 58, 59, 77, 78, 79, 82, 86, 91, 92, 109, 114, 121, 122, 126, 127, 129, 130, 133, 135, 136, 137, 138, 140, 141, 143, 144; civil law and, 2; common, 3, 5, 6, 10, 11, 23, 41, 77, 78, 79, 85, 109, 121, 122, 126, 127, 129, 130, 135, 138; contrasted with dominion and right, 11, 40; excluded by having nothing, 133; held by Christ/apostles, 1, 5-6, 23-24, 91, 92, 100, 113, 114, 121-122, 127, 128, 129-131, 133, 137, 138, 141; held by Dominicans, 16; held by Franciscans, 3-5, 6, 10, 12; held by monk, 37, 48, 137, 140; held by prelate, 136; love of things and, 52; meaning of, 40, 41, 86, 109; of monastery's goods, 42; natural law and, 126; in paradise, 144; perfection and, 53, 58, 59, 79, 86, 135-136, 143; personal, 3, 5, 9, 10, 11, 23, 86, 91, 122, 124, 127, 130, 138; poverty and, 9, 10, 23, 58; as power of licit use, 10, 53; as primary way of having things, 138, 140; of rented house, 41, 46; in religious life, 18, 33, 109; religious state and, 77-87; renunciation of, 4, 5, 10, 13, 58-59, 62, 92, 109, 127, 129, 130, 143; same as dominion and right, 11, 40; separability from use, 3, 6, 46-47,

52, 79, 137, 144; in state of innocence, 78, 144; unqualified, 46, 47,
48; use and, 9, 12, 16, 52; wealth
and, 53. *See also* dominion, whether
heretical to attribute to Christ/apo-
stles; owner; use

paradise, 38, 49, 84, 144
patience, 72
perfection* (*perfectio*), 2, 4, 5, 8, 9,
10, 16, 17, 23, 24, 25, 26, 27, 28,
29, 30, 31, 32, 33, 34, 35, 36, 37,
50, 51, 52, 53, 54, 55, 56, 57, 58,
59, 60, 61, 62, 63, 64, 65, 66, 67,
68, 69, 70, 73, 74, 77, 78, 79, 80,
81, 82, 83, 85, 86, 87, 88, 89, 91,
92, 97, 105, 108, 109, 111, 121,
122, 123, 124, 125, 126, 127, 129,
133, 134, 135, 138, 143, 144, 145;
acquiring/exercising, 81, 133; active
life and, 68; charity and, 28, 34, 50,
57, 67, 80, 122, 126; of Christ/apo-
stles, 5, 23, 80, 92-93, 97, 108, 121,
122, 123, 124, 127, 129, 131, 132,
133, 134, 135, 138; Christian, 8;
contemplative life and, 65-70, 87;
diminishment of by having temporal
things, 37, 51-53, 55-58, 61, 63-65,
67, 74, 78, 79, 85-89, 105; dominion and, 55-57, 77, 88, 135; evangelical, 105, 138; faith and, 60;
impediments to, 31, 70, 144; instrumental contributions to, 25, 32-37,
80, 89; making provision for the
future and, 62-74; of a monk, 80; of
moral life, 27; nature of, 25-28, 52,
66, 80, 82, 89, 92, 133; necessities
of life and, 53, 55-57, 58, 83, 111;
obedience and, 25, 30, 125; ownership and, 53, 58, 59, 79, 86, 135-
136, 143; personal, 34, 37, 50-62,
64, 77, 80, 81-82, 86, 88, 122, 124,
127, 130, 138; positive means to,
80; of possession, 60; poverty and,
8, 9, 16-17, 23-36, 51, 78-79, 80,
85, 89, 109, 123, 125, 138, 144-
145; in present life, 34, 56, 55-57;

privation/lack of, 26, 29-31, 32;
privative means to, 80; of religious
institutes, 82-83; religious state and,
16-17, 77-86, 133, 134; renunciation and, 2, 50, 79, 85, 89, 109,
124, 139, 143; rights and, 6-7, 55-
57, 77, 82, 88, 99; solicitude and, 5,
51, 58, 69, 73-75, 131, 134, 144-
145; of a state, 37, 53, 64, 73, 77-
87, 88, 105, 124, 135; state of prelacy and, 81, 87-91, 133; use and,
55, 57, 82; virtue and, 26-28, 53,
60-61, 80, 123, 126; wealth and, 26,
35, 53, 60, 86. *See also* imperfection
personal(ly)* (*propri-um/-e*), 3, 4, 5,
9, 10, 11, 13, 15, 17, 18, 23, 33, 34,
35, 36, 37, 39, 42, 47, 48, 50, 51,
52, 53, 56, 57, 58, 60, 62, 64, 72,
73, 76, 77, 78, 79, 80, 81, 82, 84,
85, 86, 87, 88, 89, 91, 92, 93, 94,
95, 97, 101, 102, 108, 109, 110,
111, 112, 113, 121, 122, 124, 125,
126, 127, 128, 129, 130, 131, 132,
133, 134, 135, 136, 137, 138, 139,
141, 142; advantage/benefit, 47-48,
113; authority, 15; belongings, 85;
choice, 72; dealings with things, 85;
desire for temporal things, 94, 132;
dominion, 3, 23, 33, 35, 36, 50, 58,
72, 78, 91, 122, 136; dwelling, 130-
131; having nothing, 51, 60, 76, 77,
78, 84, 92, 93, 94, 95, 108, 109,
111, 112, 121, 127, 128, 130, 131,
133, 142; having things, 50, 51, 52,
56, 88, 95, 108, 111, 141; labor, 48,
93, 95; meaning of, 79-80, 86-87;
necessity, 73, 108; ownership, 3, 5,
9, 10, 11, 23, 86, 88, 122, 124, 127,
130, 138; perfection, 34, 37-62, 64,
77, 80, 81-82, 86, 88, 122, 124,
127, 130, 138; possession(s), 18;
property, 33; renunciation, 4, 51,
62, 79, 85, 88, 101-102, 109, 110,
111, 124, 127, 128, 133, 134, 135,
136, 138, 139; right, 18, 33, 35, 42,
50, 51, 56-57, 78, 79, 87, 88, 91;

subsistence, 13, 34; use, 18, 127; wealth, 35

possess* (*possideo*), 6, 18, 23, 35, 38, 52, 54, 56, 63, 79, 92, 93, 94, 95, 100, 102, 103, 107, 109, 110, 122, 124, 127, 131, 132, 133, 135, 136, 138, 139, 146; as translation of *occupo*, 38n. 3; as translation of *habere*, 23n. 1. (Note: this verb is rarely used in a technical sense in this volume.)

possession(s)* (*possessio*), 5, 7, 11, 12, 17, 25, 35, 38, 59, 60, 61, 72, 80, 86, 87, 88, 93, 97, 110, 111, 122, 127, 141, 144; in common by Franciscan, 5-6, 17; in common by Dominicans, 7; community of, 86; contrasted with use, 9-10, 12, 127, 144; definition of by Dominicans, 7; definition of poverty and, 9; as impediment to charity, 144; licit through right to things, 60; of nothing in common defended by Aquinas, 17-18; perfection of a, 60; positive nature of, 127; when unqualified, 127

poverty* (*paupertas*), 1, 2, 3, 4, 5, 6, 7, 8, 9, 10, 11, 12, 14, 16, 17, 18, 19, 21, 23, 24, 25, 26, 28, 29, 30, 31, 32, 33, 34, 35, 36, 37, 51, 58, 72, 73, 74, 77, 78, 79, 80, 82, 85, 89, 92, 93, 94, 97, 108, 109, 110, 117, 118, 119, 123, 124, 125, 127, 129, 133, 134, 138, 139, 144, 145; absolute, 85; Aquinas's views on, 16-17; beatitude of, 26, 31; charity and, 28, 29, 31-36; of Christ/apostles, 2, 4, 5, 8, 11, 16, 23, 92, 95, 97, 100, 109, 118, 119, 124, 127, 129, 130-132, 138-139, 144, 145; compatible with imperfection, 36; contrasted with chastity, 30; defined, 9-10, 16, 28, 119; degrees of, 33, 72, 127; development of, 79, 85; as disposition of the mind, 9, 28-31, 89, 110, 111; Dominican, 7; dominion and,

28, 33, 34, 35, 37, 61, 72, 78, 79; evangelical, 93, 123, 124, 138, 144; as exterior effect, 9, 16, 28, 29, 30, 31, 32, 34, 36, 58, 89, 109; extreme, 92, 94, 108, 110; fear of, 74; Franciscan and Dominican contrasted, 7; Franciscan practice of, 1-7, 16, 119; having nothing and, 92, 123, 125, 127; impatience and, 72; instrumentally contributes to perfection, 25, 31-36, 89, 133; involuntary to be borne patiently, 72; as lack/privation of things, 26, 28, 29, 31, 33; making provision for the future and, 37; monastic, 4; necessities of life and, 10, 34, 58, 72, 85, 86; ownership and, 9, 10, 23, 58; perfect, 37, 127, 134, 139; perfection and, 8, 9, 16-17, 24-36, 51, 78-79, 80, 85, 89, 109, 123, 125, 133, 138, 144-145; possession and, 9; religious life and, 17-18, 33; religious state and, 133; right(s) and, 28, 33-34, 37, 61, 79, 100, 134; solicitude and, 145; state of, 145; state of perfection and, 25, 29; state of prelacy and, 133; unqualified, 10, 33-34; use and, 9, 28, 33; virtue and, 30, 36, 61, 92; voluntary, 25, 26, 72; vow of, 4, 12, 25, 26, 30, 125; when not to be chosen, 72. *See also* having nothing

power* (*potestas*), 10, 11, 13, 14, 26, 27, 28, 32, 39, 40, 41, 42, 44, 45, 46, 53, 55, 56, 60, 67, 72, 76, 101, 104, 106, 123, 132, 136, 140; of action (*executionis*), 11, 40, 46; of dispensing things, 136; dominion and, 40-41; in fact (*de facto*), 10, 12, 13, 40, 46; licit, 10, 11, 39, 40, 42, 45, 56; to licitly use things, 10, 11, 12, 14, 40, 41, 45, 46, 53, 55, 56, 101; ownership and, 40-41, 53; rights and, 11, 13, 39, 40-41, 44, 45, 53, 55, 56, 101, 104; of the soul, 29

precept(s)*, 32, 68, 73, 74, 80, 93, 94, 95, 100, 101, 103, 104, 105, 107, 110, 122, 128, 131, 132, 136, 138, 139, 140, 144; given to apostles not to possess anything, 74, 95, 103-104, 110, 132, 138-139, 140; love of God and, 32, 80; not to be solicitous, 73, 107; obligating apostles to evangelical poverty, 93-94, 131, 132; obligating apostles not to have rights to things, 100-101; to use things for subsistence, 100, 101, 105, 144
predication (unqualified): nature of, 91, 108
prelate*, 43, 48, 87, 88, 90, 108, 133, 136, 146; dominion and, 43, 48; in early church, 146; necessities of life accepted from faithful, 108; perfection of and having things in common, 87-90; personal ownership and, 133; study necessary for, 90. See also, state of prelates, state of prelacy
present life, 34, 35, 51, 55, 56, 67, 68, 111. See also wayfaring state
pride, 35, 57, 59, 66
privation* (privatio), 16, 26, 28, 29, 30, 31, 32, 35, 54, 62, 80; imperfection as, 54, 62; and perfection, 26, 29-31, 32, 35, 62, 80; poverty and, 16, 28, 29, 30, 35; signifies nonbeing, 32. See also imperfection
providence (divine), 64, 70, 71
purse*, Christ's, 23, 53, 62, 73, 74, 80, 92, 96, 97, 108, 114, 121, 122, 133, 135, 136, 137, 139, 142, 143, 146; condescension to weakness and, 53, 62, 92, 121-122, 142; dominion/ownership/rights and, 23, 96, 97-98, 133, 139, 143, 146; as example for humans, 73, 74, 108, 143; establishes Church finances, 74, 80; making provision for the future and, 135-137; not held from necessity, 114; use of things and, 23-24, 133,

139, 146
reckon* (computo), 38, 45, 46, 47, 48, 49, 99. See temporal things, reckoned as God's; temporal things, reckoned as someone's; temporal things, reckoned as no one's
rashness, nature of, 112. See also dominion, whether rash to attribute to Christ/apostles
religious state 25, 77, 79, 80, 81, 82, 87, 133; constituted by vows of obedience, chastity, and poverty, 25; dominion/ownership/rights and, 77-87; perfection of, 77-87; poverty of, 133; as state of acquiring perfection, 81-82, 88, 133-134; as state of perfection, 25; vows of, 25
religious: dominion held by, 33, 49; necessities of life used by, 61; ownership held by, 33, 109; rights held by, 33, 49; poverty of, 72
religious institutes. See religious state
renunciation/renounce/relinquish* (abrenuntiatio, renuntio, abrenuntio, relinquo), 3, 4, 5, 9, 10, 13, 25, 28, 35, 37, 51, 52, 58, 59, 62, 63, 77, 79, 84, 88, 89, 90, 92, 93, 98, 100, 101, 102, 109, 110, 123, 124, 127, 128, 130, 131, 132, 133, 134, 135, 138, 143; Bonaventure's understanding of, 3; charity and, 28, 33; by Christ/apostles, 3, 4, 5, 91-96, 98, 100, 101-102, 103-104, 108, 109, 123-124, 126-127, 128, 129-130, 131, 135, 138, 139, 146; common, 4, 27, 101, 109, 127, 129, 133, 135, 139; difficulty of, 52; as disposition of the mind, 28, 89, 90, 102, 110; by Dominicans, 4, 7; dominion and, 89; as exterior effect, 89, 102; by Franciscans, 3-4, 6, 10; of friends/parents, 102; of making provision for the future, 37, 63; as nakedness, 62; necessities of life and, 108, 111; of ownership, 4, 5, 10, 13, 58-59, 62, 109, 127, 129,

130, 143; perfection and, 59, 79, 85, 89, 109, 124, 139, 143; personal, 4, 51, 62, 79, 85, 88, 101-102, 109, 110, 111, 124, 127, 128, 133, 134, 135, 136, 138, 139; of possessions, 25; poverty and, 14, 15, 28, 37, 79, 124, 133; of rights, 6, 98, 100; of simple use not licit, 12-13; state of, 134; state of prelacy and, 88-89; unqualified, 127. *See also* Matt 19:27

right to use something (*ius utendi*), 12, 14

right(s)* (*ius*), 2, 5, 6, 8, 10, 11, 12, 13, 14, 15, 16, 18, 23, 28, 33, 34, 35, 37, 38, 39, 40, 41, 42, 43, 44, 45, 46, 47, 48, 49, 50, 51, 53, 55, 56, 57, 58, 59, 60, 61, 69, 77, 78, 79, 82, 84, 85, 86, 87, 88, 91, 96, 97, 98, 99, 100, 101, 103, 104, 105, 106, 107, 108, 109, 111, 112, 113, 114, 125, 127, 132, 134, 137, 138, 139, 140; to administer things, 43, 48, 113; charity and, 56; civil law and, 2, 6; common, 11, 33, 42, 49, 50, 51, 56, 78, 79, 87, 91, 108, 138; contrasted with dominion and ownership, 11n. 42, 40; debt of, 104; defined, 40-41, 45; dominion and, 61; evangelical perfection and, 105; held by an administrator, 42; held by Christ/apostles, 6-7, 11, 91, 97, 99-99, 106, 113, 138, 132, 139; held by community, 42, 43, 79, 113; held by dependent child, 37, 43-44, 46, 48; held by Franciscans, 6; held by monastery, 42; held by a monk, 37, 43-44, 46, 48, 140; held by religious, 33, 48; held by slave, 43, 46, 48; to immovable goods, 98, 105; kinds of, 41-42; perfection and, 55-57, 77, 82, 86-7, 88, 96-97; personal, 18, 33, 35, 42, 50, 51, 56-57, 78, 79, 87, 88, 91; poverty and, 28, 33-34, 35, 37, 78-79, 134; as power of licit use, 10-11, 15, 39-41,

42, 45, 46, 50, 53, 55, 56, 60, 61, 85, 98, 101, 104, 112, 113; relative, 41, 43, 44; same as dominion and ownership, 40; separability from use, 12, 15, 18, 37-50, 56, 60, 69, 82, 97, 98, 99, 114, 137; separable from dominion, 97; in state of innocence, 78, 84; taking hold of things and, 49-50; to thing itself, 41, 42, 45, 46, 56, 98, 99, 101, 106, 113; to things bought and sold, 105-106; to things consumed in use, 11-12, 44, 46-47, 56, 59, 82, 98-99, 105, 106, 113, 137; to things not consumed in use, 44, 46, 56; to transfer things, 42, 96, 98; to use things, 8, 11, 13, 16, 44, 45, 47, 48, 50, 55-56, 82, 98, 113, 137; unqualified, 41, 42, 43, 44, 46, 48, 103; use and, 12, 13, 15, 60, 100, 101; to the very use of a thing, 41, 45, 44, 56, 98, 101, 106, 113; to what is advantageous, 127. *See also* dominion, whether heretical to attribute to Christ/apostles

silver, 94, 104, 110, 131, 132, 134, 135, 139, 146. *See also* gold, money

simple use in fact* (*simplex usus facti*), 4, 6, 12, 13, 14, 15, 24, 33, 40, 57, 61, 67, 79, 82, 85, 97, 100, 105, 108-109, 121, 128, 137, 138, 142, 143, 146; by Christ/apostles, 6, 12, 24, 100, 105, 121, 128, 137, 138, 142, 143; common use and, 69, 82, 146; complete lack of illicit, 67; by Franciscans, 4, 6; can be licit or illicit, 40; nature of, 12-15, 40; poverty and, 33-34, 67, 108-109; separability from dominion/ownership/right, 14-15, 24, 40, 61, 79, 85, 100, 105, 121, 128, 138, 142, 143; by religious, 69, 82. *See also* use. (*Note:* "simple use in fact" appears equivalently as "simple use," "use in fact," or "bare use" (*nudus usus*))

sin, 8, 55, 68, 144, 153

slave*, 15, 37, 43, 44, 46, 48, 97, 137,

140

solicitude* (solicitudo), 5, 51, 58, 62, 63, 65, 66, 67, 69, 73, 74, 75, 76, 95, 107, 111, 123, 131, 132, 134, 144, 145; contemplative life and, 66, 69; love of temporal things, 65-66; making provision for the future and, 62-63, 65, 67, 75, 145; for necessities of life, 67, 69, 73, 111, 134, 145; perfection and, 5, 51, 58, 67, 69, 73-75, 131, 134, 144-145; poverty and, 5, 144; prohibition of, 63, 73-75, 95, 107, 123, 131, 132. See also making provision for the future; Matt: 6:34

Spirituals. See Franciscans, Spirituals

state* (status), 25, 27, 29, 30, 37, 53, 54, 55, 56, 61, 62, 64, 65, 68, 73, 77, 78, 79, 80, 81, 82, 83, 84, 85, 86, 87, 88, 89, 92, 105, 114, 115, 121, 122, 124, 133, 134, 135, 136, 137, 138, 144, 145; of apostles, 124, 133, 135; of Christ, 133, 135; of Christian religion, 64; defined, 81; of evangelical perfection, 138; of heaven, 78; of innocence, 78, 84, 85, 137, 144; of merit, 27; of perfection (perfectionis), 25, 29, 30, 64, 77, 80, 81, 89, 92, 133, 135, 144; of poverty, 145 of prelacy/prelates* (praelationis/parelatorum), 77, 81, 88-90, 133; "social," 61, 65, 73; of those who have nothing, 77-78, 84, 122, 133, 136; of those who have something in common, 77-78, 85

taking hold* (occupo) of things, 38, 39, 54, 47, 48, 49, 50, 99; dominion and, 49; granted by God, 38, 45, 48; meaning of, 38n. 3; rights and, 38, 45, 47-50, 99; use and, 49

tempting God, 62, 69, 70

things/goods consumed in use* (res/bona consumnuntur ipso uso), 3, 6, 7, 8, 11-12, 13, 15, 44, 46-47, 52, 55, 56, 59, 55, 56, 59, 68, 69, 82, 98-99, 100, 106, 113, 127, 137,

143, 144, 146; making provision for the future and, 69-70; rights to, 11-12, 44, 46-47, 56, 59, 82, 98-99, 105, 106, 113, 137; rights to held by Christ/apostles, 11-12, 98-99, 106, 113; separability from dominion/ ownership/rights, 3, 6, 8, 11-12, 15, 46-47, 52, 69, 79, 82, 97, 98, 99, 114, 137, 143, 144, 146, 147

things/goods, temporal* (res/bona temporalia), 3, 4, 5, 6, 7, 9, 10, 11, 13, 14, 16, 18, 23, 26, 28, 29, 30, 31, 32, 33, 34, 35, 36, 37, 38, 40, 42, 43, 44, 45, 46, 47, 48, 49, 50, 51, 52, 55, 56, 57, 58, 59, 61, 62, 64, 65, 66, 67, 68, 70, 72, 73, 74, 75, 76, 77, 79, 82, 83, 85, 87, 88, 89, 90, 91, 94, 96, 97, 98, 99, 100, 101, 102, 103, 104, 105, 106, 113, 114, 125, 128, 134, 135, 136, 137, 142, 144; capital, 7; of the church, 136; of a community, 6, 42, 43; desire for, 35, 50, 52, 57, 70, 71, 94, 132, 135; granting of (see granting, of things); held in common, 6, 34, 50, 51, 52, 56, 57, 58, 65, 77, 78, 79, 80, 82, 83, 85, 89, 93, 94, 95, 96, 102, 105, 108, 125, 128, 130, 137, 138, 140, 141, 144; held personally, 50, 51, 52, 56, 88, 95, 108, 111, 141; immovable, 98, 105, 112; in themselves not opposed to virtue, 66; love of, 29, 35, 51, 52, 57, 59, 66, 70, 97, 125, 135; moveable, 112; not consumed in use, 11, 13, 41, 44, 46, 55, 56, 69; reckoned as God's, 11, 38, 45, 48, 49, 137, 144, 146; reckoned as no one's, 38, 39, 45, 49, 99, 137, 144; reckoned as someone's, 38, 45, 46, 48, 49, 99. See also goods, temporal; things consumed in use; dominion; ownership; right(s); use

transfer (alieno), 3, 6, 11, 14, 40, 41, 42, 45, 46, 47, 48, 53, 55, 56, 69, 83, 87, 98, 99, 100, 105, 106, 119,

137, 145; of consumable things, 11, 46, 47, 68-69, 99-100; kinds of, 42; licit as right to things, 10-11, 40-41, 43, 45, 53, 105-106; of money, 46, 99, 105-106; perfection and, 55, 56, 83; for personal benefit, 47-48; of things by Christ/apostles, 98-100, 105-106, 137, 145; utility of, 56, 82-83

trust, 35, 63, 66, 76

unqualified(ly)/without qualification* (simpliciter), 10, 33, 34, 41, 42, 43, 44, 46, 47, 48, 54, 60, 88, 91, 92, 95, 101, 103, 105, 108, 109, 121, 122, 127, 130, 139, 143; blessedness, 60; blindness, 108; dominion, 33, 41, 42, 44, 48; false that Christ/apostles had something in common, 121, 130; having things, 127; health, 91, 121; imperfection, 54; lack of charity, 54; ownership, 44, 46, 47, 48, 109; perfection, 122; possession, 127; poverty, 10, 33-34; precept to use things for subsistence, 101; predication, 91-92, 108-139, 143; realization of an end, 101, 105; renunciation of things, 127; right, 41, 42, 43, 44, 46, 48, 103; sight, 108; true that Christ/apostles had nothing in common, 91, 130; true that Christ had a purse, 143; truth/falsity of a proposition, 91, 121; wealth, 10, 33, 34

use* (usus), 1, 2, 3, 4, 6, 8, 9, 10, 11, 12, 13, 14, 15, 16, 18, 19, 23, 24, 25, 27, 28, 33, 34, 35, 37, 38, 39, 40, 41, 42, 43, 44, 45, 46, 47, 48, 49, 50, 52, 53, 55, 56, 57, 58, 59, 60, 61, 67, 69, 74, 75, 79, 80, 82, 83, 84, 85, 91, 96, 97, 98, 99, 100, 101, 104, 105, 106, 108, 112, 113, 114, 119, 120, 121, 127, 128, 129, 132, 133, 135, 136, 137, 138, 142, 143, 144, 145, 146, 147; by administrator, 113; by child, 37, 43-44, 137; by Christ/apostles, 6, 11-12, 23-24, 97-101, 105, 112, 113, 121, 128, 133, 135, 137, 138, 142, 143, 145. 146; by community, 145-146; by Dominicans, 17; by Franciscans, 2-3, 4-5, 10, 14-15; by monk, 37-38, 43-44, 80, 137; by slave, 37, 43-44, 137; civil law and, 2; common, 18, 79, 80, 92, 127, 144; dominion and, 3, 10, 44, 137; granted by God, 38, 48; having nothing and, 79, 84, 108, 113; having things and, 79, 82, 85, 132; in heaven, 55; illicit, 40, 45, 56, 101; just, 8 (see also licit use); kinds of, 15; licit, 10, 11, 12, 13, 14, 15, 16, 18, 39, 40, 41, 42, 45, 47, 49, 50, 53, 55-56, 61, 69, 98, 99, 100, 101, 104, 112, 113, 114; love of temporal things and, 59; natural law and, 127, 144; necessary for subsistence, 35, 38, 53, 59, 84, 87, 100, 101, 104, 105, 107, 133, 135-136, 144; ownership and, 9, 12, 16, 52; perfection and, 55, 57, 82; personal, 39, 42, 18, 127; positive law and, 127; poverty and, 9-10, 12, 16, 28, 33, 108, 133; rights and, 6, 8, 12, 13, 15, 37-50, 100, 101, 127 (see also use, licit); separability from dominion, 6, 8, 10, 11, 15, 18, 37-50, 79, 97, 137, 143, 144, 146, 147 separability from ownership, 3, 6, 46-47, 52, 79, 137, 144; separability from right, 12, 15, 18, 37-50, 56, 69, 82, 97, 98, 99, 114, 137; in state of innocence, 38, 144; things as if just using, 132; unjust, 12, 39 (see also illicit use); vows and, 39. See also things, consumed in use; things, not consumed in use; simple use [in fact]

usufruct, 12, 137, 144, 147, simple use and, 12

usury, 146, 147

very use* (ipsius usus), 41, 44, 45, 46, 55, 56, 68, 69, 82, 98, 106. See also use virtue* (*virtus*), 25, 27, 28, 29, 30, 31, 32, 36, 40, 45, 52, 53, 55, 60, 61, 63, 66, 68, 80, 92, 94, 97, 108, 122, 123, 126, 142; acts of, 26, 27, 29, 66, 67; of apostles, 92, 123; as arduous, 52, 60; charity and, 27; dominion and, 61; ends of, 28; good of, 25, 31; habits of, 26, 27, 29, 66, 67; having things and, 52, 60; infused, 26; intellectual, 27; love of temporal things and, 31; making provision for the future, 68; mean of, 60, 61; moral, 27; nature of, 27; not necessarily impeded by temporal things, 66-67; perfect, 61; perfection and, 25, 26, 53, 60, 123, 126; poverty and, 30, 31, 36, 61, 92; rights and, 61; theological, 27; wealth and, 61; works of, 60, 80-82. *See also* virtuous

virtuous* (*virtuosus*), 25, 26, 27, 28, 29, 30, 31, 60, 61, 66, 67, 80, 81, 82. *See also* virtue

voluntary poverty, 25, 26, 28, 72

vow of poverty, 4, 9, 12, 25, 26, 30, 31, 39, 50, 93, 100, 101, 124, 131, 138, 139, 142; by apostles, 93, 100, 101, 124, 131, 138, 139, 142; cannot renounce all use, 12, 39, 50, 100, 101; by Franciscans, 4; renunciation of dominion and, 4, 39; as lack of ownership, 9; object of, 26, 31; obligations imposed by; 81, 91, 100, 101; perfection and, 26, 31; religious state and, 25; as state of perfection, 25, 30

wayfaring state, 54-56, 62. *See also* present life

wealth* (*divitiae*), 10, 26, 34-36, 53, 55, 59-61, 66, 79, 80, 86, 95, 97; apostles lived without, 95; charity and, 34, 35-36, 53, 55; love of neighbor and, 35-36; love of temporal things and, 59; necessities of life and, 10, 59, 78, 86; as opposite to poverty, 10, 26, 34, 35, 79; perfection and, 26, 35, 53, 55, 60, 79, 86; pride and, 35, 59, 66; religious state and, 80; self love and, 35; unqualified, 34; virtue and, 61

"what belongs to another"* (*alienum*). *See* expressions of ownership: what belongs to another

"what belongs to oneself"* (*proprium*). *See* expressions of ownership: what belongs to oneself

"what is held in common"* (*commune*). *See* expressions of ownership: what belongs in common

yours. *See* expressions of ownership: yours